Praise for Safety Performance Reimagi

Who Cares Wins! *Safety Performance Reimagi*   ',
'what' and 'how' of Sociotechnical Safety. The   )r
change by barbecuing some of safety's most s   d
plentiful case studies drawn from many high ...., the book then provides readers with practical tools to create the psychological safety and trust within their teams essential for work to be done well and reliably.

This book is a significant addition to the 'New View' literature and is a must-read volume for leaders from the Boardroom to the frontline.

Clive Lloyd, Author of Next Generation Safety Leadership: From Compliance to Care.

*****

Safety Performance Reimagined masterfully outlines the essentials of the 4-Dimensional approach myself and my leadership team embarked on. Prior to 2002, I managed OMV-Pakistan's green field gas field development, where we quite successfully created what I would now call a 3-Dimensional HSEQ System.

When I took over the role as GM of OMV's Austrian Exploration & Production Operations in 2002, I learned a different approach—a 4-Dimensional approach. With 50 years of operations of mainly very mature oil and gas fields and injury rates many times the industry average, the challenge in Austria was different to Pakistan. With the support and leadership insights of Rod and Brett, myself and my team went from looking for what went wrong to asking ourselves what was missing. Through a new leadership approach and the safety culture it created the overall quality of our work reached a new level where our people were the solution.

This book brilliantly shares the lessons we learned. Lessons about relationships, trust, common purpose, commitment, and outstanding performance. I am forever grateful to Brett and Rod for their leadership development and help in understanding the power and importance of leadership in organisations of any size.

Reinhart Samhaber, Senior Vice President, OMV, Engineering and Production (Retired)

*****

The authors set out to answer, "*Why are leaders not seeing the issues in safety for what they are, and why is it that many leaders 'just don't get it'?*" They not only answer those questions; they also provide the solutions based on their hard earned experience. This is a profound book that bears reading many times as you grow in your leadership capabilities.

If you want to get excited about reading this book start with Brett and Rod's personal stories in the introduction. Their experience in high risk situations, what they learned from their failures, and their eventual success will grip you and establish their credibility.

Rosa Antonia Carrillo, MSOD, Author of The Relationship Factor in Safety Leadership

*****

Safety Performance Reimagined is a hard hitting, compelling and decisive call to action to make a step change in the way that we approach safety in the workplace.

What makes this book stand out is the clear conclusion from the compelling selection and analysis of real world case studies—of failures and of successes, to demonstrate the clear need to challenge the status quo and create change.

The experience, professionalism and passion of the authors comes through strongly. They recognise the profound impact of effective leadership as the single most important ingredient for success. The authors explore how good leaders cultivate sustainable performance based on common purpose, trust, ownership, empowerment and care.

The authors have done much more than just critique the current state of safety. They provide a framework and a kitbag of tools to enable the reader to approach the change needed across multiple fronts.

This is an excellent publication as it seeks to help industries and organisations create safer work operations. It is thought provoking, at times challenging and comes at a time when we need to stop and review where we are heading.

John Kempe, ex-special forces Lieutenant Colonel, 18 years Oil & Gas as GM, VP and CEO.

*****

In this book Brett Read and Rod Ritchie take us on a journey of the good, the bad and the ugly of safety. In reimagining safety performance they identify the one key variable that can lead to better outcomes at all levels within a company—Leadership.

The authors help the reader understand the power of leadership in safety and how the key elements of leadership—openness, honesty, trust, communication, motivation, and execution—create great performance and sustainable outcomes for safety and also for good corporate practice, from the shop floor to the Board Room.

Jeffrey Foster, Executive Chairman, Latitude 66

*****

What do you get combining an ex-special forces soldier and an ex-oil and gas engineer? Well, anything is possible. With the authors Brett and Rod, you get an engaging, thought-provoking and inspiring book written through a mindful exercise of reflection and shared learning on safety leadership and culture.

Traversing both the art and science of safety, the authors canvass counter-intuitive aspects and debunk old-thinking, before presenting a compelling case for change, from control and compliance to commitment and care. Their reimagined 4-Dimensional approach paints leadership as omnipotent in creating and sustaining safe work. A must read for any organisational leader.

Michael Morgan, ex-special forces medical specialist, certified work health and safety professional and practicing WHS lawyer.

*****

Safety Performance Reimagined

Safety Performance Reimagined

A 4D Approach to
Organizational Performance

Melanie,
        I hope you find
this book useful.
Who Cares Wins!

Brett

Brett Read & Rod Ritchie

i

ISBN: 9798597745855

Published by Pale Horse Media Co.
Phoenix, Arizona

Table of Contents

Table of Figures

Acknowledgements

Many people have contributed to creating the final version of this book. This book is the culmination of 20 years of work, that included research and application in many companies and countries. A special thank you must go to Dr Keith Owen for working with us and sharing and analysing his original research into the leadership practices that create high performing teams. His work was instrumental in helping us to develop the CARES Framework and the models in this book.

Clients often very graciously acknowledge the learning and benefits they have gained both professionally and personally from working with us and the material in this book. But the flipside of that is the learning that we have gained over many years of seeing these leaders skilfully and uniquely apply what we teach to create inspiring levels of engagement, ownership and self-directing teams. They are the people who inspired us to coin the phrase – Who CARES Wins.

Several clients and colleagues have been very generous with their time to review drafts and provide invaluable insights and feedback. Among the many who have supported us and contributed, we would specifically like to acknowledge the contribution and efforts of Bruce Webb, Reinhart Samhaber, Jeff Foster, John Kempe, Warren Ford, Michael Morgan, and Peter Neal.

Thank you also to our network of connections on LinkedIn who have provided inspiration and insight and contributed in a variety of ways to reimagining safety performance.

Within Safety Leaders Group we would also like to acknowledge the unwavering support of Jennifer Schuiling over the several years that it took to create this final edition. We would also like to thank Melanie Read who has been very supportive and resourceful as our ever willing research assistant.

Safety Performance Reimagined

Forward

This book is not just a great treatise in what it means to lead high performing teams. It is also a call to action, a call to adventure and discovery and in the true sense of the word – it is iconoclastic. Long held icons of the way safety is discussed, reported, and lived will be strongly challenged and criticised … and a new way of safety performance reimagined.

On the 14th of September 2017 I was promoted to Chief Operating Officer of an independent oil and gas production company on the sudden departure of my predecessor.

Six days later a series of events played out that I remember in detail – and so much of what happened is central to the message of this book.

On the morning of the 20th of September, I saw that we had achieved a safety milestone …a year since the last recorded lost time injury.

At 7:32 a.m. I wrote to the CEO with the words *"this is a tremendous achievement in any business and in particular in the context of three drilling rigs, multiple projects, turnarounds and new fields opening up. Could I suggest an email to staff and a message on the corporate website? Happy to work on some appropriate text for both"*. As per the conventional approach to safety performance, I was of the view that we should celebrate a year of people not reporting being injured. This book proposes a different approach and supports the message of a growing number of safety professionals who argue that the current approach to safety leadership is flawed and even toxic.

At 10:59 a.m. I received an email entitled *"EXERCISE EXERCISE EXERCISE Sitrep Number 1 Tanker Incident"* indicating we were practicing and exercising the emergency response capabilities across three countries. The scenario indicated two injuries requiring hospitalisation.

The exercise escalated over the morning to include *"reports on multiple social media with news about a bombing that took place at the oil export terminal"*. I followed the protocols and for the purpose of the exercise I had the legal team draft a holding statement to be used 'if asked'.

At 12:09 The exercise escalated further, as they do, and I received an email entitled: *"EXERCISE EXERCISE EXERCISE name of deceased person"*. A simulated reply from HR came next *"Please can you reconfirm the name of the deceased person, there is no match of the name on HR database. Please check and reconfirm the first name. We do have someone with the second name as stated below"*. Despite this being a fabricated practice scenario, I still got a chill thinking about it. At the time, I felt it was right for the emergency response team to have a sense of chronic unease …this was serious business. But this is the wrong way round, as I later learned through Brett and Rod there is a different mindset that serves us better.

For the next part of the exercise there was a debate about how to communicate internally, with the head of health and safety proposing town hall meetings in the major locations. Text for an email to all staff was agreed. We worked the scenario a bit further and then called time, the exercise was stood down and we held a debrief and wash up.

At 15:15 as the weekend was approaching, I sent the second of what became a weekly note to all staff with the following:

"In the morning we mobilized the Crisis Management Team (CMT) for a drill and exercise. This was a three-hour commitment to test the response team's support for the in-country teams. I learned a lot about our capability and about myself. Being part of the on-call organization is a significant responsibility and commitment. It is also a great development opportunity, is a requirement for many senior positions, is great training and ultimately in a real situation can make an immediate difference to friends and colleagues who need help. Thanks to J and the HSSE team for coordinating. Thanks to D for honest feedback and great CMT leadership."

At 17:29, just before heading out of the office for the weekend, I received another incident email – the type that as a COO, you certainly do not want to receive. This email did not have the word EXERCISE repeated three times. This one was for real:

"We had an incident this afternoon resulting in possible injury to a contractor (IP). A grader was reversing, and the IP apparently walked into and was knocked down by one of the grader's tyres. It was an open area and witness account says the IP walked into the scene despite the reverse warning signal and other vehicles sounding horns to warn him away. More details to come. We understand the IP was a 'banksman' – watching out for mobile equipment and people movements. The IP was assessed by the Medic, and whilst nothing obvious on vital signs or pain (?), the tyre did hit/(roll?) across his pelvis area and abdomen. The IP has been moved to hospital for x-ray etc.

More to follow when investigated in detail."

21:05 update *"The IP is in critical condition. Internal abdominal injuries and pelvic break/fractures. J headed to hospital after updates from M indicated serious condition at hospital. J indicated IP has had surgery for very serious abdominal injuries. Doctors say next two days critical. J spoke with family. Not requiring support at this point. Seems more to this incident than initial reports/assessment. Team assembling 0800 at office."*

In the early hours I received the call one no wants to make or take:

Mr. MHM, a 32-year-old supervisor, from a local village had been moved to a central emergency hospital. At approximately 02:00 on 21st September he succumbed to his injuries.

My third weekly note started with this:

"The absolute worst thing that can happen in our industry is someone we work with in our business doesn't go home to their family. I still cannot put into words what this means to us. We will follow up in three ways. W, General Manager is leading the immediate response, with family, the worksite and the relationship with the company involved. S has today returned from site with the rest of the Incident Investigation team. Many thanks to S, J, K, L and the rest of the team. Secondly, we are committed to learning from and acting on their findings which we will review next week. Thirdly, we are focusing on Safety Leadership and Culture. By now you should have had a conversation with your line manager on this and many thanks for the feedback received to date. You will see in the coming weeks and months that this is a consistent theme …safety leadership rests with all of us, it is measured in both words and actions and fundamentally it means looking out for each other, following up on what we know we should do and finishing what we start."

What happened next is the subject of this book. We invited the Safety Leaders Group (SLG) to come and work with us in three countries, to run workshops, to get under our skin, to help us reimagine safety performance.

I developed a relationship with Brett Read and Rod Ritchie (SLG) who coached and guided us on our new journey into 4D Safety. Through this process I deepened my relationship with my teams, my people, my leaders, and my front-line workforce. During the Safety Leadership workshops, I also developed a sound understanding and appreciation for what they mean by a 4D approach to organizational performance. Brett and Rod are deeply committed to the mission they are on; they have thought hard about the case studies they present. They have a message that every Board member and senior leader responsible for safe operations should understand.

On that day in September, I was on the roughest part of the journey you will read about in this book and I am still on that journey.

I began the day with a classic failure of conventional safety. I focused on what was wrong, not what was missing … I wanted to celebrate a year of people not reporting being injured.

I was then pleased to be working on a practice drill with a real sense of chronic unease. The idea that this is healthy will be challenged in this book.

Following twenty-five years of safety inductions, safety training and company safety programmes I had come to rely on safety metrics. On this day, our numbers were telling us we were operating safely at the same time that we had just had a fatality in our operations. Clearly, something needed to change. The team came together, and we committed to do the only thing you can do in this situation – we got into action and embarked on a journey of doing safety very differently. We created trust, engaged in dialogue and shared meaning to identify a common purpose. It is an enduring regret that the catalyst to do this had to come as the result of a fatality on my watch.

Who cares wins.

Bruce Webb BEng CEng CEnv FIChemE
Aberdeenshire, Scotland

Preface

This book has been written as a result of our commitment to help organizations and industries create safe operations. Its intended audience is any leader who, through their decisions and leadership practices, influences how safely an organization or team operates.

In this regard, the focus for this book is far reaching and its audience extends from senior safety managers and operational leaders up to the executive managers and board members making decisions about where, how, and with whom the organization will operate. It also includes decision makers who control budgets and determine procurement and contracting decisions.

As a Board member or a leader in an organization, what keeps you awake at night?

A generation of managers have been taught that they need to live in an environment of chronic unease—constantly concerned about how they ensure that their company operates safely? This is not a healthy or sustainable approach to managing the operational risks in business.

The expectations and obligations placed on the most senior leaders in organizations has never been greater. The mantra of zero accidents and the threat of punishments that are possible under Industrial manslaughter laws creates a fear response in many. The psychological need to protect oneself has created a demand for safety professionals to provide a solution. Unfortunately, the conventional approach to managing safety is flawed and is not creating sustainable results.

The current approach to safety has morphed from an ethical responsibility to keep operational workers safe to a bureaucratic accountability to report up the organization to nonoperational people.

The conventional safety approach is based on a misguided view that sees people as a problem to be controlled, and errors and accidents as anomalies that must be controlled through ever increasing layers of systems and volumes of rules and procedures that must be complied with. This approach has resulted in the ratios of HSE compliance jobs increasing dramatically over the last two decades. But our industries are not getting safer; serious injury and fatal accident rates are actually going up![1]

As Albert Einstein stated, the definition of insanity is to continue to do the same things and expect a different result. The conventional approach to safety, which we refer to as a 3-Dimensional, COP-Safety approach needs to change.

The authors have over 60 years combined industry experience leading and implementing Health, Safety and Environmental management and performance improvement initiatives in over 30 countries. In the early 2000's as we were successfully implementing leadership driven, people centric, safety performance improvement in different companies and countries, we also observed the rise of Behavioural Based Safety (BBS) driven approaches which were the antithesis of our thinking and approach.

These approaches which relied on a—talk at you, not with you—endless monologue of safety posters, *"thou shalt"* inductions, notice board campaigns, entry gate safety scoreboards tracking the number of days since someone screwed up, gained incredible uptake and momentum globally as a result of slick marketing. It's important here to recognise that not everyone freely chose to *"drink the Kool-Aid"* that was being pushed by the BBS, *"people are the problem,"* find & fix approach to safety devotees. Many companies resisted what they instinctively knew was not a good approach to leading and influencing people. Unfortunately, these companies were invariably smaller operators or service companies who—in the absence of a well-defined and clearly articulated alternative approach—were coerced and conscripted via joint ventures or contracts and fear of regulators to adopt and provide evidence of their *"best practice"* BBS approach to safety.

Our initial concern with this direction in safety thinking has turned to frustration and prompted us to write this book. What we believe is necessary, is a refocus based on the awareness of a fourth dimension of performance which is ever present in every operation where people are involved. That 4th Dimension is based on effective safety <u>leadership</u> and leveraging the incredible performance capacity that people bring to any operation. This approach is however vexed by the dilemma that people have an amazing ability to adapt but can also at times be unpredictable and at worst unreliable. In this book we invite the reader to reimagine safety performance and the leadership practices that help companies realise the performance gains to be had. At the heart of this approach is compelling evidence that when leaders trust their people and provide support and guidance, real transformation happens.

Over the last 20 years the authors have worked together on many successful safety performance improvement initiatives that have seen organizations completely transform how leaders engaged, influenced, and inspired their teams. Many of the organizations that we have been invited to work with have had significant performance and safety challenges. In the most challenging cases, lost time injuries and fatalities had come to be regarded as a regrettable but unavoidable part of high risk work.

In every engagement we have worked on, we started with leadership—what the organization's leaders focused on, what they valued and cared about. Performance improvement always came through realigning the focus and creating a more caring approach where people were seen as the solution and not the problem. Many leaders were willing and able to change how they thought and acted; some were not. Those that were not willing or able to reimagine their role and do safety differently did not create a sustainable safety performance. Sadly, some leaders just don't "*get it*."

Several years ago, we asked ourselves: Why are leaders not seeing the issues in safety for what they are, and why is it that many leaders "*just don't get it*"? As we discussed the issues and our answers to these questions, we considered how we could share what we had learned. How could we provide operational managers, executive managers, their supervising Boards, and other people who choose to be responsible for safety with a profound, yet easy to understand framework for explaining and practicing sustainable safety leadership? 4-Dimensional Safety and the Who CARES Wins Framework was born from that desire to share what we have learned and what we know from experience works. In the interest of saving lives and keeping people safe we hope that you can learn from this book and become part of an ever increasing cadre of leaders who have chosen to make a difference in terms of the way safety is 'done'. A positive additional benefit of making this change is significantly better operational efficiency. But there is one catch, the leadership practices that we explore in the book require leaders to be able to put their teams and people first, to be willing to build meaningful relationships and not be self-oriented or purely ego driven. This journey takes time and courage, but we know that if you are prepared to go the distance, you and everyone that works in your organization will be the better for it.

This book is a mix of experience, applied research, discussion of industry failures and catastrophes and the lessons we have learned from successful change programs in multiple operating companies around the world.

Endnotes:

[1] Safe Work Australia (2018). *Fatality Statistics by Industry.* [online]
https://www.safeworkaustralia.gov.au/statistics-and-research/statistics/fatalities/fatality-statistics-industry#figure-1-worker-fatalities-proportion

Introduction

A Journey of Experience and Collaboration

The two authors of this book share a common purpose and desire to improve safety performance in business through great leadership.

We discuss a wide cross section of case studies ranging from BP Texas City, BP Macondo, the SAS Black Hawk tragedy, the VW Dieselgate Scandal and Boeing 737 Max Aircraft. Our experience, the investigation findings and the lessons learned highlight that the seeds for many of these catastrophes were laid years before the final event. The common thread running through these catastrophes is that they were all created by decisions to operate a certain way or continue to operate, knowing that things were not being done well. The challenge is to understand why the decisions were made and to know how to create better outcomes. In a very few cases those in charge were just rolling the dice and relying on luck that things did not go wrong. In these cases, the remedy does not require much contemplation. But what about the other cases? What is the solution for the majority of cases where good people were just trying to do their job? In many of the case studies presented in this book, the accepted wisdom and norms for how to create safe performance failed to cope with the increasing levels of complexity and expectations for leaner and more agile operations?

Over the last 20 years, the field of safety has continued to build layer upon layer of things that don't work. Researchers and leaders in the field are now reconsidering and testing the efficacy of many of the systems and processes that have crept into the conventional safety approach and are not finding links between these practices and improved safety performance. As a result, commonly held views about the role of the safety professional and what companies should ideally track and focus on to improve safety performance are being questioned. A recent post from David Clarke the CEO of the Australian Institute of Health and Safety (AIHS) flags 2021 as the year that the AIHS will *take this issue on once and for all.*[1] We hope this book can help create the change needed and the development of a more effective approach that creates sustainable safety performance.

While the authors share a common commitment, we also have quite different backgrounds and life experiences. Our models and recommendations are all based on our experiences and knowledge gained from working in many different countries and companies. These experiences unfortunately include dealing with disabling injuries and fatalities.

The purpose of this book is to share what we have learned from studying safety and operational performance and successfully helping companies steer a course and implement those leadership and work practices that improve their performance.

Organizations are finding that their people increasingly desire and look for meaning and purpose in their work. This is understandable when viewed in context of Maslow's Hierarchy of Needs[2], which puts self-actualization and the pursuit of your life's purpose at the top of a pyramid of human needs.

As the world is developing, standards of living in much of the industrial world are improving and the imperative of feeding the family is less of a challenge. It is therefore not surprising that the current generation of workers is looking for more—in a variety of different ways (some effective and some not) they are asking, "*Why—What's the purpose of the work I do?*"[3] Our education systems and business systems are not doing a good job of answering this question and need to do a much better job of addressing this need.

What would we like this book to achieve? Firstly, we hope that it will serve as a wake-up call to inspire the leaders who control the resources and systems within organizations to think more broadly and not just rely on those systems and processes to keep people safe. Secondly, it should provide insights and tools for leaders to design and create safe workplaces. Thirdly, the insights and ideas we share, when properly applied, will create more efficient and cost-effective operations.

In the chapters of this book, we will mostly speak with one voice that is born out of a common passion and understanding of the need to make a change. In the first chapter, to help the reader understand why we do what we do, we share aspects of our personal journeys and experiences in safety leadership. In the subsequent chapters, we will at times speak in the first person as we share stories from our personal experience. In these instances, for the sake of continuity, we do not identify the speaker; but whose story it is should be obvious to the reader.

Structure of the book
The book is structured into three parts which enable an organization to work with it as a road map to guide them through the process of creating sustainable safe operations.

Part 1. The Failure of Conventional Safety—Focusing on What's Wrong instead of What's Missing
Part 1 consists of 3 chapters. Chapter 1 outlines some of our personal experiences and WHY we believe safety needs to change. Chapter 2 discusses the shortcomings in the conventional approach to safety. Chapter 3 explores the current 3-Dimensional approach to managing performance and introduces a 4th dimension, which is about people and safety leadership.

At the end of Part 1 you should be clear about WHY change needs to happen and WHY you should be leading that change.

Part 2. Who CARES Wins—What Effective Leaders Do to Create Performance

Part 2 consists of 5 chapters that map out WHAT the most effective leaders do to create sustainable safety performance.

Chapter 4 explores the 'new view' of safety and revisits the sociotechnical paradigm that sits at the heart of making the optimum decisions about risk management; by understanding the relationships and interconnectedness between ourselves, others, technology and systems.

Chapter 5 looks at the leadership understanding, and skills required to make the shift to become a more caring leader—a leader who is able to engage their people so that they want to work safely and effectively.

Chapter 6 introduces the CARES Framework and Chapters 7 and 8 explore CARES in more detail. CARES is not simply something that we dreamt up; it is the result of long-term research to establish the leadership practices that create sustainable high performing teams. The leadership practices that are outlined in the CARES Framework have been tried and proven in many different cultures and environments over the last two decades.

CARES makes it easy to understand the specific things that highly effective leaders do. Furthermore, it explores the mindset and purposeful approach needed to apply these leadership practices.

It is also a call to action that asks leaders to rethink and reimagine their approach to creating organizational performance. CARES is unique—it provides a very effective set of leading performance indicators that can be used to measure, monitor, and effectively track the development of the leadership practices that create sustainable safety performance.

No properly run business would ever conduct operations without having an effective set of KPI's in place to track financial and production performance. Increasingly we are understanding that the human side of performance provides the greatest opportunities for performance improvement. With CARES it's possible to bring the same level of sophistication to the sociological side of the business.

To understand why you should be applying the CARES Framework as leading Key Performance Indicators (KPI's), it is worthwhile considering that more that than two thirds of a team's performance is driven by leadership practices—the things that CARES measures.

Part 3. The 6 Factors that Create Relationships and Achievement

Part 3 explains HOW effective leaders do WHAT they do. It consists of 4 chapters, Chapter 9 introduces the 6 Factors that create relationships, achievement, and sustainable performance. Chapter 10 deals with trust, shared meaning, and common purpose. It outlines HOW these are used to build the foundation of relationships that outstanding achievement is built on. Chapter 11 looks at the commitment, responsibility, and accountability, that achieve sustainable performance. Chapter 12 brings it all together and discusses how to create sustainable 4D Performance, including putting 4D Performance into practice.

Endnotes:

[1] Clarke, D. (2021). *LTIFR's.* [post] LinkedIn. https://www.linkedin.com/posts/david-clarke-07348214_ltifrs-we-understood-the-problem-before-activity-6754181711271206912-jvgb
[2] Wikipedia (2021). *Maslow's hierarchy of needs.* [online]
https://en.wikipedia.org/wiki/Maslow%27s_hierarchy_of_needs
[3] Villa, D. (2018). *All you need to know to motivate millennials.* [online] Forbes.
https://www.forbes.com/sites/forbesagencycouncil/2018/03/30/all-you-need-to-know-to-motivate-millennials/#3371914f60ae

Part One

The Failure of Conventional Safety – Focusing on What's Gone Wrong Instead of What's Missing

Wait ... Wait ... Wait ...
Let's rethink, and we'll
try this one more time!

Chapter 1

Safety Performance by Design or by Default

As a leader you get to make choices. You either become a leader, someone who influences and designs the world around you (Mastery)[1] or you accept the circumstances and events in life and become a passenger. You get to choose whether you live your life by design or by default—self leadership.

Organizational cultures (the way things are done around here) are created and developed in the same manner. They can be purposefully designed and developed by the leaders of the organization or they can be allowed to develop and morph under the influence of any number of factors and not be created to any particular design. The point to note here is that you don't get to choose whether or not your team or organization has a culture— every organization has a culture of some type. What you do get to choose is whether you are influencing them and guiding them to your design and purpose.

This is true for safety; it is always the case that safety performance is either created by design or by default. However, this is not the same thing as *"all accidents are preventable"*. They're not, and we will discuss why we say that in Part 3 of this book. But for now, what we will say is that we know it's possible to operate year after year after year with no one being hurt working in your operations. But that only happens by design, and a very clear leadership intent—safety leadership.

Confucius said that people learn wisdom in three ways:

1. By meditation
2. By imitation
3. By experience

He said that meditation was the noblest way to gain wisdom, imitation was the easiest and experience was the bitterest. We think he must have had safety in mind when he spoke these words.

Imagination goes beyond imitation

Imagine a highly successful company, one that people dream of working for. Just imagine working for a company that:

- understands the difference between leadership and management and constantly challenges how they think about leadership and performance

6

- understands the art of leadership in walking the fine line between order and chaos

- sees people as the solution and not as the problem and subsequently enables their employees to tap into autonomy, mastery and purpose

- has successfully changed its safety paradigm and has engaged all stakeholders in a commitment to a sustainable safety approach

- has a framework to help identify where the gaps are and uses that framework to guide and influence their decision making to achieve the desired change

- recognises the need for a sociotechnical approach which successfully navigates the complex interplay between people, technology, systems, the structures, and the markets they operate in

- embraces a learning culture versus a blame culture

- is focussed on what's missing instead of what went wrong

- ensures everybody understands where their role fits within the organization, what is expected of them and is provided the information and resources needed to do their job well

- creates the psychological safety where everyone is supported to have a voice and to make hard decisions

- Focuses on commitment not compliance—because they understand that compliance is an outcome, created by engaged people committed to doing what they have all agreed is the way they work

A company like this is led by leaders who:

- understand that they are responsible for creating the performance climate

- understand that they need to constantly evolve and create the way forward

- understand that their company's current performance, including safety, is a testament to their leadership

- understand the importance of building strong, positive relationships with themselves, others, their environment, and purpose

- are in constant dialogue with their teams and people to create shared meaning, shared values, shared reality, and trust

- provide leadership that meets people's needs for respect, belonging and purpose

- create psychological safety—the ability to speak openly without fear of negative consequences

The large majority of people (both leaders and workers) do not work for a company like this and would happily leave their present employer if offered the opportunity to join such a company. The truth is that most people are prepared to work hard for a leader and an organization that meets their needs for respect, belonging and purpose. The sad part is that few leaders are currently leading their companies this way. The reality and positive message is that any leader can make this change; this book explains how.

Research on engagement in North America, Europe and Australia is all reasonably similar and shows that engagement levels have been consistently low for the last 20 years. The research is telling us that typically only a third of workers are actively engaged and committed to their employer and enthusiastic about their work. Another third are ambivalent about their work and typically describe themselves as just there for the pay. A final third are actively disengaged and will describe themselves as having no regard for delivering a good outcome for their employer. A subset of this last group consider that their employer doesn't care about them and even mistreats them. Even more concerning is the observation that a fair proportion of this group of workers can actually have a malicious and malevolent attitude towards their employer.[2]

It falls on executives and senior leaders to change this. Think of this book like a recipe. Like the ones you see that get your mouth watering. It first has a stunning picture of the amazing culinary delight that you, with a bit of effort and learning, can create.

Figure 1 below is that picture. Through our research of the leadership practices that create sustainable performance we have developed the leadership efficacy chain. Part 1 of this book introduces you to that.

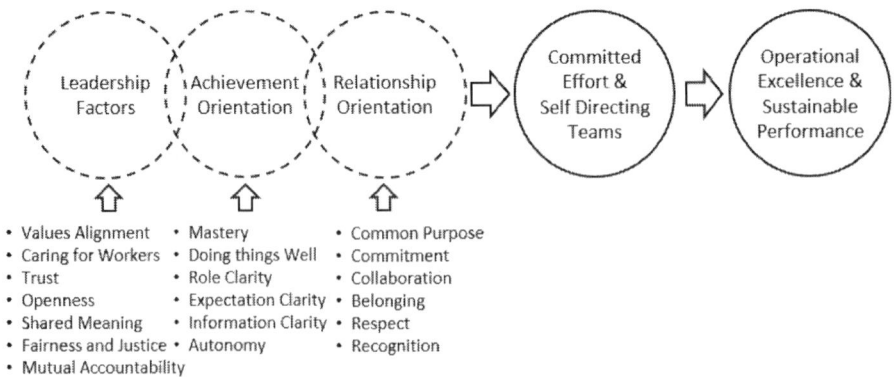

Leadership Factors	Achievement Orientation	Relationship Orientation	Committed Effort & Self Directing Teams	Operational Excellence & Sustainable Performance

- Values Alignment
- Caring for Workers
- Trust
- Openness
- Shared Meaning
- Fairness and Justice
- Mutual Accountability

- Mastery
- Doing things Well
- Role Clarity
- Expectation Clarity
- Information Clarity
- Autonomy

- Common Purpose
- Commitment
- Collaboration
- Belonging
- Respect
- Recognition

Figure 1. The Leadership Efficacy Chain

In addition to the picture of the delicious creation, a recipe lists all the ingredients, what you need to have, and third it steps you through how to create the final result. Part 2 of the book outlines WHAT you need—the key ingredients needed to create the change. But, to take on this creative challenge, you will need your WHY for safety that gives you the commitment to making this happen.

The last part of the recipe are the instructions that step you through how to create the masterpiece. The third part of this book outlines the 6 Factors that Create Relationships and Achievement. This is about How leaders create sustainable safety performance. Think of these factors as the 6 steps that all successful leaders take.

Where My Journey in Safety Leadership Started
By Brett Read

In my time in the Special Air Service Regiment (SASR) I learned to free fall parachute and did many demanding high-altitude high opening (HAHO) and high-altitude low opening (HALO) jumps. When I left the Army, I moved into a business unit manager role for a multinational company and on weekends I continued to skydive and became a senior instructor responsible for running the drop zone.

On a cold winters day in Victoria, not long after I qualified as an instructor, I had a malfunction with the deployment system on my main parachute that saw me almost hit the ground with a perfectly good reserve chute on my back. It was, like many accidents, a combination of several factors all combining to create the conditions where my near miss was the outcome.

Someone who was not familiar to me had packed my chute. Another instructor had asked me if he could use my second rig to qualify another packer on packing round reserve parachutes, which is what I had in the older of my two rigs. I knew my fellow instructor well and knew that he would supervise the student packer to ensure that he packed my reserve perfectly. Also, if the student packer failed the pack or if for any reason my fellow instructor was not happy with the job, he would pull it and repack my reserve himself.

The packing of the reserve went fine, my friend checked it off and then left the packer to close the container for my main and re-stow the deployment chute unsupervised; something that was routine in his mind. What he didn't realise was that the packer made a serious error when packing the pilot chute that deploys my main chute. He was unfamiliar with the particular type of pilot chute and instead of asking for advice he had assumed it would be OK. He continued and unknowingly stowed it in a way that it would jam in the pocket when it was pulled. The error was not detectable in a visual inspection.

Later in the day, I took my second rig and went up with three jumpers to do an *"easy"* jump. There had been clouds building at height over the afternoon, and they had started to form at our 10,000-foot planned jump height. As we climb it's clear that the cloud base is descending and we can't make 10,000 feet, so we circle skirting the clouds and descend until we have a clear view of the target. We are now at 6,000 feet. We make the call to change plan and not do the planned 4-way manoeuvres, and instead just do a link up before breaking off and opening our chutes. I'm last out and dive down to the lowest guy and link up. We hold on and look around and see that the other two guys are a distance away and still higher—they are not going to make the formation. By now we're under 3,000 feet. We break off and I turn and track to get a clear bit of air to open in. As I am completing my track and look up to clear the airspace above me before opening my chute, I see that one of the other jumpers has tracked in the same direction as me and is a couple of hundred feet above me. I curse as I change direction and track further to get clear air, but all the time I'm losing altitude. As I come in to deploy my pilot chute, I check my altimeter I am under 1,800 feet and falling at 200Kph. I should have been more concerned at this point, but I had become over-confident. Hell, it's just a fun jump—no heavy combat gear, no 45kg pack, no assault rifle strapped down my side.

I attempt to pull my chute, but the pilot chute jams. I pull harder but it won't come out. It doesn't make sense. I tug on it again and pull as hard as I can, but in doing so I delay too long in my effort to pull the pilot chute. I go for my reserve and by now I'm getting ground rush and my adrenaline is pumping at max! I pull my reserve and a wave of relief comes over me as I feel the reserve leave my back and open. I check my altimeter and I'm well under 500 feet! Less than 3 seconds of free fall! My sense of euphoria is rapidly drowned out by a loud scream of condemnation from my inner self as I realise how seriously low I am and how much I screwed up.

Later, as I reflect on the jump, I realise that there were numerous things that were not routine. But, right up until my attempt to pull my main chute, it had not registered, and it almost killed me.

I learned a lot from this incident, and it provides several lessons for safety leaders, both in managing your understanding and risk awareness and your ability to understand and influence the people you work with.

However, the current conventional approach to safety would not have identified the most important lessons from this incident. The reasons for this are increasingly being identified and discussed by academics, practitioners and safety leaders who can see the limitations of the conventional approach.

Erik Hollnagel in his book *Safety-II in Practice* explains it as follows:

> *"An unintended, and usually overlooked, consequence of conventional safety management is that the basis is made up of snapshots of how an organization functions – or rather, snapshots of how an organization*

does not function, of how it fails, or has failed. The conventional wisdom is that accidents and incidents provide opportunities to learn and the basis for taking steps to make sure that the same or similar will not happen again. Indeed, one of the seminal works in safety is a book entitled Learning from Accidents in Industry (Kletz, 1994). Yet consider for a moment that accidents are events that occur infrequently and irregularly and lead to serious adverse outcomes. Accidents are therefore not typical of how an organization performs; on the contrary, they represent unusual situations where an organization has failed either in part or in whole. Yet safety management focuses on and analyses such situations in order to improve safety, following the 'find-and-fix' approach. Without being facetious, it would actually be more appropriate to call it the management of nonsafety."[3]

The conventional approach to safety as it has evolved, focuses on eliminating accidents by identifying hazards, investigating accidents, and focusing on human error. It would have focused on what was wrong—the gaps in the training of the packer that packed my reserve parachute and incorrectly closed my main chute. And it would have focused on me being low at opening. These are facts and they contributed to the incident. But they are not the key lesson.

As I reflected on the jump and the circumstances leading up to it, I came to understand that this incident was years in the making. It is human nature that if we do something, or we work with hazardous conditions, for long enough with nothing bad happening, we can start to take them for granted. I had lost sight of the basic fact in skydiving that every time you jump out of a plane you need to do certain things correctly or you will die. I had lulled myself into a thought process that graded jumps in my mind. I was of the mindset that, this was an easy jump.

As Hollnagel says, and I had to learn the hard way, we need to focus on making sure we are doing things well. This involves understanding the critical things that leaders do to create safe and sustainable high performing teams and organizations. I was not blatantly cutting corners, but I had become accustomed to pushing the envelope and operating close to the edge of performance. What I had not kept in mind was that on the other side, on the outside, of the performance envelope is failure.

I had allowed myself, as Sidney Dekker would later come to identify, to drift into failure. Dekker in his book *Drift Into Failure* (2011) brilliantly captures my journey and the path that has led to the majority of catastrophes that I've reviewed. Dekker describes it as,

"Drifting into failure is a gradual, incremental decline into disaster driven by environmental pressure, unruly technology and social processes that normalize growing risk."

This is a leadership issue which still very much needs to be addressed if we are to create sustainable safety performance.

Complacency is a symptom of drift and something that can happen to anyone involved in high risk activities if they don't guard against it. It must always be remembered that past success does not guarantee future performance or safety.

Avoiding complacency requires good training, great leaders and coaches and self-leadership. Following my reserve parachute ride, I had a different attitude to risk and how I dealt with it personally and as an instructor. I looked for students or inexperienced jumpers who were becoming complacent. For jumpers it typically happens around 50 jumps. For pilots it happens around 500 flying hours. Skill levels are increasing, confidence is increasing. Nothing bad has happened, the initial fear of the activity has been replaced with a sense of competence and confidence in your ability. The real challenge is for this to not become over-confidence and complacency.

We had a saying in skydiving, which following the experience of my lucky escape had a new and very personal meaning for me, *"Learn from other people's mistakes; you won't live long enough in this sport to make them all yourself."* This has some value but it's not the whole picture. What I have learned from my own experience and studying and meditating on the writings of authors like Hollnagel and Dekker is that we need to avoid the temptation to just focus on what went wrong. Hollnagel advises that we need to broaden our view to focus on success—all the things we do to make things go well. In our research of teams and performance which we discuss in this book, we focused on the leadership practices that cause things to go well. They proved to be quite different to the conventional safety approach which focuses on things going wrong. We think of it as a problem focus versus a solution focus.

It's also important to note that there is a difference between things going well and going right. Hollnagel makes the point that the concept of things going right infers that there is a right way and a wrong way to do things—which he points out is too limited. One of the things that I learned from my time in Special Forces, operating in demanding and dynamic environments that require a high level of skill and adaptability, is that performance is highly nuanced and a linear gauge with a binary measure of right or wrong is too simple and is inadequate. Understanding these concepts at an intellectual level is one thing, living them, practicing them every day in an organization requires leadership and commitment.

There is no doubt that the lessons we learn by experience are invariably the ones that stay with us and influence us the most. However, for us to become effective safety leaders, we must be willing and able to learn at all three levels as Confucius defined them. One of the challenges in learning by meditation or imitation is that as someone who has not had the experience—you don't know what you don't know. And more importantly, it's typical that you don't know that you don't know. It is easy to stumble into the minefield if you don't know that it exists. This book provides leaders and teams with the leadership practices to help them learn from each other's experiences as well as the critical information, lessons, and wisdom they need to commit to creating safe and sustainable operations.

Drift erodes resilience

Hollnagel in his work focuses on resilience engineering and initially tended to focus more on resilience from a management and organizational perspective.

> *"Resilience engineering recognised from the very beginning that it was necessary not only to prevent incidents and accidents but also to ensure resilience—defined as an organization's ability to function as required under expected and unexpected conditions alike. Resilience engineering thereby offered a new interpretation of safety management."[4]*

Over time Hollnagel's focus changed from a safety engineering and management perspective to include the need to anticipate and the capacity to adapt. This brought in the human aspect of resilience and saw the definition change and the scope broaden to include resilient performance.

> *"Resilience is an expression of how people, alone or together, cope with everyday situations—large and small—by adjusting their performance to the conditions. An organization's performance is resilient if it can function as required under expected and unexpected conditions alike (changes/disturbances/opportunities)."[5]*

Dekker in his work has also captured the importance of people and the complexities of sociotechnical organizations. Dekker's view of resilience as it applies to safety is,

> *"Resilience sees safety as a presence of capacities, capabilities, and competencies to make things go right. No longer should we define safety as the absence of things that go wrong, no longer should it be seen as an absence of negatives (such as errors, violations, or incidents)."[6]*

Resilience and robustness

David Sterling founded the first SAS unit during the Second World War. The effectiveness of SAS tactics was made patently clear in their first year of operations against General Rommel's Axis forces in North Africa in 1942. Rommel's forces had steamrolled their way east from Tunisia across Libya and Egypt capturing the vital oil fields of North Africa. Major David Sterling was an unconventional thinker who could see the flaws in the Allied Forces tactics that had allowed Rommel to dominate them. Stirling convinced his superiors to support him to do things differently—his small group of highly robust and resilient soldiers raided Rommel's airfields, ports, and rail lines with devasting effectiveness. His biggest success came on the night of 26–27 July 1942 when his SAS squadron with 18 jeeps raided the Sidi Haneish landing strip and destroyed 37 Axis aircraft, mostly bombers and heavy transport, for the loss of one man killed. For many months in 1942 the SAS destroyed more enemy aircraft than the Royal Air Force in North Africa.

Today SAS units exist in Britain, Australia, and New Zealand. They pride themselves on their ability to rapidly respond and operate anywhere in the world in all climates, terrain, and environments. My time in the SAS in the 1980's and 90's taught me about resilience and robustness.

I hear people use the term resilience as if it is a synonym for robustness, but there is a difference and as leaders it is essential that we understand the distinctions and the connections. Resilience and robustness can be applied to both things and people, teams, or organizations.

The SAS selection course is designed to look for and test resilience and robustness (both mental and physical robustness). To better understand the difference between resilience and robustness, it is useful to consider their opposites. The opposite of robust is fragile. While the opposite of resilient is brittle. When expressed like this they even seem to be mutually exclusive. The human mind and by extension the organizations that people create have the capacity to be both.

Robustness is associated with strength and the will and capacity to withstand stresses—to persevere in the face of adversity. It is a characteristic that the thing or person has. Be wary though—there is a fine line between perseverance as a positive trait and bloody mindedness or what can be termed target fixation, which can lead to winning the battle and losing the war.

Resilience is about capacity and potential and is associated with what an organization does, it is the ability to adapt and do something different. Continuing the conflict metaphor, it would be expressed as, do we even need to fight, or do we not fight this battle and live to fight another day?

When resilience drifts outside of the current performance envelope the brittleness is exposed, you get catastrophic failure—things and people snap, they fracture, they shatter. Robustness fails differently, when you reach the limits of robustness, things and people get distorted or twisted, they get bent out of shape, they melt down.

A metaphor that works for the physical world is Damascus steel, which was created when sword makers blended steels that had different qualities. The best steel for sharpening and holding an edge had a downside, it was brittle and would break in combat. So, they folded it in layers of more flexible and therefore more resilient steel, this steel was softer and didn't hold an edge but the combined steel, Damascus steel was better than anything else.

Understanding and developing both robustness and resilience is also highly correlated with sustainable high performance and is what distinguishes organizations like the SAS.

The Petrochemical industry, and many other high risk industries, have suffered from a lack of both resilience and robustness as a result of poor leadership and management. The BP Texas City explosion in 2005 is a good example of where a lack of resilience and robustness allowed complacency and risk-blindness to creep into the running of the operation. Complacency typically affects one's ability to see things as they are and leads to risk-blindness and a failure to adapt as and where needed. The result is a lack of robustness and resilience.

When you investigate failure and accident causation do you make the distinction between failures in robustness compared to failures in resilience? The remedial actions are often quite different, especially in regard to people. The capacity for robustness can be developed through education and training, whereas resilience is a factor of intelligence and character and is best achieved through firstly selecting the right people.

Unless we maintain situational awareness and stay real to the risks of whatever it is that we are doing, the outcome can be very different to the expectation. In a work environment this is the role of leaders. It falls upon the leader to create the shared understanding and commitment to doing the necessary things to create safe operations.

The SAS Black Hawk Tragedy
On the 12th of June 1996 I got in my car to drive to work at the Special Air Service Regiment in Perth, Western Australia. I had left the regular Army and the SAS four years earlier but had been invited to join the small Reserve component of the SAS to work on a special project. I started the short trip to work expecting that day to be much like the day before. I turned on the radio to catch the news and was hit by the report that there had been a crash involving Black Hawk helicopters and the SAS. Details were sketchy, but the report confirmed that two helicopters had crashed and that there were many fatalities.

When I got to the front gate of Campbell Barracks, the home of the SAS Regiment (SASR), news vans and reporters were everywhere. Once I was inside the barracks, I went to the headquarters and arrived just in time to attend an update briefing on what was known at that time. The critical incident response team had been there through the night. The enormity of the catastrophe and the emotional roller coaster that they were on showed on their faces.

What was known was that two Black Hawks on a counter-terrorism training exercise had collided on approach to the target and had crashed to the ground in a fireball. Fifteen SAS soldiers and three army aviators were dead. The details of the injuries of the survivors were still coming through, but it was clear that several of the survivors were not in good shape. What became blatantly clear was that the lives of the families of those killed and the five SAS soldiers and three aviators that survived the crash were changed forever.

Just after the briefing the Commanding Officer of the SAS met with me and asked me to develop a plan to coordinate the various support agencies in order to make sure that the families of the victims got the support they needed.

It was still less than an hour since I had first turned on the radio. A sense of stunned disbelief was still present, and that was then overlaid with a barrage of questions that go through your mind – How could this happen? What had gone wrong? Would the injured all survive? How bad were they hurt? What about the families? There were no quick answers to many of these questions. We all had things that we could do to look after the survivors and all those who were affected by this tragedy, so we got busy and focused on the things that would make a difference.

After the funerals and the temporary shift in focus to care for the families of the fallen and the injured, the SAS regiment got back on with doing what it does. A while later, I was at a barbeque having a beer with several of the soldiers who were on that ill-fated training exercise and were in the helicopters following the lead choppers that crashed. *"How do you feel about the risks in the work you do?"* I asked. One of the soldiers responded *"We all knew that the risks were real. It has been a big kick in the guts to lose so many mates and to see all the pain that follows when it goes bad. But I have a job to do and I believe what we do is important, so I just have to get back on with it and make sure I do everything I can to the best of my ability and trust that everyone else does the same."* The other SAS Troopers nodded in agreement with the summation of what they had been through and how they felt about their purpose.

Training in the Australian SAS is incredibly real so that when individuals and teams are called upon to perform, they can do so. The consequence of this is that the SAS Regiment has lost more soldiers in training than it has in combat.

When it was revealed over the months that followed that this wasn't just a tragic accident and that it was preventable, it changed the way I thought about the incident and the loss of those lives. The board of inquiry identified that the events that laid the foundations for this accident went back seven years to when the Army acquired the Black Hawks in 1989. Between the Air Force and the Army, they got the spare parts and maintenance planning wrong and, in the years preceding the accident the defence force struggled to have sufficient serviceable helicopters to carry out the required aircrew training.

What was most shocking was that the consequences of this were identified in a review conducted by the 1st Division, the Army Command responsible for the operation of the Black Hawks. The report was released just 10 weeks before the accident and it identified that the aircrew in 5th Aviation Regiment had not been getting a great deal of practice, and their skills had degraded. It stated that the decrease in capability can be categorised in three areas—currency, proficiency, and safety. It specifically warned of degraded skills in formation flying, and support to special forces operations. It further warned that crews will not be fully proficient to undertake those demanding tasks.

Hollnagel states that resilience engineering proposes that four resilience potentials are of primary importance:

- the potential to monitor,
- the potential to learn,
- the potential to anticipate, and
- the potential to respond[7].

He highlights that these four potentials should not be rank ordered but are instead a continuous process that describes how a resilient organization functions.

The four resilience potentials—failing on the last hurdle
The Army system and the leaders, from the sharp end up to Formation Command level, had been monitoring all aspects of Black Hawk helicopter operations. They were learning and adapting how they operated and what they needed to do in an environment that had been allowed to drift to the very edge of the safety envelope. The 1st Division's formal review of the Black Hawk issues was provided to the Chief of the Army. It identified the deficiencies for what they were and advised that the deviations from good practice were no longer tolerable. But the Chief of the Army didn't respond and act on this report. The SAS and 5th Aviation were still tasked to train and be prepared to meet the Australian Government and Defence Force requirements for counter-terrorist response.

The accident was anticipated and, consistent with the characteristic of brittleness when resilience is pushed to the limits, the failure occurred in a catastrophic manner.

The board of inquiry report in the Black Hawk Tragedy stated explicitly that *"the systemic problems contributed to the tragic outcome, and that the shortage of serviceable aircraft, the reduction in aircrew proficiency, and the high resignation rates of trained pilots, were part of the conditions and environment in which the accident became inevitable."* [8]

However, after the crash, the Army blamed five operational level officers for the tragedy and commenced court martial proceedings against them.

No Generals were ever held responsible for the outcome.

The 12 months after the Black Hawk Tragedy was a defining time for me and its effect was to set me on the course that I continue to be on today. When you experience a catastrophic event like the Black Hawk accident it changes you. When you work in a high-risk environment, you know that the work you do is dangerous, but it is common to think *"it won't happen to me."* Or, to think that the training and the hard work you've done to develop and maintain competency and proficiency is enough. You think you've got the risks covered. You look out for yourself and you look out for your mate's safety and you trust everyone else to do the same. That works and can be effective for creating personal or individual safety at the sharp end, but it doesn't address the process safety issues or the organizational issues that create catastrophes—what industry calls Major Accident Events. The SAS Black Hawk Tragedy, NASA Challenger Disaster, BP Macondo, Boeing 737 Max are all examples of organizations failing to effectively manage the interconnection between technology and the people employing it.

Situational awareness and risk orientation

To achieve a change, it is imperative that Boards and senior leaders who are making the decisions about the quality and integrity of the operations must maintain situational awareness and a realistic risk orientation. In this book we discuss how the current approach to safety is failing to meet this need and how organizations can do a better job of:

1. Giving leaders at all levels the tools and understanding to properly evaluate and manage the risks,

2. Ensuring that the KPI's and feedback mechanisms used keeps leaders accurately informed as to what is happening at the job site, and

3. Creating the psychological safety where leaders at all levels are supported to make hard decisions.

I have given a lot thought to my journey in safety leadership and count myself lucky to have survived the personal near misses that I had in the first half of my life. Some may say that this is just a factor of getting older and that may in part be the case. But there is more to it than the wisdom gained through experience. There is a crucial role for leaders at all levels to provide the education and guidance needed to create the climate where operational risk does not get taken for granted.

As I studied accidents and understood more about why and how they happen, I have changed my perception and attitude towards risk. I am still OK with taking on an activity that involves risk, but I make sure that I understand the risk and make sure that my whole approach is safe. A question that I have learned to ask myself and one I recommend to anyone evaluating risk (basically every one of us at some point in time) is to ask ourselves, *"What's the worst thing that could realistically happen as a result of my actions, or my decision to allow an activity to start or continue?"* If I am not willing to accept that consequence, then the decision becomes an easy one. Don't do it or take action to better manage the risk!

My Safety Leadership Journey Through a Lifetime of Oil and Gas Operations
By Rod Ritchie

I started working for a company called Schlumberger in 1974 as a young field engineer.

Today Schlumberger unites 100,000 people representing 140 nationalities with products, sales, and services in more than 120 countries. It is the world's leading provider of technology for reservoir characterization, drilling, production, and processing in the global energy industry.

The first 14 years of my career with Schlumberger consisted of working in many countries in west Africa, in France and then in the Amazon basin in Peru, before working in Balikpapan in Indonesia. Working in these environments necessitated a vertical learning curve. It was, as I have come to understand, a masterclass in learning to be robust and resilient. We were expected to deal with chaos and the unexpected and be able to perform. I observed that while other companies at times had a culture of *"just get it done and I won't ask how you did it"* the expectation from Schlumberger to not take shortcuts and do things in a proper and orderly manner was always there. I also learned about company culture and a commitment to quality; we were expected to challenge our processes and strive to be innovative.

It is worth noting here that unlike other companies that simply promoted good operators and technicians into leadership roles, Schlumberger provided very good formal training and lots of mentoring to help me develop as a leader.

The formative lessons for me during this time were that shared meaning, trust and empowerment were critical to our success. I learned that as a leader it was my job to ensure that my whole team understood and were aligned to a common purpose and secondly from task to task, they understood my intent and expectations. I came to realise that my job was to provide the right support and encouragement and ensure they had the right resources and skills to do the job; they did the rest.

My next assignment was based in Dubai in the Middle East. With the commitment and endeavour of my team we created a highly profitable business. It wasn't the equipment and resources, the systems and processes, or rules that created this improvement—it was people.

I have always been passionate about HSE and so when offered the newly created role of Health, Safety, and Environment (HSE) Manager for the Middle East region I jumped at the opportunity. I believed there was so much more that had to be achieved in this field. Little did I know just how much needed to change in HSE, not only in Schlumberger but the Industry as a whole.

The First Gulf War
One of the biggest challenges that we faced in my time in that role was in 1991 in Kuwait following the Gulf War. In January and February 1991, the Iraqi military set fire to 700 oil wells as part of a scorched earth policy while retreating from Kuwait.

This catastrophic act of terrorism presented some mammoth challenges for the Kuwait Oil Company (KOC). This was not a normal oil well blow out, this was 700 Oil wells on fire in a recent war zone, so along with the typical risks associated with a well blow out they also faced the risk of Oil clouds, unexploded ordinance, oil lakes, smoke, and extreme driving risks.

KOC was desperate to extinguish these fires so the call went out to the industry for assistance in extinguishing the fires and getting the wells under control. Schlumberger was well positioned to be able to respond and was the first company on the ground in Kuwait. Being the *"first in"* also means high risk and the need to manage and adapt as the gaps between work as imagined and work as done become apparent.

Boots on the ground
As the Middle East HSE Manager, I was responsible for the HSE planning for how we were going to look after our people while undertaking this highly dangerous but essential work. The Kuwait Country Manager and I visited many sites to conduct risk assessments and planning before putting our people in the field. There were many hazards to be managed, Land mines had been placed in areas around the oil wells, and a military cleaning of the areas was necessary before the fires could be put out. It was a mammoth task; the fires were started in January and the last one was not extinguished until November.

The KOC were under pressure to extinguish the fires and control the environmental damage. It was evident that very few company background checks were carried out before the many companies started working in this high-risk environment. Our job was to support the many firefighting companies from every corner of the globe with equipment, technology and chemicals. It was soon obvious that there were widely varying degrees of experience, and more importantly safety leadership capability among the responders.

Our first challenge was to ensure that our crews remained safe while working with the firefighting crews. It was critical that we were aligned, and all had a shared meaning on just how our part was to play out.

Our teams had to be resilient and focussed on the right way to execute our part. We were clear that, in a novel situation everyone is a novice—we needed to create the right learning environment and support our people to manage the *"influence"* from some of the firefighting companies; some of which were called cowboys because of their unhealthy risk appetite.

Executing the response

We assembled our crews in Dubai to participate in two days of risk management training pertaining to Kuwait, before they were deployed to fight the fires.

These sessions were not just basic Safety recalibration but more about trust. We had to trust one another as the decisions of others could affect our safety in the field. So, agreements around trust and the empowerment for our crews to make decisions that they believed were correct were always supported by the leadership. This included knowing they had our full support to STOP the job to better manage the risk.

During our time in Kuwait our teams managed to extinguish 50% of the fires, but sadly this came at a cost. Our focus and diligent operational standards and leadership approach meant that we had no serious injuries at the well sites, but we unfortunately still lost two employees during this campaign. This was the result of one of our heavy vehicles inadvertently following a car carrying journalists who were completely lost and drove into a lake of crude oil which then ignited.

This tragic loss of life was gut wrenching for me. Informing the families that their loved ones were not coming home is a very tough thing to do.

This tragic accident helped me understand that there is always more to do with the way we lead and support our people. Don't ever think that the job is done, as good safety leadership is a journey not a destination.

While Kuwait presented very real and pressing challenges, the biggest challenge we faced in terms of the safety of our people in the Middle East was related to vehicle operations and safe driving. As a result of my experiences at the time, I wrote my first Society of Petroleum Engineers (SPE) paper titled *"Journey Management"* which turned out to be a game-changer for the industry. My passion for this subject probably stemmed back to my childhood when I lost my oldest brother in a car accident and that loss has always stuck with me. It is hard at any age to try to get your head around the reality that a life has been lost unnecessarily due to an error in judgment and lack of understanding that driving is, for most people, the greatest risk they will face during their life.

Based on this SPE paper we introduced a very strict driving policy in the Middle East, a couple of key elements were the use of seat belts and driving to the conditions. Amongst drivers and supervisors, I quickly became known for my unrelenting campaign on the commitment to this policy. Driving for many of us is very personal and not just work related. Most young men tend to think they are above average at it. So, telling someone that they are not doing it right is not the answer. To successfully change people's attitude to driving risk and their ability to manage the risk we had to change their understanding and their awareness.

Schlumberger were an industry leader in the introduction of In Vehicle Monitoring Systems (IVMS). When we introduced IVMS it was a part of a coaching and development program, where it was a useful tool to provide real-time and unbiased monitoring and feedback on driving behaviour to help drivers understand the driving practices that helped them remain safe. Sadly, for most companies it is currently used as a policing tool. For too many companies their approach involves very little coaching and development of drivers. They simply apply a three-warning process that results in people being sacked. This is symptomatic of the failings of the conventional approach to safety that just focuses on what went wrong and human error instead of training and developing people to create the capacity for things to go well.[9]

Following my time in the Middle East I headed up several Schlumberger operations headquartered at different times in Jakarta and Perth. In each case by focusing on creating shared meaning we were able to create teams that were aligned and committed to a common purpose. Once we got this, we were able to give people more autonomy. It never ceases to inspire me when I see how much people will step up and work hard for something they care about and where they feel that they can make a difference.

The work that we had done in leadership development, building of trust and a sense of being part of a supportive team really paid off in 1998 as my team responded to the very difficult and chaotic time when President Suharto was overthrown. In the midst of military action to put down civil unrest we evacuated all of the expat Schlumberger staff and the 425 members of their families. I am very proud of how well our people pulled together and looked out for each other through that chaotic time.

After several years in Indonesia, I was transferred back to Perth as the Oilfield Services HSE Manager for Australasia. It was in this role that I met Brett Read who I engaged to deliver safety leadership training for Schlumberger managers and supervisors.

In my various corporate roles, I continued to engage Brett and his company, Safety Leaders Group (SLG), and we have been very successful in creating leadership driven safety performance improvement. When I retired from my corporate role, I welcomed the opportunity to again work closely with Brett to share our understanding with other organizations. The results we have achieved while working together over the years in multiple countries around the world gives us a sense of pride to know that we have played a part in keeping people alive and safe. We will share some of these results in this book in the hope that we can continue to advance current thinking and safety leadership practices.

In 2002 I was offered the opportunity to work for an Oil and Gas company called OMV, headquartered in Vienna Austria.

Working for an oil company was very different and I thought at length about what I had learned working for a service company. In a service company, you get to work with a wide variety of clients and experience many difference cultures. I found it very educational to observe different cultures and approaches to leadership or flat out lack of leadership across different organizations. Schlumberger has a very strong focus on safety performance and we closely tracked our various team's performance working for different clients. It became very clear to me that all of the training and systems that we gave our people was not the major determinant of safety performance.

This was brought home loud and clear a number of years later by a Schlumberger presentation to the Drillsafe Forum in Australia. They presented HSE Performance results of the various service teams total recordable incident frequency rates (TRIF) by client. The 80/20 rule was very evident here. The results showed very clearly that 80% (41 out of 52) of Schlumberger teams and operators were working safely and not experiencing recordable incidents. The statistic that was even more insightful when examined, was that broadly, 90% of all incidents were experienced by teams working for just ten percent of clients.

Discussions with the Schlumberger crews working for these clients confirmed that the differences were subtle, they felt they were constantly pushed to just get the job done and to take shortcuts. They also felt that it was not safe to speak up and voice their concerns to the client. It is a rare individual who as a team leader will stand up to a senior client manager who is pushing them in this way. And it is a rare individual operator who, when working in this environment, will maintain the work practices and disciplines that create the situational awareness needed to proactively intervene and prevent an incident.

In the next chapter, we discuss in detail the huge impact that culture and direct leadership has on performance and how a management approach doesn't create change.

During my time in OMV Australia, I was also involved in the Australian chapter of the Society of Petroleum Engineers (SPE) to help with the HSE conferences. This was to be the start of a much greater involvement in both the SPE and the International Oil & Gas Producers Association over the next 10 years to try to change the way we approach safety in the Oil & Gas industry.

As previously mentioned, after working with Brett in Schlumberger, I engaged his company, Safety Leaders Group (SLG), to work with us on our approach to safety leadership in OMV. At the time we had a drilling campaign and an onshore gas plant development project in Australia and an offshore FPSO project in New Zealand. The challenge was to bring leadership teams together and to create a level of aligned performance as quickly and effectively as we could. Working with Brett we were able to combine and apply our expertise to develop a shared language and a framework that identified what leaders do and how they do it to create sustainable performance improvement. Our experience in these projects and operations reinforced that the leadership practices that drove safety performance also drove all other areas of performance in the business. Good leadership doesn't just affect one aspect of the business, safety performance is simply a clear and objective measure of how well we are performing from a leadership perspective. Our excellent results in HSE in the business in Australia and New Zealand attracted attention from OMV's management in Europe. Our operations were performing better than the rest of the company and in recognition of this I was offered the job as HSE Manager for the global Exploration and Production (E&P) Division of OMV located in Vienna, Austria. This decision was easy as it presented me with an opportunity to change a company culture. From what I had been able to observe of the broader company, I was clear that the HSE focus and knowledge of the line management in OMV at the time was certainly lacking and needed some serious influencing.

> The leadership practices that drove safety performance also drove all other areas of performance in the business.

Changing from a conventional safety approach

The first part of the business that we set our sights on was Austria. Safety performance in our Vienna basin operation was not good.

Up until 2004 OMV Austria had been engaging a well-known, large global safety consulting firm whose solution required significant ongoing investment in layer upon layer of their safety systems including, the ZERO slogans, STOP Cards and Safety Performance Curves. The result was an ever-increasing safety bureaucracy and what we later would come to see as a management approach to a leadership issue. They closely tracked lost time accident rate (LTI), which was running at 14 compared to the International Association of Oil and Gas Producers (IOGP) average which was 1.0 at the corresponding time. To put this into context—for every hour worked an employee was 14 times more likely to be hurt badly enough to be unable to return to work the next day compared to the *average* of the industry. We weren't average at safety; we were 14 time worse than average.

So, the statistics told us how bad we were doing, but they didn't tell us how to change this. In fact, focusing on these did the opposite. When leaders (who are getting paid bonuses for low safety statistics) talk about the number of incidents and errors, the only thing that workers hear is—your failings are costing me my bonus. I knew we needed to change the focus, so that it wasn't about the numbers. It needed to be about caring for people and their safety.

Once we recognized that our current efforts were not leading to sustainable safety performance improvement, we started to see the shortcomings for what they really were.

The root cause here was a lack of two things: firstly, a lack of leadership focus and secondly, a lack of clarity i.e., an understanding of what created great performance and a leadership commitment to doing those things well.

A leadership driven approach to safety

Based on the successes that we had in Australia and New Zealand, I knew that whatever we did needed to be driven by leadership. So, I again engaged Brett's company to help us create the change we needed. With SLG's guidance we embarked on a safety leadership development program across OMV's Austrian operations. The focus was on ownership of safety, making it personal and engaging people through shared meaning and autonomy. The message was initially met with scepticism from a jaded workforce who had grown tired of 4 years of *"the latest program."* However, this quickly changed as the GM in Austria and his leadership team embraced the Who CARES Wins approach and were seen by the workforce to be walking the talk. Over the next two years we made significant improvements in our safety performance. The third year saw OMV Austria achieve its first year of lost time injury free operations—an LTI frequency rate of zero.[10]

I headed the HSE function in the E&P group for five years and enjoyed the role as we managed to have a huge impact on the way we did business. Although not everyone in the company (at the time) appreciated where we were going on this HSE journey, no one could dispute the results that were achieved.

Safety performance improvement on a grand scale

The greatest challenge during this time was the merger and acquisition of Petrom the Romanian Oil and Gas company. At the time of the M&A Petrom had a headcount of 60,000 compared to OMV's headcount of 6000, plus a soviet based culture. The HSE culture was seriously lacking to the extent that every year more than 10 people were being killed while working for Petrom. It was very obvious to me that the root cause of the problem was a lack of leadership understanding and commitment. So again, aided by Brett and SLG we embarked on a two-pronged approach; the first was to educate the managers and the workforce on what was expected from them in terms of committing to the journey of change; the second was to develop a level of understanding with the leaders about how they could contribute to create the change needed.

Like any cultural change, this paradigm shift took several years of hard work and dedication. This focus paid off in 2010, when our Petrom business had its first year without a fatality.

In 2010 I was promoted to the role of Senior Vice President of HSSE which allowed me to have direct access to the executive board and the chance to help influence their decision making in terms of the long-term effects on performance and the safety of our stakeholders. The additional "S" in my title referred to Security which was added to my remit with promotion to Senior Vice President.

During my corporate tenure, I was heavily involved with the Society of Petroleum Engineers (SPE) and was the Chair of the Safety sub-committee for the global SPE HSE conferences. This involved the selection of all the papers and the panel sessions. At the same time, I was also involved with the international Oil & Gas Producers Association (IOGP) where I had several members of my HSSE team involved in improving the industry global standards that many companies use to this day.

In 2012 I decided it was time to retire from the corporate world and I was approached by SLG to help with some projects that included a Coal Seam Gas business in Queensland Australia and a leadership and cultural change program for a European Oil and Gas company operating in the Kurdistan region of Iraq.

I must admit that after 40 years in the Oil and Gas industry and having worked in many countries and different cultures it never ceases to amaze me that so many companies lack the basic leadership to enable a workforce to perform to its full potential.

The journey continues, and I refuse to give up on my quest to make a difference to the performance of companies wherever I am able to do so.

Key Takeaways from this Chapter
1. Resilience and robustness are key factors in safety performance.

2. Resilience is about capacity and potential and is associated with what an organization does, it is the ability to adapt and do something different.

3. Robustness is associated with strength and the will and capacity to withstand stresses—to persevere in the face of adversity. It is a characteristic that the thing or person has.

4. There are four resilience potentials are of primary importance: the potential to monitor, the potential to learn, the potential to anticipate, and the potential to respond.

5. When resilience drifts outside of the current performance envelope the brittleness is exposed, you get catastrophic failure—things and people snap, they fracture, they shatter.

6. Robustness fails differently, when you reach the limits of robustness, things and people get distorted or twisted, they get bent out of shape, they melt down.

Reflection Questions

1. Is your safety performance created by design or by default?

2. What percentage of your organization are actively engaged, committed and enthusiastic about their work, and how do you know?

3. When you investigate failure and accident causation do you make the distinction between failures in robustness compared to failures in resilience? The remedial actions are often quite different.

Endnotes:

[1] We discuss mastery as a part of Orientation in Chapter 6.

[2] Mann. A., and Harter, J. (2016). The Worldwide Employee Engagement Crisis. *Gallup Business Journal*, 7 January 2016

[3] Hollnagel, E. (2018). *Safety-II in Practice*. CRC Press. Kindle Edition. p.4.

[4] *ibid*. p. xiii.

[5] *Ibid*. p.14-15.

[6] Dekker, S. (2015). *Safety Differently: Human Factors for a New Era*. 2nd ed. CRC Press. Kindle Edition. p.269.

[7] Hollnagel *op cit*. p.24.

[8] 4 Corners. (1997) *Black Hawk Disaster, Australia, 1996 (Part 1)*. [video] https://www.youtube.com/watch?v=R3sD2TMwlEk
4 Corners. (1997) *Black Hawk Disaster, Australia, 1996 (Part 2)*. [video] https://www.youtube.com/watch?v=5042ShkHUo0

[9] Hollnagel *op. cit*. p.24.

[10] Read, B., Zartl-Klik, A., Veit, C., Zamhaber, R., and Zepic, H. (2010). Safety Leadership that Engages the Workforce to Create Sustainable HSE Performance. In: *SPE International Conference on Health Safety and Environment in Oil and Gas Exploration and Production*. Rio de Janeiro, Brazil, 12-14 April, 2010. SPE. https://onepetro.org/search-results?page=1&q=SPE-126901-MS

Chapter 2

A Common Thread of Industry Catastrophes

It is an unfortunate situation that when it comes to process safety and major accident events and catastrophes, such as the SAS Black Hawk Tragedy, BP Macondo Blow Out, the Pike River Mine Disaster, Volkswagen Emissions Scandal or the Boeing 737 Max crashes, the trust that we place in senior managers, government legislators and regulators is often misplaced.

Esso Longford Gas Plant Explosion

On 25 September 1998, Esso experienced a Major Accident Event (MAE) when a heat exchanger at its Longford Gas Plant, in Australia exploded. The resulting explosions and fire killed two workers and injured eight others. A safety audit conducted by Esso's parent company Exxon only months before had given the plant a clean bill of health. Esso subsequently blamed four operators for the accident and sacked them.

The Royal Commission into the Longford Explosion came to a very different conclusion. It found that years of cost cutting had resulted in deficiencies in the skills and competency required for those operators to make the necessary risk management decisions.

BP and a decade of catastrophes

On 23 March 2005, an explosion at the BP Texas City Refinery killed 15 workers and injured 170. BP initially blamed six operators and supervisors for the accident and sacked them. The US Chemical Safety Board (USCSB) investigation into the accident found the ultimate cause for the accident could be traced back to management decisions about cost cutting, resourcing levels and lack of accountabilities for safe operation of the refinery. The sacked BP workers subsequently won payouts for damages from BP for their dismissal.

Tony Hayward, the CEO of BP when the Deepwater Horizon accident happened on the Macondo Well in the Gulf of Mexico in April 2010, asked the question *"What did we do to deserve this?"*

A better question would have been – *What did we do to create this?* Or, *What were we missing that allowed this to happen?*

Over a 10-year period BP had multiple MAE's that in every case have been linked back to poor safety leadership in the form of cost cutting and putting production ahead of safety or environmental concerns.

1. 2000 BP Grangemouth Refinery, Scotland. Major explosion and asset damage.

2. 2005 BP Texas City Refinery, Texas. Major explosion and asset damage, 15 fatalities and more than 170 injuries.

3. 2006 BP Pipelines Prudhoe Bay, Alaska. Major corrosion and loss of containment resulting in a huge environmental disaster.

4. 2010 BP Macondo Well, Gulf of Mexico. Major blow out on the Transocean Deepwater Horizon drilling rig. 11 fatalities, the loss of the Deepwater Horizon and the largest offshore environmental disaster in US History.

BP makes for a powerful case study in terms of individual MAE's and their causes. But there is another lesson in BP's performance post Macondo. BP seems to have addressed their issues and is a good example that reinforces that the solution starts with leadership. It is ten years since Macondo and Bob Dudley stepping in as CEO. BP has had a very different second decade of this century compared to the first.

After each MAE BP made assurances to their stakeholders that they were effectively addressing their shortcomings. However, the recurring nature of these MAE's in BP's operations suggested a fundamental lack of understanding of the debilitating effect of fundamental inconsistencies between management rhetoric and effective leadership actions. The result has been the very sad loss of life of many people working for BP and major environmental disasters in Alaska and the Gulf of Mexico. The financial impact for BP shareholders has been enormous. BP has incurred repeated convictions in UK and US courts, paid out more than $60 billion dollars in fines and compensation which eroded shareholder value.[1] The reputation of the oil and gas industry has also been severely damaged as highlighted in the National Commission on BP Deepwater Horizon and Offshore Drilling Report to the President which stated:

> "The immediate causes of the Macondo well blowout can be traced to a series of identifiable mistakes made by BP, Halliburton, and Transocean that reveal such systematic failures in risk management that they place in doubt the safety culture of the entire industry."[2]

The media in the aftermath of the Macondo Blowout tried to paint BP as reckless and Tony Hayward as not up to the job as CEO. The truth is not as simple as that. Loren Steffy in his book *Drowning in Oil,* points out the mammoth job that Hayward faced when he took over as CEO.

Many authors have written about the reckless cost cutting that occurred in BP in the period before Tony Hayward was appointed to the CEO role. There is no doubt that BP management became complacent about the risks of running complex facilities and operations and convinced themselves that they could effectively operate at lower costs than their peers.

Steffy points out that, *"Hayward also took office amid three criminal investigations and jump-starting the huge cultural change that his fundamentally staid company needed fell squarely on him."*[3]

Since he took over in 2005 after the Texas City refinery explosion Hayward had instigated a lot of change in BP. He replaced John Manzoni who was the Global Head of Refining in BP and instigated several programs aimed at changing the leadership practices and culture. However, the complexity of creating a unified culture is highlighted by BP's results. At the same time that BP was having these MAE's in the UK and US it ran world class operations in many other parts of the world. The issue for BP was that there were clearly pockets of resistance within their global operations that just didn't get it. The managers who were running the Macondo field in the Gulf of Mexico clearly were not running those operations to the standard that Hayward and BP wanted. Had the highest levels of BP been aware of the shortcuts and poor decisions being made on Macondo they surely would have intervened; but they weren't aware. The BP salary structure was heavily biased towards individual bonuses which undoubtedly influenced the decision-making process and contributed to the factors that led to the MAE's. The managers of Macondo either could not understand or did not want to buy-in to what Hayward was trying to achieve.

We believe the biggest factor that limited Hayward's effectiveness in changing the BP culture was that BP had no effective measures that proactively highlighted the poor leadership practices on the Macondo operation. This is not a problem that is unique to BP. Steven Newman the President and COO of Transocean who owned and operated the Deepwater Horizon drilling rig that exploded and sunk on the Macondo well was grappling with this issue as well. In an email to his managers, he criticised the Key Performance Indicators being used to report to him. Newman wrote in an email:

> *"I am not convinced at all that we have the right leading indicators. The leading indicators we report today are all just different incident metrics — they have nothing to do with actually preventing accidents. What if we asked our OIMs to report the number of tasks that proceeded without a think plan discussion? Their first response would obviously be zero — which would then be the start of an interesting conversation (how do you KNOW that?). This is by no means a scientifically measured leading indicator, but the nature of the discussion would get the OIMs thinking about the culture on the decks — and the only way they could really meaningfully answer the questions would be to get out on the decks."*[4]

Newman clearly understood that what he needed in the field were leaders that got out on the decks and confirmed—that what they expected was being done. And what he needed was a set of leading indicators that confirmed for him that this was being done. Unfortunately, he didn't have them. This is a failing on the part of the organizational managers and the experts that advise them which we will explore further in the discussion of case studies in this book.

This goes to the heart of the problem arising from the conventional approach to safety. Even when you have leaders like Newman who want to do the right thing, the current safety system lets them down. On the one hand he is being told that the Deepwater Horizon is a very safe rig—they've had 7 years without a lost time injury. His senior managers and auditors are visiting the rig and are not highlighting major concerns about how things are being done. How are leaders like Newman supposed to provide the necessary leadership, that is required to make a difference in safety when the system is flawed and doesn't give them what they really need?

What Newman was effectively saying to his organization was that, I want us to work safely. I want us to be a safe organization. I want to make sure that the things we are doing are going to create this. But what you are giving me does not fill me with confidence and basically, he is asking: Is this all we have? Is this as good as we can do?

At the time of the Macondo blow out, the Oil & Gas industry in general was also in the early stages of implementing process safety indicators and the BP drilling team on Macondo had no effective measures of process safety; there was a blinkered concentration on personal safety.

You can blame or learn

There is a very clear need for better leading indicators on the people side of safety, coupled with a better understanding of how people interconnect with technology and systems. To do this effectively will require a rethinking and reimagining of how organizations work with the human and social factors relating to leadership and team performance.

The common thread with the above MAE's is that each of them was years in the making. Often from the boardroom down, decisions that are made "*today*" can have the ability to kill people in the years to come.

Todd Conklin has written extensively on the topic of blame and the detrimental impact it has on learning.[5] Conklin is renowned for the axiom of, "*You can blame, or you can learn; you can't do both.*"

It is easy to blame the individuals who were filling the various positions at the time the accident occurred. But blame doesn't fix things, it often incorrectly makes it seem like the error was a choice. In some cases, the leaders in charge of the operations were just the unfortunate souls who were in the hot seat when someone triggered the booby trap that had been laid years earlier by decision makers somewhere in the management structure.

The explosion at the BP Texas City Refinery that killed 15 people is a case in point. BP took over the refinery from Amoco in 1999 and applied continued costs cuts over a six year period until the explosion and fire in March 2005. The plant had five refinery managers in the six years that BP owned it. The refinery manager at the time of the explosion was deeply concerned about the safety performance of the refinery he had recently taken over. He reviewed accident records from the plant over the preceding decades and was dismayed to find 22 fatalities from an ongoing series of accidents. In late 2004 he flew to London to present his findings to the VP of Global Refining and to plead for budget relief to address his many concerns.[6] One of the previous cost-cutting decisions, made in 2002 by the refinery manager at the time was to not connect a flare to the unit that later exploded and killed 15 people and injured 180 others. That decision saved $150,000. Had the flare been installed the explosion would not have happened.

Our observations and the experience gained through too many years and instances of MAE's is that it is not an effective approach to make people the problem. We need to focus on our attitude and understanding of the art of leading and the science of managing safety in our operations if we are to improve.

The fact that the individuals, at any level of management, did not see these events for what they were, also highlights the challenging issue of dealing with the complexity of modern-day sociotechnical operations. If your organization does not have an effective methodology for measuring the leadership practices, skills and competencies required to maintain operational integrity, these can degrade over time without the issue being recognised. When this decline in operational integrity goes unrecognised and not addressed, it lays the foundations for a catastrophe. In the above cases, many of the managers and operators that were filling their role when the event happened were not the decision makers who laid the foundations for the accidents. Just as in the case of the SAS Blackhawk Tragedy, they became part of the weakened fabric of operational integrity that made the event possible.

What we know from studying these catastrophes is that it is rarely one event or one single cause that leads to the accident. There are typically multiple causes that come together to create the event. This is a double-edged sword, as it can make it difficult to identify the weak signals that forewarn of an impending catastrophe. However, it also means that there are usually several opportunities to stop the accident from happening; in the majority of incidents someone will have seen the issue developing but all too often because of a lack of psychological safety or a flawed ineffective bureaucratic approach, they do not speak up or are not listened to—this is where caring leadership can help have these (weak) signals recognised and acted upon.

The challenge is to create the trust and psychological safety, that allows the workforce to feel they can speak up without repercussions from management. This is undeniably a leadership challenge. Accepting this challenge starts with recognising that the current conventional approach to safety is not meeting this need. Organizations, educational institutions, and regulators need to change if we are to move safety beyond the current level of performance.

Changing our view of safety

The term *chronic unease* has been used to capture the sense of awareness needed to maintain safety in high risk work environments. In our work with high performing teams, we have noted that the best teams, the best performers, have a more positive mindset about their role and how they create outstanding performance. This was summed up by a drilling manager who said, *"Unforeseen events or difficult situations can and do happen and they happen for a variety of reasons. It is up to everyone involved in our work to make sure that these events don't happen to us or if they do, we have a plan to deal with them. Myself and everyone that works here, needs to maintain constant vigilance to ensure that what we set out to do, is done and what we expect to happen, does happen. The moment we see that this is not the case we need to respond and act."* Constant vigilance is the positive mindset that outstanding performers bring to the game to make sure that things go well. This is the mastery mindset that high reliability organizations use to create robust and resilient organizations.

Here's how James Reason, describes high reliability organizations. He highlights how they have incorporated their awareness of the ever-present nature of risk into the functioning of their systems.

> *"High reliability organisations are the prime examples of the system approach. They anticipate the worst and equip themselves to deal with it at all levels of the organisation. It is hard, even unnatural, for individuals to remain chronically uneasy, so their organisational culture takes on a profound significance. Individuals may forget to be afraid, but the culture of a high reliability organisation provides them with both the reminders and the tools to help them remember. For these organisations, the pursuit of safety is not so much about preventing isolated failures, either human or technical, as about making the system as robust as is practicable in the face of its human and operational hazards. High reliability organisations are not immune to adverse events, but they have learnt the knack of converting these occasional setbacks into enhanced resilience of the system."[7]*

Constant vigilance means having the wisdom to focus on what is needed to make things go well.

But this is contrary to the conventional industry safety approach with its focus on lagging indicators, in the misguided perception that not having an incident in the past is a predictor of future performance. The Deepwater Horizon Drilling Rig which was celebrating seven years without a lost time incident when it exploded, killing 11 workers, rang alarm bells for many. Unfortunately, there is still more work to be done to bring about the paradigm shift required for authentic, leadership driven, safety performance.

A sad reality that we see played out in business, organizational and government scenarios is that accidents continue to happen as a result of completely predictable and preventable circumstances. Over the years as we have witnessed and researched accidents and catastrophes, one aspect of flawed human behaviour and decision making stands out. It is the propensity for the responsible people to not act on the warning signs. To ignore the risk and to fail to prepare or change course. It seems that there is never enough time or resources to do it right the first time around, but once the catastrophe happens there is always enough to fix it then.

Prior to the 2005 explosion at the Texas City Refinery BP failed to spend the money to fix the degraded refinery they acquired in the 1999 Amoco merger.[8] After the explosion and after paying the record fines and compensation to the victims, BP came up with more than $1billion to fix the previously identified problems at the refinery.

We have spent the last 25 years researching and studying safety performance and looking at both ends of the spectrum. We believe it is important to understand the thinking and the leadership practices that make an organization more likely to have a MAE. However, it is more important to understand the leadership and work practices of the best performing organizations—to understand and focus on doing what's needed to ensure things go well.

The top performing organizations know that outstanding performance is not created through fear and moving away from what they don't want. Focusing on the negative, tracking lagging indicators that measure failure and errors, doesn't create the performance mindset needed. Rather than focusing on what they don't want, the best performers are clear about their purpose and focus on moving towards what they want and what it takes to create this culture.

In every successful case of organizational performance improvement that we have helped create, this shift in thinking and what was driving motivation was at the heart of the change. This is about creating psychological safety based on a powerful Why. Figure 2 below is a model that we use which has been adapted from Peter Fuda's concept of motivation and moving from a burning platform to burning ambition.[9]

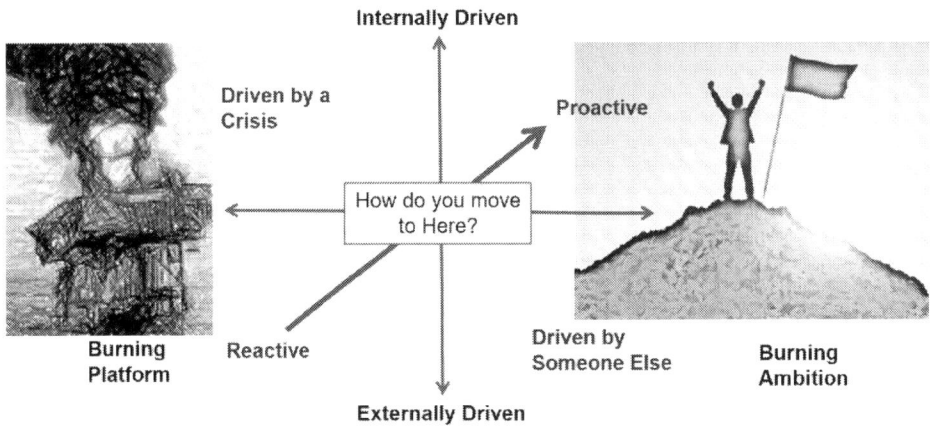

Figure 2. From Burning Platform to Burning Ambition

The burning platform metaphor which was linked to the decision of Andy Mochan to jump from the Piper Alpha Oil Platform in the North Sea in 1988 has been used by numerous authors.[10]

Fuda highlighted the shortcomings of being driven by a fear of crisis or impending doom. He noted that moving towards what you want in a purposeful way brings with it a completely different energy to backing away or shielding yourself from what you fear. This is the mindset of leaders who choose to accept the responsibility for creating the psychological safety that creates sustainable performance. They and every leader in their organization actively designs it and orients their performance focus towards achieving this balance.

We are not saying that you can control everything that happens in the workplace or in your life for that matter. But you can choose to be a resilient safety leader and decide how you respond to circumstances and events. A problem can be seen as an issue to worry about and fret over, or a situation that is either dealt with or accepted; that is the decision a true leader can take.

To quote Jim Rohn, *"In the process of living, the winds of circumstances blow on us all in an unending flow that touches each of our lives.... It's not about the wind that blows, it's how you set the sails."*[11]

Sometimes the seas and the weather are in your favour. You have a good tail wind and flat seas, and you can get to your destination on a screaming reach that has you there in good time and feeling comfortable. But there are also times when everything is against you, you are faced with a howling head wind and rough stormy seas. You can give up and forget about your plans or you can choose to reset the sails and steer a different course to get to your planned destination. Effective safety leadership is fundamentally about having the courage to make the difficult choices and do the hard yards to achieve your goals. Choices and actions have consequences but having experienced the pain and suffering of the victims of major accidents we are very clear which are easier to live with in the long term.

We discussed at the start of this book that meditation was the noblest path to wisdom. Developing the concepts in this book has helped us gain new levels of clarity. It's important here to note that none of the things we recommend in this book are hypothetical or based on theoretical concepts developed by people who have never led teams in real high-risk work environments. The solutions we put forward have been developed through experience, they are leadership driven and are based on enabling workers and teams who genuinely just want to do a good job and stay safe to work effectively. The solutions don't need external rule enforcers playing Cop or people offering prizes and rewards to make people work. They just need authentic leadership focused on creating trust, shared meaning, and common purpose.

This understanding and the insights that come from it, has enabled us to help leaders we have coached and developed to reflect and meditate on what's possible and to become better safety leaders.

Performance is either created by design or by default. In business, the end game is to improve the performance and competitiveness of our organization. Leadership is the key here; it creates sustainable safety, but it achieves much more. All areas of performance are driven by the same things. You don't see a safe company with bad results in other measures of performance.

Key Takeaways from this Chapter

1. Effective safety leadership is fundamentally about having the courage to make the difficult choices and do the hard yards to achieve your goals.

2. Constant vigilance instead of chronic unease. Moving towards what you want in a purposeful way brings with it a completely different energy to backing away or shielding yourself from what you fear.

Reflection Questions

1. How often do I ask myself: What did we do to create this? Or, What were we missing that allowed this to happen?

2. As a leader do you choose to accept the responsibility for creating the psychological safety that creates sustainable performance?

3. As a leader am I driven by fear of things going wrong—the burning platform? Or

4. Am I driven by an intention to proactively create something that is values based—a burning ambition?

5. Do I focus on what is needed to make things go well?

Endnotes:

[1] Hopkins, A. (2009). *Failure to Learn: the BP Texas City refinery disaster*. CCH Australia Ltd. Print.
Steffy, L. C. (2011). *Drowning in Oil: BP and the Reckless Pursuit of Profit*. McGraw Hill. Print.
[2] National Commission on the BP Deepwater Horizon Spill and Offshore Drilling., (2011). *Deep Water: The Gulf Oil Disaster and the Future of Offshore Drilling: Report to the President*. https://www.govinfo.gov/content/pkg/GPO-OILCOMMISSION/pdf/GPO-OILCOMMISSION.pdf
[3] Steffy *Op. Cit.*
[4] Newman, S. (2009). *FW: Preliminary thoughts and supplementary info*. [email]. p.TRN-MDL-03999532.
http://www.mdl2179trialdocs.com/releases/release201303211200016/TREX-26032.pdf
[5] Conklin, T. (2019). *The 5 Principles of Human Performance: A contemporary update of the building blocks of Human Performance for the new view of safety*. Kindle Edition.
[6] U.S. Chemical Safety and Hazard Investigation Board. (2007). *Investigation Report: Refinery Explosion and Fire*. [online] BP Texas City March 23, 2005. USCSHIB.
https://www.csb.gov/bp-america-refinery-explosion/
[7] Reason, J. (2000). Human error: models and management. *BMJ*, [online] 320(7237), pp.768–770. doi:10.1136/bmj.320.7237.768
[8] U.S. Chemical Safety and Hazard Investigation Board. (2007). *Investigation Report: Refinery Explosion and Fire*. [online] BP Texas City March 23, 2005. USCSHIB, p.153.
https://www.csb.gov/bp-america-refinery-explosion/
[9] Fuda, P. (2013) *Leadership Transformed*. Profile Books. Print.
[10] Connor, D.R. (1992) *Managing at the Speed of Change: How Resilient Managers Succeed and Prosper Where Others Fail*. Random House. Print.
[11] Rohn, J. (2004) *The Set of the Sail*. [online] http://www.appleseeds.org/Rohn_set-sail.htm

Chapter 3

A Management Approach to a Leadership Issue
A 3D Vs a 4D Approach

> *"A good intention, with a bad approach, often leads to a poor result."*
>
> — Thomas A. Edison

There is something missing in the way many businesses currently approach their safety performance and performance in general. Their mindset towards performance and failure plays a key role in what they focus on, how they lead their people and the results they get.

The science of management has taught us to manage and track 3 Dimensions in our business. These 3 Dimensions are:

1. Production and schedules,

2. Costs and resources,

3. Systems and processes using a mixture of lagging and leading indicators.

The increasing complexity of business means that it is essential that we get these 3 Dimensions right. If any of these dimensions are not adequately planned or managed to create robust systems, then performance will suffer or possibly fail all together.

What seems to not be understood by too many business managers is that getting the first 3 Dimensions right is not enough. These 3 Dimensions are merely enablers of performance; they are based on systems thinking and they focus on compliance with that system. But they don't create commitment.

> *"A system or a procedure never achieved anything, it is people being committed to implementing the system that achieves the performance needed."*
> — *Safety Leaders Group*

Creating the commitment to follow procedures and to do things well is the role of leaders. The occurrence of workers not following established procedures is not because of poor workers, it is the result of poor leadership. In the words of Clive Lloyd, *"Behaviors are not the problem—they are expressions of the problem."*[1]

In the conventional approach to safety, huge levels of resources are expended measuring and monitoring the first 3 Dimensions. Managers of these systems can tell you the cost of every aspect of the system—but they can't tell you the value of much of it. Typically, they have a technical focus on the robustness of the system, while very little attention is given to track and monitor resilience and the effectiveness of the 4th Dimension—people and safety leadership.

In the 3D management approach and even more so if there is a Behavioural Based Safety (BBS) program running in conjunction with it, we count what we can count—we don't count what counts.

In 2015 Professors Erik Hollnagel, Robert Wears and Jeffery Braithwaite published a White Paper titled *From Safety-I to Safety-II* highlighting the current limitations and issues in safety. In the White Paper they described the issues that they identified with the current approach to safety as follows:

> *"Most people think of safety as the absence of accidents and incidents (or as an acceptable level of risk). In this perspective, which we term Safety-I, safety is defined as a state where as few things as possible go wrong. A Safety-I approach presumes that things go wrong because of identifiable failures or malfunctions of specific components: technology, procedures, the human workers and the organisations in which they are embedded."*

> *"Humans—acting alone or collectively—are therefore viewed predominantly as a liability or hazard, principally because they are the most variable of these components. The purpose of accident investigation in Safety-I is to identify the causes and contributory factors of adverse outcomes, while risk assessment aims to determine their likelihood. The safety management principle is to respond when something happens or is categorised as an unacceptable risk, usually by trying to eliminate causes or improve barriers, or both."[2]*

The issue is that the way the conventional approach to safety currently functions, it creates safety managers not safety leaders. Of course, not everyone who comes through this system thinks like this. There are many good leaders out there, but when we talk to them, we are more frequently hearing that they are observing and experiencing a growing lack of leadership in industry. Regulators and companies are increasingly relying on a management approach, resulting in more and more complex systems and audits attempting to create a safe workplace.

4-Dimensional Performance and Safety

The 4 dimensions that create sustainable safety are:

1. Production and schedules,

2. Costs and resources,

3. Systems and processes using a mixture of lagging and leading indicators.

4. Safety leadership practices that create a commitment to a common purpose—ensuring that things go well.

The conventional approach to safety must move beyond compliance to focus on a commitment to do the things that create and drive safety performance.

That requires us to move beyond the realms of systems thinking and management and into this 4th Dimension of performance—which requires a mastery orientation and is about human factors, emotional intelligence, leadership, Open Systems[3], Complex Adaptive Systems (CAS)[4] and Complex Responsive Processes (CRP)[5].

A fundamental principle of human performance is that everyone makes mistakes—people are not perfect. Todd Conklin provides some insight here, *"... if you design and create a process that demands perfection from an imperfect and normal human operator and your designed process fails because of an operator error or mistake, this failure is the product of the system design and not of the human operator."*[6] People don't choose to make an error or mistake, it's not about choice. Errors and mistakes happen because people are fundamentally fallible. It's why the KISS principle (keep it simple, stupid) was created.

Companies and the managers that are responsible for protecting shareholders' funds face a very real dilemma. They must be able to show that they have taken appropriate actions to ensure they have created a safe workplace. When it comes to dealing with regulators or the courts the conventional Safety-I approach to this is to be able to show compliance or at least the expectation of compliance with a very detailed and prescriptive management system. We call this *"a management approach to a leadership issue."* It is increasingly being shown to not work and is being called out by a growing number of authors,[7] academics[,8] and practitioners[9] who are showing this approach for the fallacy that it is.

The Zero Injuries Fallacy and other credibility destroying mantras

All of the authors referenced in the preceding paragraph have written about and provided detailed accounts and discussions of research that highlights the limitations and flaws with the zero injuries/zero harm/all injuries are preventable mantra, so we will not spend more time on this, except to say that we absolutely agree.

*"**To be** persuasive, We must be believable,*
***To be** believable, We must be credible.*
***To be** credible, We must be **truthful**."*
— *Edward R. Murrow*

The leadership and specifically safety leadership that creates 4-Dimensional Safety is not a prescriptive, binary, on or off issue. Human interaction and influence is much more complex than that. Effective leadership is nuanced and dynamic and must be crafted to suit the context and the audience. Prescriptive mantras that on even superficial analysis are seen to be fanciful do nothing whatsoever for the leader's credibility, respect, and effectiveness.

The *"Safety First"* and *"Safety is our highest priority"* mantras that we hear from so many companies are clear examples of where Safety has been led down the garden path by people who clearly don't understand the importance of leaders being credible in what they say and do. Let's just explore the statements of safety first and safety is our highest priority to see how credible they are. There is no company in the world that manages operational risk to zero, it's not possible—your risk register confirms this fact, and your workers and the public know that. The best companies manage risk to the accepted principle of ALARP, As Low As Reasonably Practicable. Plenty of companies actually manage risk to a tacit standard of ALARA— As Low As the Regulator Allows. Given that you don't and can't manage risk to zero, it stands to reason that you can't guarantee that the low probability risk that you've accepted causes an incident. If the *"Safety First"* and *"Safety is our highest priority"* devotees really meant what they said they would never start work. We have had companies who have said to us that, *"We don't mean it that way."* Or the proponents of Zero Harm that have contested *"It's more of an aspiration."* From a leadership perspective, any statement that you make that can't stand on its own veracity, that needs qualifying is hugely damaging to your credibility.

Please understand that the gap between the mantras, the management speak, and the reality is like a huge spotlight on what is perceived by many workers as serious integrity and credibility issues. Is it any wonder that when these same managers then say to their workforce that they care about their safety that it falls on deaf ears.

This is also where a behaviour-based safety approach which is based on the behavioural psychology principles of operant conditioning is incomplete and doesn't work in complex work environments—we will speak more on that topic in Part 2.

Our advice is that the preferred statement should always be along the lines of:

The Safety of our workers and stakeholders is a core value. Wherever Safety comes into conflict with schedule, production, costs or any other business metric, Safety must always take precedence.

41

The issue with the conventional approach is that young operators, engineers, supervisors, and managers get taught to focus on KPI's that measure and reward compliance with the 3D systems. Remember we said earlier getting the first 3-Dimensions right only creates the conditions for safe operations; it does not guarantee safety. The issue is that the leaders and those making risk management decisions do not effectively understand the 4th dimension, the people and leadership, which is what actually creates and drives safety performance. Consequently, too many people are not clear what a real commitment to safety and the appropriate safety leadership practices look like. When the gaps in their thinking and understanding result in an accident, the powers that be, blame the individual instead of addressing the shortcomings in the overall approach.

Greg Smith the author of *Papersafe: The triumph of bureaucracy in safety management (2018)* is a lawyer specializing in Employment Law and Workplace Health & Safety. Smith expressed his concerns for the current direction of safety as follows:

> *"At some point health and safety management seems to have lost its way. Rather than being concerned about protecting workers and others from the hazards associated with business, health and safety management has devolved into a self-perpetuating industry which has driven a wedge between management and the workforce. Health and safety management has become synonymous with trivial rules and burdensome, never ending paperwork."*

Smith called for the need for change to reduce bureaucracy, expressing his concerns as:

1. *"Safety management can become too bureaucratic to work effectively.*

2. *Bureaucracy hides the true state of safety and creates an illusion safety is well managed, when it is not.*

3. *Much of what we do in the name of safety management, especially the bureaucracy and administration, is unnecessary and ineffective – it adds nothing to the 'safety' of workplaces.*

4. *Bureaucracy makes life harder for workers and more difficult for them to understand the health and safety risks in the workplace.*

5. *Bureaucracy distracts organisations, so they do not pay proper attention to what they say they do in the name of health and safety. They do not analyse their information and they do not know if their health and safety initiatives 'work'."*[10]

Sustainable safety is not created by tracking accidents and focusing on eliminating errors—the conventional, performance-oriented approach to safety. It is created by leaders doing specific leadership practices (that we know create performance) as well as they possibly can—what we call a mastery orientation (see Chapter 6 for a more detailed discussion of mastery orientation).

Hollnagel (2015) when he discusses the change in safety that is needed uses the phrase "*doing things well*" as distinct to "*doing things right*". It's important to understand this distinction and why we should think of and focus on doing things well as opposed to—just doing things in the right way. To focus on "*doing things right*" would imply that safety is created by doing things a specific way—this is systems thinking and is more aligned to conventional or Safety-I thinking. It would only be dealing with the technical aspects of safety and would be ignoring the social or Human and Organizational Performance (HOP) aspects of safety.

Increasingly, industries such as health care and aviation are starting to shift the focus from just looking at accidents and what went wrong.

Marit de Vos a researcher from Leiden University Medical Centre uses a powerful analogy,

> *"It's like we've been trying to learn about marriage by only studying divorce."*[11]

The analogy is insightful. If you were starting out on a marriage you wanted to last for the rest of your life ...wouldn't you be well served by talking to couples who have been married for decades ...or would you only focus on the train wrecks?

Safety is no different, the behaviours and conditions that cause things to go well are quite distinct from what causes things to go wrong.

Pilot and aviation safety expert Stuart Lau says that,

> *"Research suggests there are many opportunities to learn from the behavior of those pilots that excel in very complex and dynamic operating environments."*

> *"For pilots, this concept moves from identifying the occasional human error to finding those practices where, day-in and day-out, crews adapt and adjust to successfully mitigate threats and trap errors."*

> *"Recognizing that sound operating procedures are the basis of safe operations, there are those scenarios that take a flight crew 'off script' or are displaced from center. The strength of the resilient pilot is to recover from these distractions caused by weather, mechanical delays, system malfunctions, or other factors. Cognition—the ability to learn, adapt, and adjust—is a strength of the human mind."*[12]

Balancing the good and the bad

It is important to recognise that many of the improvements in safety performance over decades have been delivered by improvements in systems used for controlling and managing the 3-Dimensional enablers of performance i.e., better trained and more competent frontline operators, better processes, safer equipment etc. We refer to this as 3D safety. These developments are important and the management focus on refining the enablers of safety performance needs to continue. However, in order to successfully confront the current shortcomings, we need more than processes and systems. In parallel to these we must focus on the safety leadership practices that actually drive safety performance. We need a triumph of mastery over bureaucracy—4D Safety.

Applying a 4-Dimensional Safety approach effectively operationalises Safety II. It allows for an important mind shift from as few things as possible go wrong to ensuring that as many things as possible go well.

Sustainable improvements in safety performance will only come about by changing the current industry approach which is not effectively focusing on and addressing the complete picture.[13]

Simon Sinek in his book *Start With Why*[14] describes the difference between US and Japanese auto design and manufacturing:

> *"We can continue to slice and dice all the options in every direction, but at the end of all the good advice and all the compelling evidence, we're left where we started: how to explain or decide a course of action that yields a desired effect that is repeatable. How can we have 20/20 foresight? There is a wonderful story of a group of American car executives who went to Japan to see a Japanese assembly line. At the end of the line, the doors were put on the hinges, the same as in America. But something was missing. In the United States, a line worker would take a rubber mallet and tap the edges of the door to ensure that it fit perfectly. In Japan, that job didn't seem to exist. Confused, the American auto executives asked at what point they made sure the door fit perfectly. Their Japanese guide looked at them and smiled sheepishly. 'We make sure it fits when we design it.' In the Japanese auto plant, they didn't examine the problem and accumulate data to figure out the best solution—they engineered the outcome they wanted from the beginning. If they didn't achieve their desired outcome, they understood it was because of a decision they made at the start of the process."*

> *"All this for no other reason than they ensured the pieces fit from the start. What the American automakers did with their rubber mallets is a metaphor for how so many people and organisations lead."*

This is the same issue that safety is plagued by. When things go wrong the conventional approach to safety is to put a fix in place instead of going upstream to ensure that things go well at that point, so that the failure never happens.

Confronting chaos and creating order

Managers who live in the world of 3D performance think of their organization like a machine and are locked into systems thinking which focuses on creating order and stability. They cling to their policies and procedures and expect that they can maintain order through good management and control. There are multiple issues with this approach. Firstly, people do not like to be controlled. Controlling people does not create commitment and when they are not committed many people will choose to not follow the rules when they believe they can get away with it. The flaw with this approach is often expressed as: Forced compliance creates defiance. Secondly, people are human, they make errors. Even with the best intent, people make mistakes that can completely derail the nicely planned and carefully controlled system.

The 2020 global Covid-19 pandemic highlighted the flaws in the 3D focused management approach. Early in the pandemic, there was an immediate unwillingness of some organizations to let people work from home. Unfortunately, there are many managers who are not comfortable letting go of the control and order paradigm. The 2020 Covid-19 pandemic is just an example, it was preceded by SARS, 911, the Millennium Bug and more. The ability to adapt and create resilience in the organization in the face of a rapidly changing world should be a focus for Boards and executive managers.

It is important to understand that the world is not just order and it is not just chaos. It is order continuously confronting chaos and from that interaction a new state of order comes to exist.

The concept of chaos and order can be understood through the Taoist Yin-Yang symbol. Jordan B. Peterson in his book *12 Rules for Life* explains it this way. *"The symbol represents the balance and the constant tension that exists between the two forces. The Taoist symbol is a circle enclosing twin serpents, head to tail. The black serpent, chaos, has a white dot in its head. The white serpent, order, has a black dot in its head. This is because chaos and order are interchangeable, as well as eternally juxtaposed"*.[15]

The concept of chaos and order applies to both personal and process safety. We create order (3-Dimensional Safety) and that gives us an effective level of control, however the order that we create is continuously being confronted by chaos. Machines wear out or fail catastrophically, humans make errors, systems have latent design flaws that create glitches and throw us back into chaos.

Effective leaders are those who walk the fine line between order and chaos. There is a need to respect and value both, too much or too little of either is not good.

Catastrophes and times of chaos provide an opportunity to understand the distinction between leadership and management and embrace new mental models for how organizations perform. Managers manage things and by definition those things are objective and already exist in the present. Leaders create things that didn't exist before them and their influence. They deal with novel situations. Ideally, they do this by influence and inspiration not by coercion or manipulation. The experience of the 2020 global Covid-19 pandemic is just the latest example that a rigid management approach isn't effective. Relying on policies and procedures in the view that they can eliminate chaos, by controlling people through carrot and stick accountability and maintaining order through good management is totally inadequate. Times of chaos serve to highlight the flaws in the system. People in the safety and health field need to be first and foremost safety and health leaders—managing is a secondary function.

In summary, the conventional approach to safety has steered us down a particular path that is not delivering sustainable results.[16] It's now time for a course correction and to recognise that what we have been told and come to believe as the wisdom of the conventional safety and BBS *"experts"* is not the complete picture and is now holding us back.

4-Dimensional Performance explored

The icon on the cover of this book (shown in Figure 3 below) is the Logo of 4-Dimensional Performance. It can be viewed two ways. What most people see when they first look at the logo is 3 cubes that have tenuous connections at the edges with a void in the centre. This represents the 3-dimensional approach that a conventional management focused approach to safety creates. Viewed at the edges or when you look at the pieces individually, they look solid but when you get to the centre the gaping hole that is the absence of safety leadership becomes clear.

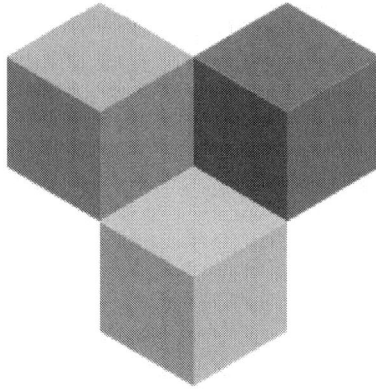

Figure 3. 4-Dimensional Performance

The other way to view the logo is to allow your mind to picture the three coloured cubes as transparent. You can look through these cubes and see a solid or opaque cube that forms the base, sitting behind the three transparent cubes. Each of the coloured cubes is solidly connected to the base. Imagining the 4 dimensions this way provides a powerful insight into one of the key characteristics of the subjective world of leadership, shared values, common purpose, and culture. That is, you can't directly see these things, you have to view them through the objective things, the work practices, systems and processes, that exist in the organization—the first 3 dimensions.

Warren Black from the industry research collaboration Complexus says that we are now living in the age of perpetual disruption. Black discusses how, "*the telephone (1876) took almost 70 years to attract 100 million users, Facebook (2004) achieved that in five years, Candy Crush (2012) in only three and TikTok (2018) in less than one.*" He highlights what this means is that, "*we are now living in a working world whereby an organization's biggest competitor a year from now, could be one that doesn't even yet exist.*"[17] No matter how clever an individual or even entire management teams are, the pace of change and disruption in today's world makes it impossible to predict how and where our current approach or our planned strategy will fail.

The solution is to ask your people to tell you what they are experiencing in terms of the 4 Dimensions—and to do that effectively it helps to know what you are expecting and what questions to ask. We need to change the question from, "*What went wrong?*" to a better question, "*What was missing that allowed this to happen?*" Asking this question changes the relationship, between people and to the error. It moves the focus from a 3D blame game to a 4D collaboration that engages the subject matter experts—the workers. In every case where we asked this question, the people at the coal face had the answer, or understood the issues sufficiently well that their input was instrumental in developing a solution. The opposite of this is thinking you already know. When you think you know the answer, you will fail to ask the critical questions.

The Boeing failures with 737 Max is a sad example of an organizations failure to effectively manage innovation and change in the face of threats from the competition.

The limitations of 3D thinking

Taking a 3-Dimensional view of performance is limited in its understanding and is highly problematic—it's about as enlightened and as safe as going swimming at a beach in Australia with a nosebleed.

In a 3D or conventional management approach people are viewed as unreliable and inconsistent—a problem to be managed and controlled.

From a dimension 1 view people are a factor of production, something to be managed and optimised using management techniques founded in the principles of Taylorism, scientific management and systems thinking. This approach views people as units of production who just need to be trained to a defined level of competency with the expectation that they will comply and consistently perform a defined function in an expected timeframe.

From a 2nd dimension point of view people are regarded as *resources and a cost* to be minimised. Unfortunately, the HR departments of many companies function this way. They overlook the significance of leadership principles such as relationships and commitment to a common purpose. When you get HR and HSE departments that function this way, the result is low levels of engagement and commitment, poor productivity, quality, and safety.

The 3rd dimension is about *systems and processes*. From a 3D perspective people and their expected level of performance are managed through the training matrix, job descriptions and organizational charts that define how the organization should function. People are managed purely objectively and the role of leadership as a driver of performance is disregarded or very much undervalued.

The 3D approach can be made to function in very stable environments like manufacturing and production plants[18]. However, it has proven to only create very low levels of performance and have detrimental impact on objective measures such as quality, cost and wastage, innovation, and schedule delays. It also negatively impacts subjective areas such as morale, engagement, commitment, and psychological safety. These factors in turn create increased absenteeism, worker turnover, and hostile industrial relations. The problems and failures in the auto manufacturing industries in the US, UK and Australia are examples of the ineffectiveness of the 3D approach. In highly dynamic and complex environments an overly simple or flawed 3D approach often fails in catastrophic ways.

History is littered with examples of these catastrophes, NASA and the loss of Challenger and Columbia, Piper Alpha, Bhopal, Exxon and the Longford Gas Plant explosion are some examples. BP's safety and environmental catastrophes which included, the 2005 BP Texas City Refinery Explosion; the 2006 major corrosion and loss of containment resulting in a huge environmental disaster at BP Prudhoe Bay, Alaska; and the 2010 BP Macondo Well, Gulf of Mexico provide an example of an organizations failure to learn.[19]

Moving to a 4D view of performance

In every successful engagement we have worked on, it was always the 4th Dimension—leadership that drove the change. Leaders who recognised people were the solution and applied leadership practices that were consistent and congruent with the team's values were the ones who engaged people, made them feel safe and that they belonged. These were the key factors that drove the care and discretionary effort that created the improved performance. When we talk about a successful company, we mean a company that performs in a professional and virtuous manner, is cost effective and safe.

A 4D approach does not ignore how people fit into and function across the first 3 dimensions. Leaders who understand a 4D approach just see people in a different light, they view workers and operators not as problems, but as problem solvers.

From a 4D View people are seen as having huge potential, people bring an inherent adaptive capacity to create exceptional levels of performance and to dramatically influence schedule and timeframes (D1 – Production and Schedule). In terms of the 2nd dimension, recruiting or developing the right people and rewarding them by paying them what they are worth is seen as a critical element in creating sustainable performance. Good leaders understand how much energy and time goes into creating high performing teams and value this investment in capacity. 3D Managers just see the numbers and look at adding or dropping people simply as a business transaction. Finally, good leaders understand how systems and processes, the 3rd dimension, supports and enables people and teams to perform at a sustainably high level.

Entrepreneur Cindy Gallop, who is famed for being *"The Most Provocative Woman in the World"* masterly describes what is in effect a 4D leadership approach as follows:

> *"There is a formula for success in business, and it goes like this: You set out to find the very best talent in the marketplace, and then give them a compelling and inspirational vision of what you want them to achieve for you and the company. Then you empower them to achieve those goals using their own skills and talents in any way they choose. If, at the same time, you demonstrate how enormously you value them, not just through compensation, but also verbally, every single day, and if you enable that talent to share in the profit that they help create for you, you'll be*

successful. It's so simple, and virtually nobody does it, because it requires a high-trust working environment, and most business environments are low-trust. In order to own the future of your business, you have to design it around trust."[20]

Key Takeaways from this Chapter

1. The occurrence of workers not following established procedures is not because of poor workers, it is the result of poor leadership.

2. From a 4D View people are seen as having huge potential, people bring an inherent adaptive capacity to create exceptional levels of performance.

3. A 4-Dimensional Safety approach effectively operationalises Safety II. It allows for an important mind shift from as few things as possible go wrong to ensuring that as many things as possible go well.

4. It is important to understand that the world is not just order and it is not just chaos. It is order continuously confronting chaos and from that interaction a new state of order comes to exist.

Reflection Questions

1. How well do I know my people?

2. Are your people the problem or your problem solvers?

Endnotes:

[1] Lloyd, C. F. (2020). *Next Generation Safety Leadership*. CRC Press. Kindle Edition. p.23.
[2] Hollnagel E., Wears R.L. and Braithwaite J. (2015). *From Safety-I to Safety-II: A White Paper*. The Resilient Health Care Net. Published Simultaneously by the University of Southern Denmark, University of Florida, USA, and Macquarie University, Australia. [pdf] https://resilienthealthcare.net/wp-content/uploads/2018/05/WhitePaperFinal.pdf
[3] Mink. O.G., Mink, B.P., Downes, E.A. and Owen, K.Q. (1994). *Open Organizations*. Jossey-Bass. Print.
[4] Miller, J. H. and Page, S. E. (2007). *Complex Adaptive Systems: An Introduction to Computational Models of Social Life*. Princeton University Press. Print.
[5] Stacey, R.D., Griffin, D. and Shaw, P. (2000). *Complexity and Management: Fad or radical challenge to systems thinking?* Routledge. Print.

[6] Conklin, T. (2019). *The 5 Principles of Human Performance: A contemporary update of the building blocks of Human Performance for the new view of safety.* Kindle Edition.

[7] Carrillo, R. A. (2020). *The Relationship Factor in Safety Leadership: Achieving Success through Employee Engagement.* Routledge. Kindle Edition.

Lloyd, C. F. (2020). *Next Generation Safety Leadership*. CRC Press. Kindle Edition.

Conklin *op. cit.*

Long, R. (2012). *For the Love of Zero.* Scotoma Press. Print.

[8] Dekker, S. (2017). Zero vision: Enlightenment and new religion. *Policy and Practice: Health and Safety.* [online] 15(2), pp.101-107.

https://www.tandfonline.com/doi/abs/10.1080/14773996.2017.1314070

Hollnagel *op. cit.*

[9] Bown, S. (2019). *The London Luton Airport safety differently journey.* [online] safety differently.com. https://safetydifferently.com/the-london-luton-airport-safety-differently-journey/

[10] Smith, G. (2018). *Paper Safe: The triumph of bureaucracy in safety management.* Wayland Legal. Kindle Edition. p.3.

[11] Kiernan, K. (2019). *In Focusing On What Pilots Do Wrong, We May Be Missing Valuable Lessons From What They Quietly Do Right.* [online] Forbes.

https://www.forbes.com/sites/kristykiernan/2019/11/14/new-nasa-research-explores-contribution-of-pilots-to-aviation-safety/?sh=d583d1d2ac37

[12] Lau, S. (2020). *AINsight: Safety Differently, by Learning from the Good.* [online] AINonline. https://www.ainonline.com/aviation-news/blogs/ainsight-safety-differently-learning-good

[13] Hollnagel *op. cit.*

Dekker *op. cit.*

Conklin *op. cit.*

Carrillo *op. cit.*

Lloyd *op. cit.*

[14] Sinek, S. (2011). *Start With Why*. Penguin Books Ltd. Kindle Edition. pp.14-15.

[15] Peterson, J. B. *12 Rules for Life*. Penguin Books Ltd. Kindle Edition. p.12.

[16] Hollnagel, E. (2018). *Safety-II in Practice*. CRC Press. Kindle Edition.

Dekker, S. (2015). *Safety Differently: Human Factors for a New Era.* 2nd ed. CRC Press. Kindle Edition.

Dekker, 2017 *op. cit.*

Hollnagel et. al. 2015, *op. cit.*

[17] Black, W. (2020). *Risk 4.0 – Video Blog Ep.2 – The Age of Perpetual Disruption* [video] https://www.youtube.com/watch?v=9CpbmGx7kF8&ab_channel=WarrenBlack

[18] Pink, D.H. (2009). *Drive: The Surprising Truth About What Motivates Us*. Riverhead Books. Print.

[19] (Hopkins, A. (2012). *Disastrous Decisions: The Human and Organisational Causes of the Gulf of Mexico Blowout.* CCH Australia Ltd. Print.

[20] Gallop, C. (2018). Facebook, 4 January 2018, https://www.facebook.com/253998061318016/posts/there-is-a-formula-for-success-in-business-and-it-goes-like-this-you-set-out-to-/1688834981167643/

Part Two

Sociotechnical Safety—Let's not throw the baby out with the bath water

Chapter 4

*"Don't throw the baby out with the bathwater" is an idiomatic expression
for an avoidable error in which something good is eliminated when trying
to get rid of something bad, or in other words, rejecting the favourable
along with the unfavourable.[1]*

The 'New View' of Safety—what is it?

We said in the last chapter that there is a need to change the current approach to safety and safety leadership. We have been writing papers and speaking at industry conferences on what that change looks like for two decades. Increasingly authors and thought leaders such as Carrillo,[2] Lloyd,[3] Busch,[4] and Gantt[5] are contributing and adding layers of wisdom to the work of the authors we have already cited.

One thing that all of these authors are agreed on is that the, *"new view of safety changes the definition of success. Safety is not the absence of accidents; safety is the presence of capacity. We don't improve safety by eliminating bad things, we make safety better by improving our systems, processes, planning, and operations."[6]*

Clive Lloyd in an article on the Safety Differently website discussed the *'new view"* in safety.[7]

In the article Lloyd raises a concern about challenges he sees *"that could potentially inhibit the 'new view' from reaching the potential that the safety field so badly needs and deserves."* The main thrust of his article was the need for a common term (a name) that industry can use which embraces all of the concepts, approaches and thinking included in the *'new view'* of safety.

In the article Lloyd pointed out that, *"labels ARE important!"* In psychology, *"names set frames"*. He further states that, *"Part of the success (in terms of prevalence and popularity) of Behaviour Based Safety (BBS) is the simplicity and brevity of the label."* Lloyd goes on to say that BBS, *"sets up a clear frame of 'this is about focusing on people's behaviours to improve safety'."*

Lloyd, raises several important points in the article, stating:

> *"Sidney Dekker states that Safety Differently is not prescriptive, and that there are no checklists to follow in order to successfully implement the approach. In fact, he suggests that dogmatically following a recipe would indicate a regression to traditional safety thinking. Hence, people ...— who intuitively find the new philosophy appealing—may be disappointed*

at the lack of a New View User's Manual and beat a hasty retreat to the comfort of BBS. On the other hand, Dekker himself offers a highly prescriptive approach to facilitating a Restorative Just Culture – a central element of the 'new view'. This apparent contradiction possibly arises because Safety Differently, Safety II and HOP are centered around leaders inviting their people in, and therefore the output from such a collaborative methodology will necessarily be unique to a particular leader and his/her team – it is not a one-size-fits-all approach."

In discussions following the article the term Sociotechnical Safety (ST-Safety) was proposed as an umbrella term that would encompass the approaches which are based on the principles of: people as the solution, creating trust and trusting relationships, psychological safety, resilience engineering, and focusing not on what goes wrong but on doing things well.[8, 9]

Sociotechnical Safety

The use of the term sociotechnical safety has been around for a while, however from a review of the available literature it would seem that there is no common agreement on what the term means.

The concept of sociotechnical safety is based on sociotechnical theory and sociotechnical systems which was first coined by Fred Emery and Eric Trist from the Tavistock Institute in London based on studies of changing workers relationships with the introduction of new technology in British coal mines in the late 1940's and 50's.[10] This approach recognizes the complex interaction between people and technology in workplaces. The term also refers to the interaction between society's complex infrastructures and human behaviour. According to sociotechnical theory all societies and most of their substructures, are complex sociotechnical systems.

Sociotechnical theory is about optimization, with a shared emphasis on achievement of both excellence in technical performance and quality in people's work lives. There are two main principles of sociotechnical theory:

- The first is that the combination and interaction of social and technical factors creates the conditions for successful (or unsuccessful) organizational performance. This interaction consists partly of *"linear cause and effect"* relationships, as per systems theory, and partly from *"non-linear"*, complex, even unpredictable relationships. Whether designed or not, both types of interaction occur when socio and technical elements are put to work.

- The second of the two main principles, is that optimization of one aspect, independent of the other (socio or technical) tends to increase both the quantity of unpredictable, un-designed relationships, and also possible relationships that are injurious or detrimental to the system's performance.[11]

So how can sociotechnical systems theory help our understanding of safety? The concept of 4-Dimemsional Performance and 4-Dimensional safety is based on sociotechnical systems theory. In line with the second principle of sociotechnical theory it recognises that you need an integral balance between both the technology and the people that engage with that technology.

Sociotechnical Safety defined

We define Sociotechnical Safety performance as:

> *Sociotechnical Safety performance is making the optimum*
> *risk management decisions through understanding the relationships and*
> *interconnectedness between ourselves, others, technology, and systems.*

When we talk about Sociotechnical Safety, we sometimes get asked which is more important—the social or the technical or is the technical aspect relevant to process safety and the social to individual safety. The answer as the above definition identifies, is that they are both important. Safety is both a social and technical science, hence Sociotechnical Safety. Which is more important? Ask the highly experienced acrobatics pilot whose wings come off because of poor design or maintenance. Or the family of the victims of a crash caused by pilot error and organizational cultural issues. The answer will vary.

Many catastrophes can be traced back to a failure to understand and properly manage the complex interplay between the organization, technology and systems and the people interfacing with them.

The SAS Black Hawk Tragedy has been discussed as an example that highlights the complexity involved in leading and managing sociotechnical safety.

Boeing 737 Max

The Boeing 737 Max crashes in 2018 and 2019 which killed 346 people are a further example of the need for better sociotechnical safety which is based on a 4-Dimensional approach. Boeing had been faced with the challenge of rival Airbus with their more fuel efficient A320 aircraft. Boeing decided that to avoid the huge capital investment of developing a new airplane (cost factors – Dimension 2) and for speed of getting a competitive product to the market (schedule factors – Dimension 1) it would redesign the 737 aircraft.

Boeing made significant changes to the design and repositioning of the engines on the wings which meant that the 737 Max would not handle and respond like previous 737 variants. Boeing introduced a new system to manage those changes so that the new 737 Max felt like the earlier 737's to fly.

That solution was a software fix called the Manoeuvring Characteristics Augmentation System (MCAS). This system (Dimension 3) controlled the pitch of the 737 to make the 737 Max feel like earlier versions of the 737. This meant that pilots could fly the 737 after completing an online training program—approximately one hour—instead of having to requalify for a new aircraft variant in a simulator.

The intricacies of the complex interplay between people and the technology that was central to the upgrading of the 737 aircraft to develop the 737 Max are beyond the scope of this book. But we will explore these in a second book that we are writing which will be called *Safety Leadership Reimagined*. In that book we will fully explore the role of leadership in creating sustainable safety performance in sociotechnical systems i.e., any modern day organization. For now, let's just understand the complexities and consequences of where technology and design decisions on the Boeing 737 Max let the operators, pilots, and passengers down.

The project managers, designers, and test-pilots were aware of the schedule and competition pressures to get the 737 Max in the air. This coincided with a gradual shift by the Federal Aviation Authority (FAA) to divest more authority to Boeing and allow them to carry out self-assessment of design changes—allowing the FAA to reduce costs (cost factors – Dimension 2) for their numbers of technical experts and inspectors.

Shortly after the first crash in 2018, the FAA realised they did not fully understand the automated system (MCAS) that helped send the plane into a nose-dive, killing everyone on board. Boeing subsequently admitted in court documents that two of its 737 Max Flight Technical Pilots deceived the FAA about the details of this MCAS system tied to both fatal crashes.[12]

After both accidents, the flight-data recordings indicated that the most likely cause was an Angle of Attack (AOA) sensor failure. The Manoeuvring Characteristics Augmentation System (MCAS) relied on this single sensor input to control aircraft pitch. The 737 aircraft is fitted with two AOA sensors, but the 737 Max MCAS was originally designed to take input from only one sensor. One of the changes made to the 737 Max design that enabled it to be recertified in November 2020 as safe was to have the MCAS respond to data inputs from both AOA sensors.

Prior to the crashes, Boeing believed the 737 Max MCAS system to be so innocuous, even if it malfunctioned, that the company did not inform pilots of its existence or include a description of it in the airplane's flight manuals.[13]

Boeing also decided that the aircraft operators did not need to understand the nature of those design changes which included the MCAS. However, when this new system malfunctioned—which is what happened in both crashes—the fact that the pilots were not even aware of the system made it virtually impossible for them to understand what was malfunctioning and to take appropriate action in the short time they had before they lost control of the aircraft.

Boeing managers of the 737 Max seemed to lose sight of the inherent adaptive capacity of people and the additional resilience that skilled and competent people (the 4th Dimension) bring to every sociotechnical system. Had the pilots been 1. aware of the presence of the MCAS system and 2. trained in the simple override procedure in the event of a system malfunction they could easily have switched off the system and reverted to manual flight which would have avoided the crashes.

It is hard to understand why Boeing designers decided to have a single sensor input for the original MCAS design. A factor could have been to do with unrecognised safety implications of design creep in the MCAS design and functionality. The original MCAS design allowed for 0.6 degree trim adjustments and the safety assessment of the system was based on that functionality. Subsequent design changes allowed the MCAS to adjust trim in 2.5 degree increments—a fourfold increase—but a new safety assessment of the implications of this change was never carried out.

In Oil and Gas drilling it is standard safe practice to always have two barriers to prevent uncontrolled loss of hydrocarbons from the well. The logic being that any piece of equipment can fail, hence there always needs to be a backup that prevents that failure bringing the system down.

Boeing had already learned this lesson with the 767 design more than 20 years earlier. In 1991, Lauda Air Flight 004 crashed shortly after take-off from Bangkok, Thailand. That crash was caused by a faulty sensor that allowed the thrust reverser on the No.1 engine to deploy in flight without being commanded, causing the aircraft to spiral out of control, break up, and crash, killing all 213 passengers and the 10 crew members on board. Boeing's fix for that fault was to take input from the landing gear sensor, to prevent the operation of the thrust reversers when the landing gear was not down. The designers of the 737 Max MCAS clearly did not understand the lessons learned from the 767 and the design principle of two sensors on critical systems.

Boeing said *"the F.A.A.'s rigor and regulatory leadership has driven ever-increasing levels of safety over the decades,"* adding that, *"the 737 Max met the F.A.A.'s stringent standards and requirements as it was certified through the F.A.A.'s processes."*[14] But the US Committee Report on the Boeing 737 Max found fault with both Boeing and the FAA, including the functioning of the relationship between the two organizations.[15] The 737

Max is also an example of an organizations achievement orientation drifting from mastery and doing things well—an inherent principle of ALARP (As Low As reasonable Practicable)—to one of just *"get it done"* or ALARA (As Low As the Regulator Allows).

In addition to the loss of 346 lives, the failures with the 737 Max has cost Boeing in excess of US$20 billion. In January 2021 Boeing was also fined US$2.5 billion but according to the US Justice Department will not be forced to plead guilty to criminal charges.[16]

The nature of the change needed

Currently, conventional safety and the field of management in general focuses on failures and errors—what's gone wrong. Sidney Dekker in his book *Safety Differently* describes the problem as follows:

> *"Burgeoning safety bureaucracies preoccupied with counting and tabulating lagging negatives (e.g., 'violations,' or deviations, incidents) tend to devalue expertise and experience. They turn safety from an ethical responsibility for operational people into a bureaucratic accountability to nonoperational people."*[17]

When seen from a management viewpoint, this is not that surprising. In most operations, the technical aspects, systems and processes are relatively static and tractable, so the errors are not to be found there. People on the other hand are dynamic, they are much more intractable and varied in their actions and responses to different scenarios. The conventional approach to safety and in particular BBS has focused on controlling people and attempting to manipulate their behaviour to eliminate these errors and faults. More than two decades of this approach has not led to sustainable safety performance. Sociotechnical theory and the better understanding of sociotechnical systems that it leads to can help us understand where the focus needs to be to advance this new view of safety.

We have been in an ongoing conversation with several authors and thought leaders in the 'new view' of safety and all agree that revisiting the field of sociotechnical systems to better understand the complexity of this human-technology interface is where we need to focus. In effect Safety-II, Safety Differently and HOP all fall under the umbrella of sociotechnical safety. Notably, what they have not done to date, is provide practitioners with the clarity and a concise picture of what a sociotechnical safety approach is and what is required to implement such an approach in the workplace.

We believe that taking a Sociotechnical Safety (ST-Safety) approach which encompasses the complex relationships that exist between people, technology, and the organizations they operate within is critical for creating sustainable safety performance.

Lloyd[18], Carrillo,[19] Busch[20] and Read & Ritchie[21] have all offered insights and guidance on how to interpret and understand what's needed to create sustainable change and create sociotechnical safety. What is needed for ST-Safety to become effective is for senior leaders in organizations to stop treating people as another part of the mechanism and structure of the organization—this is a leadership challenge which too many of the management and sciences schools of education are not currently addressing very well. Dan Little says,

> "One of the most important findings of safety engineering is that organization and culture play critical roles in enhancing the safety characteristics of a given activity—that is to say, safety is strongly influenced by social factors that define and organize the behaviors of workers, users, or managers." He further states, "safety is a consequence of a specific combination of technology, behaviors, and organizational practices." [22]

Moving to a sociotechnical safety approach which recognises the complex interplay between people, technology, the structures, and the markets they operate in, will need a paradigm shift across industry, regulators and academia if we are to achieve the performance improvement that we know is possible. Clearly this is no minor feat, this requires us as leaders to recognise the deficiencies in the current approach and focus our resources on creating the change.

Creating Sociotechnical Safety as an integral part of business

Many years ago, we adapted Ken Wilber's Theory of Integral Consciousness and created a model for integral performance. The Integral Model (see Figure 4) is a relatively simple yet very powerful model to aid the development of a balanced and effective approach to the challenge of managing sociotechnical systems to achieve sustainable organizational performance.

The left side of the model is the **objective** view. It is observable and measurable. It includes the technological aspects, systems and processes in our business. It is where managers focus their attention and where they need to influence and control. Most organizations understand and are proficient at working on this side of the model.

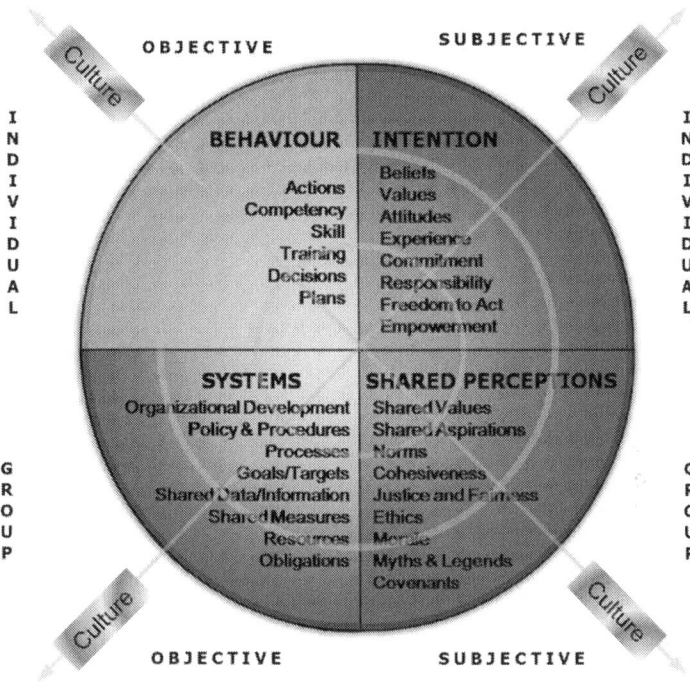

Figure 4. The Integral Model, adapted from Ken Wilber 1997

The right side is the **subjective** view. It cannot be observed or measured directly; it needs to be perceived. It includes the human and sociological aspects in our business. It is influenced by effective leadership, but it cannot be controlled. Many organizations struggle to understand this side of the model. For these organizations, this lack of understanding prevents them from seeing the big picture.

The Integral Model allows for an understanding of the difference between 3D and 4D thinking, which is at the heart of the competing paradigms that we see in safety. Safety-I, which sees people as a liability or a hazard—a problem to be managed and controlled—is rooted in the 3D systems thinking of the left side of the model. Safety-II, Safety Differently and the principles of HOP all seek to leverage the 4D performance potential that exists in the right side of the Integral Model.

Communication

Access to the left side of the model is typically via monologue, one-way communication. It is the documents, emails, policies, procedures, training manuals, observable behaviours, etc. that flow out of the headquarters. It's all the things that tell people (one directional communication) how things are to be done, what's important, how to act, operate and behave. It is important to note that buy-in and engagement are not part of the quadrants on the left side on the model. These factors sit on the right side of the model.

Access to the right side is via dialogue. In real life, it may contradict the monologue and tell people how things are really done around here. While the subjective aspect of this side cannot be observed or measured the dialogue can be observed, recorded and reported upon. However, what the dialogue means, what motivated it and what the expected or anticipated outcomes of the dialogue are, is also subjective. The subjective side of the model is the focus of leadership. Effective leadership always has a strong grounding in dialogue and is typically focused on a view or vision of the future. What the possibility is for that future is expressed by leaders in their dialogue and their conversations in the organization. Good dialogue is distinct to a monologue because it involves two-way communication, good listening is a critical component of dialogue as it confirms that what the leader was meaning to say was perceived correctly.

Behaviour Quadrant

The upper left quadrant of the Integral Model is the domain of **Behaviour**—the view of the individual from the exterior. Improvements in this area come from training, upskilling or working with individuals to influence and align their behaviour. This quadrant includes all the things that you see the individual doing or working with, however it is purely just the observable, measurable, objective aspect of behaviour.

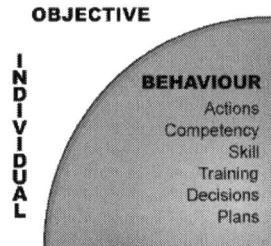

OBJECTIVE

INDIVIDUAL

BEHAVIOUR
Actions
Competency
Skill
Training
Decisions
Plans

People are more than just their behaviour and that is the part that behavioural based safety doesn't take into consideration. To understand why a person does what they do, you need to look at the intention and behaviour as two parts; but we also need to be aware that the What and Why are integral. We can look at behaviour and the components of behaviour: skill, competency, planning, decision making—all the things that are part of behaviour, but to understand how people do those things and why they do them, you have to go to the right side of the Integral Model and look at intention.

Intention Quadrant

The upper right quadrant is the domain of **Intention**, the view from the interior of the individual (consciousness). It includes the values, standards, purpose, commitment, and the listening (meaning) the individual brings to all situations. Improvements in this area come from working with individuals, through leadership, and creating a sense of belonging. People who feel they belong, are committed and willing to have skin in the game. Change in this area is typically perceived as difficult and requiring time. In reality, a change in intention can happen in an instant. Trust is a good example of this. The moment you realise or decide that you can't trust someone, it completely changes your intention towards them.

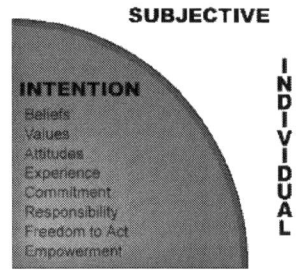

Systems Quadrant

The lower left quadrant is the domain of **Systems**, the view of the group from the exterior. It includes the organizational and management structures, formal and informal leadership system (does your organization have one?), formal and informal metrics, and formal/informal systems of acknowledgement, recognition and respect. This quadrant is Dimension 3 in our 4-Dimensional Performance approach. Change and improvement in this domain is driven by good management. And any good manager will understand that simply having systems and procedures in place doesn't keep us safe—it is people using the systems and procedures effectively that keeps us safe; and that is created through leadership.

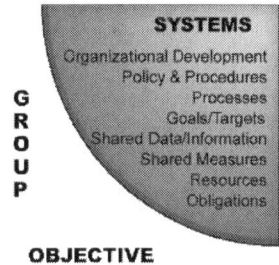

Shared Perceptions Quadrant

The lower right quadrant is the domain of **Shared Perceptions**, the view from the interior of the group. It includes the actual or perceived shared values, norms and standards of the group. It is here we find the ethics, morale and sense of justice that is commonly held by the group. Positive change in this domain has its genesis in leadership. This quadrant should be firmly in the focus of the company board and the executive leadership team. Sadly, that is often not the case.

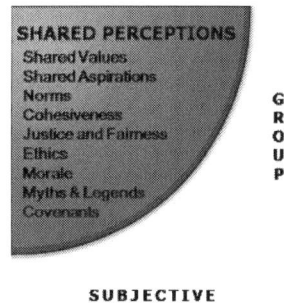

The left side of the model is where most organizations focus their attention.

Summary of Key Concepts and Insights from the Integral Model

- The right side cannot be observed or measured directly; it needs to be perceived.

- The right side is influenced by effective leadership, but it cannot be controlled.

- The left side is about management and where managers focus their attention and where they need to influence and control.

- Access to the left side of the model is via monologue, one-way communication through policies, rules and procedures, safe work method statements, etc.

- Access to the right side is via dialogue. In real life, it may contradict the monologue and tell people how things are really done around here.

- No one quadrant is more important than another.

- Our performance is only as good as our weakest quadrant.

- Shared perceptions and intentions drive behaviour, but you can't have a shared perception or intention about a system that is outside of your paradigm. So each quadrant is truly integral to every other quadrant.

A sad indictment of the current state of management understanding is the fact that while most accidents occur as a result of human behaviour(s) (or more accurately sociotechnical factors) which are driven by factors that sit on the right side of the integral model, most recommendations from incident investigations are focused on the left side of the model—more systems, more training, audits and reviews.

A fact that reinforces this is that we are now seeing industry statistics that tell us that the majority of incidents that occur are happening because people are not implementing and following established systems and procedures properly. If you want to verify the veracity of this statement, we recommend that you do a review of your last 2 years of incidents. Our experience is that it is always the majority, i.e., more than half of all incidents are *"happening because people are not implementing and following established systems and procedures properly."* In many companies the figure is in excess of eighty percent. Like the Schlumberger experience discussed in the introduction of this book, the problem here is invariably not one of training or a lack of systems; it has to do with commitment. The solution to a lack of commitment is a leadership challenge not a management one. Why are workers not committed to implementing and following the existing procedures that you have? If you can't answer that question, you can't create the solution.

Rosa Carrillo in her book *The Relationship Factor in Safety Leadership* puts it this way, *"Traditional safety-performance improvement efforts—assessment, gap analysis, action planning, implementation and measurement—aren't lowering the fatality rate because they don't address the socio-emotional issues we face on the human side of safety management. This deficiency affects technological issues as well because in retrospect so many of the failures could have been prevented in an environment that enabled people to speak up and to listen in spite of uncertainties."*[23]

The need for an integral approach is supported by Andrew Hopkins and James Reason. James Reason in an article entitled *Beyond the limitations of safety systems* put it this way:

> *"There is a widely spread misconception …. That somehow systems sit apart from culture. It is this belief that drives managers' over-reliance on systems on the one hand, and an insufficient understanding of, and emphasis on, workplace culture, on the other. They believe, mistakenly, that compliance with such rules and procedures can be achieved simply by the imposition of systems, while ignoring the crucial cultural dimension. Yet it is the latter that ultimately determines the success or failure of such systems."*[24]

Thinking of the organization as a machine

The paradigm described on the left-hand side of the Integral Model essentially views the organization as a machine. This view evolved from the Newtonian perspective of the universe. Which, when applied to organizations leads to the traditional management approach we call *"COP"*—Control, Order, and Prescribe. From the COP perspective, organizations are just an assemblage of parts that can be understood by known methods of analysis such as the scientific method. The machine works through detailed specification of requisite roles and then strict enforcement of the rules of engagement and operating procedures. This paradigm works reasonably well in cases in which the system is closed, change is slow, interdependencies are low, certainty is high, and variability is low. But this approach fails in complex systems where the performance is more than the sum of the parts.

The leader's role is so much more than just the manager of a closed system. The team members input, and influence, can be so much greater if they are led well and are committed to a common approach where safety is a value and not just a priority.

We suggest that it is time for Industry leaders to critically review what's driving their safety performance. Are the majority of your efforts simply focused on the left side of the Integral model (the enablers—3-Dimensional safety) or do they also include measuring and effectively developing the leadership practices that drive safety (4D safety)? If, despite your best efforts you are still having unacceptable incidents and injuries and struggling with frontline commitment, it is time to look beyond the limiting mindset that you can *"manage"* people's performance. Your people need to be led not managed.

This concept of the complex interplay between culture and systems compliance is core to sociotechnical systems theory and captured in the Integral Model. It is shown as arrows in each quadrant. Culture in the Integral Model can be understood to develop like concentric waves that start at the centre of the model and spread outward.

Reason understands that for a system to be used and even developed in the first place there needs to be a culture that supports it. Hopkins supports this view and quotes Reason in his book *Safety, Culture and Risk* and reiterates the need for an integral approach, *"To repeat, the cultural perspective does not replace the systems perspective, it augments it. No one is saying 'ignore systems, all we need to do is get the culture right'; on the contrary, the right culture is necessary to make safety systems work."*[25]

What does it take to create an Integral Approach?

To change the current approach, we need to start at the top of the organization. Based on our experience in the board room and working with executive teams, we have witnessed some board members, who don't have the necessary levels of experience or understanding of the whole subject, pushing the leadership team (via the CEO) to obtain better, faster financial results. These directors can be dangerous if not influenced and where needed, overruled by other more experienced or better qualified board members. The natural tendency of a non-operational director can be to show a level of frustration when an operational event, e.g., drilling or construction is behind schedule and over budget. This is often perceived by the CEO as pressure to speed up and reduce costs. Macondo is a great example of what can happen when this sort of mindset is pushed down the organization.

David Michaels discussed just how disastrous this approach can be *"During my years at OSHA, where I served as the Assistant Secretary of Labor from 2009 through the beginning of 2017, I received several reports of safety system failures at DuPont facilities. I watched with concern as the company, under pressure from activist shareholders to increase profits, cut costs and let its safety program deteriorate. Needed repairs and upgrades were delayed, worker training postponed, and risk assessments overlooked. The culmination was an incident at an insecticide plant in LaPorte, Texas, where, as a result of a basic process safety management failure, an extremely toxic chemical—methyl mercaptan— was released and two workers were overcome. With inadequate equipment, others rushed in to save their colleagues. In all, four workers were killed."*[26]

Our experience has shown that when this style of management is prevalent there is an element of fear-based acceptance/agreement so the middle management will not question the approach and therefore the pressure is quickly transmitted to the work site.

The Pike River coal mining accident in New Zealand in 2010 is another example of pressure from the board room being pushed down the chain of command quite literally to the coal face. This tragic accident was not a matter of if it would happen but just when. The senior management had several opportunities to stop the job and create a safe work environment but decided to push on to make money at the expense of the lives of 29 miners.

This has changed, to a degree, in some countries (UK, Australia) due to the more recent legislation. Legislation like the Corporate Manslaughter Act mean that directors can be prosecuted for negligence in the event of a fatal accident if the board is deemed to have not done enough to help avoid that accidental event. But this approach is still a management approach (regulations and legislation) to a leadership issue. It will help get the attention of company directors and senior managers, but it does not provide the solution.[27]

From our time organising and presenting at many industry conferences over the last 20 years it has become increasingly clear that knowing our current paradigm is flawed, i.e., understanding the need for a new paradigm to drive different safety performance doesn't of itself achieve much. To be effective this understanding needs to be linked with an effective approach and committed action.

What is happening is that safety performance is improving in various industries in pockets, but not currently across the board. While BP experienced the catastrophe of Texas City in 2005, it was also achieving very good safety performance in many other parts of the organization. These improvements are always driven by leaders who "*get it*" and have the courage to make a stand. The problem is that the solution does not fit with conventional "*find & fix*" management approach to safety. It doesn't fit the current paradigm that drives many companies at the executive level. This paradigm needs to change.

The way to create an injury free workplace is understood by some but not by your typical CEO or board level executive. This problem does not just apply to Safety. Industry is in general failing to understand how they can achieve sustainable performance.

Our premise is that the current approach is not sustainable—it is not working. It is based on current thinking—that does not get it. A different approach is needed and until a company embraces that solution, they will not achieve sustainable safety performance improvement.

Creating an Integral Approach to Behaviour and Performance
An Integral Approach is driven by intent, the top right quadrant in the Integral Model as shown in Figure 4.

1. It is a Values proposition.

2. It is created through Leadership.

3. It is achieved through sound Management.

It is widely quoted that as much as 90% of all accidents are a result of human behaviour which is driven by factors that sit on the right side of the integral model.[28] However, as we have said, most recommendations from incident investigations are focused on the left side of the model—more systems, more training, audits and reviews. When we discuss this issue with operational managers, they express a common frustration that executive teams and boards don't accept recommendations and remedial actions that sit on the right side of the integral model. They regard these as too hard to measure and track. They want measures that can be easily quantified and put in a report; even though they don't produce a sustainable solution.

Trying to redress issues that sit on the right side of the integral model with more systems or more training will never work. An organization that only views their operations through a 3-Dimensional or left side of the integral model perspective can invest time and energy on systems and can write volumes of manuals and procedures, but if their workers have not *"bought in"* to the need for them, if there is no ownership and no commitment to them, they will never be integrated into the work practices on the frontline. All you end up with is a situation where workers begrudgingly comply with the rules while they are being watched and checked up on. The moment they are not being watched they will do what they really want to do. This reduces the role of your frontline leaders to being COPs, looking to catch people breaking the rules. This compliance approach is very costly, inefficient, and ultimately not sustainable.

Leadership not management changes behaviour

The ineffectiveness of a management driven approach was highlighted very effectively in a review conducted by several US universities and published in the EHS Today e-magazine. The authors reviewed the effectiveness of the introduction of mandated electronic logging devices for heavy transport vehicles. Their findings highlight the fallacy of management approaches that are focused on changing behavioural outcomes.

> *"We recently analyzed detailed data from the Federal Motor Carrier Safety Administration (FMCSA) to assess how the electronic logging device (ELD) mandate has affected three important transportation safety-related outcomes: hours-of-service (HOS) compliance, accident counts and the frequency of unsafe driving. Our results show that the ELD mandate clearly achieved its first goal: HOS compliance improved considerably, with the frequency of the most egregious violations dropping by roughly 36% shortly after the mandate and by more than 50% when the FMCSA strictly enforced the mandate. Compliance rates of small carriers and independent owner-operators improved the most, with*

large asset-based carriers practically unaffected because they already used ELDs (and had very few HOS violations).

Surprisingly, the number of accidents for the most-affected carriers did not decrease, and our research indicates, may have increased relative to large asset-based carriers. Finally, the number of unsafe driving violations for these same carriers increased considerably, which could explain why their accident counts did not decrease. This suggests that small carriers and independent owner-operators made up for productivity losses due to stricter HOS compliance by working more rapidly." [29]

If we are to continue to improve safety performance, we need to move beyond 3-dimensional systems thinking and just focusing on the enablers of safety and start proactively tracking and developing the right side of the Integral Model, safety leadership – the 4th Dimension of safety performance.

To repeat, what is needed to make the change is an integral approach that blends all four quadrants of the Integral Model.

George Clason, in his book *The Richest Man in Babylon*, said:

"Our acts can be no wiser than our thoughts, our thinking can be no wiser than our understanding." [30]

This is such an important concept to understand—it is our understanding that enables our thinking. Abraham Maslow knew this, and he stressed the importance of this concept when he said, *"Two people who do not share a common paradigm, cannot have a meaningful conversation about that topic."*

Einstein warned about the pitfalls of the other end of this spectrum, of not thinking broadly enough, when he said: *"A problem cannot be solved from the same level of thinking that created it."*

High performing leaders understand the 4-dimensions of performance, they are always focused first on creating meaning and alignment and then turning those thoughts and intention into action. The best performing companies are very clear that safety needs to be an integral part of their business and they focus on the leadership practices required to achieve that commitment. They are also aware that their performance is only ever as good as their weakest quadrant.

Giving Sociotechnical Safety wings

A good analogy to help us understand where we are on this journey to creating safe workplaces and to understand how much still needs to be understood is to compare the current approach to man's early attempts at powered, manned flight. Before the Wright brothers there was no established paradigm for what was required for sustained manned flight. The many videos of man's early attempts to fly that are on YouTube highlight the bizarre contraptions and constructions that people dreamt up in their efforts to achieve man's dream to fly. The Wright brothers established the fundamental principles that were based in the laws of physics that allowed them to understand and create sustained flight. Any pilot, regardless of whether they fly a commercial passenger jet, a fighter plane, a hang glider or a ram air parachute can tell you the five principles of aeronautics that control flight. They are lift, drag, pitch, roll and yaw. Understanding these principles (the paradigm) is what allows a hobbyist to build a plane in their own garage.

These principles guide the design of every aircraft, get them wrong and you are headed for a crash. Over time the complex interplay between these five factors is being understood to deeper and deeper levels and this allows aircraft to achieve levels of performance never thought possible. Managing this complexity is becoming progressively more demanding and increasingly relies on computers to assist the pilot to manage the aircraft performance.

The 2018 and 2019 Boeing 737 Max air disasters are examples of a catastrophic failure to adequately manage this complex interplay between the computer controls, pilot competency and the basic laws of aeronautics.

Safety performance is no different. If we are to achieve sustainable and injury free operations, we need to understand the fundamental principles that drive such performance. In terms of our journey in safety many organizations are in the era of the Wright brothers, with people still coming up with clumsy "*solutions*" that are not based on sound principles. Many of the aspects of Safety-I and Behaviour-Based Safety (BBS) are prime examples of this which we discuss in more detail in Chapter 8.

The BP Texas City Refinery disaster is a perfect case study for understanding how a 3D approach which suffered from a lack of effective leadership from the top down can lead to a catastrophe. BP failed to combine the human, technology and systems components required for the operation of a complex sociotechnical system such as a refinery.

Texas City is clearly an example of what not to do as a leader. However, it is useful to study and understand these negative examples from history because that is fundamentally how the human brain works. We take note of and remember things that caused us pain or grief. The lessons then become part of our knowledge and experience and help create a higher level of understanding and situational awareness in our operations.

Unfortunately, the conventional approach to safety has taken a 3D approach to the lessons to be learned from these accidents. This thinking has led to a misguided reactionary focus on what's gone wrong and a focus on controlling the human behaviours that this approach believes creates accidents. In recent years several authors have highlighted the shortcomings of this approach.[31]

Andrew Hopkin's book, *Failure to Learn: the BP Texas City refinery disaster,* explores the gaps in current thinking and the approach that lead to the Texas City disaster. As Hopkins says, *"What is remarkable about this case is the amount of information that has come to light on the causes of the accident, most importantly, information about the internal workings of the corporation. These workings have been laid bare, in an almost unprecedented way."* [32]

Thanks to the courageous stand made by Eva Rowe, who lost both parents in the Texas City explosion, a remarkable amount of information about this case is now available at a website that Eva Rowe fought to create – www.texascityexplosion.com.

At the other end of the performance spectrum, we have observed that the best performing organizations are increasingly focusing on ensuring that their organization is following a 4-Dimensional approach. An approach that ensures that not only are the first 3 dimensions managed well, but that the leadership practices which are needed to support and implement management best practice are happening.

This enables them to respond to avoid the impending danger. Accidents can and do happen, but they don't just happen overnight, there are always signals. Often these signals are weak and when viewed individually may not trigger alarm bells, however they do forewarn that things aren't what they should be. The best operators put in place the leadership practices, measures and the disciplines that enable them to identify these signals and proactively respond and stop these events before they become a catastrophe.

As we researched and studied what the best performers did, we were able to identify what sets them apart from the herd. The best performers understand the leadership practices and the team behaviour necessary to create injury free performance. We have studied the leadership practices that make a difference and distilled them down to an understandable framework which is captured in the CARES acronym, which we discuss in Part 2. We have then applied this learning with many clients and coached leaders in many different countries and across a variety of cultures. In every case, when leadership commitment to safe operations is authentic, improved performance across the board will follow.

Safety is an outcome of excellent operational management and courageous leadership committed to doing things well.

Safety is designed and delivered through our choices and actions. However, for many people (and organizations) this seems to be a difficult concept to grasp. In the case of BP Macondo, the managers responsible for that operation deviated from good design and drilling practices in the drilling of the well. BP identified in their own investigation of the blowout that eight (8) critical well control barriers were breached. The reasons for these breaches can be traced back to poor leadership and non-technical skills leading to complacency and/or risk normalization resulting in a lack of situational awareness.

Like the Australian Army in the Black Hawk tragedy, the senior managers responsible for managing the Macondo operations lost sight of the inherent risks in what they were doing. They seemed to think that even though they were cutting corners resulting in well barriers and controls not being in place, things would still turn out all right.

The tragic aspect of the different BP cases was that BP had failed to learn from their past failures and provide the leadership needed to create effective change.

Carolyn Merritt was the head of the US Chemical Safety Board (USCSB) at the time of the BP Texas City Explosion. In a media interview she discussed the USCSB findings in the investigation of the explosion. *"The problems that existed at BP Texas City were neither momentary nor superficial. They ran deep through that operation, of a risk denial and a risk blindness that was not being addressed anywhere in the organization."*, she said. Later in the interview when asked about the preventability of these types of events, Merritt said *"These things do not have to happen. They are preventable, they're predictable … people do not have to die because they are earning a living."* We would go one step further and say that people should not die because they are earning a living.

Key Takeaways from this Chapter

1. The gaps in current thinking and lack of understanding of what truly drives performance has led to an imbalance between leadership and management.

2. Conventional safety creates safety managers not safety leaders.

3. Leaders are different to managers.

4. Leaders create something that didn't exist before them.

5. Managers maintain the status quo; they keep things functioning and performing as they were designed and are expected to be.

6. Both management and leadership are critical functions.

7. Having systems and procedures in place does not keep us safe – it is people using systems and procedures effectively that keeps us safe.

8. Unfortunately, too many senior managers only want measures that can be easily quantified and put in a report.

9. There is no question—it is leadership, not management that creates outstanding performance.

10. We need a new paradigm and achievement orientation which embraces mastery and focuses on the safety leadership practices that actually drive safety performance—4D Safety.

11. In terms of leadership (the 4th Dimension of safety performance), our industry has been steered down a path that is not delivering sustainable results.

12. Safety is an output of excellent operational management and courageous leadership committed to doing the right thing.

Reflection Questions
1. Am I managing or leading?

2. How well is my leadership group performing? How do I know?

3. How is our leadership monitored and evaluated?

Endnotes:

[1] Wikipedia (2020). *Don't throw the baby out with the bath water.* [online] https://en.wikipedia.org/wiki/Don%27t_throw_the_baby_out_with_the_bathwater
[2] Carrillo, R. A. (2020). *The Relationship Factor in Safety Leadership: Achieving Success through Employee Engagement.* Routledge. Kindle Edition. p.68.
[3] Lloyd, C. F. (2020). *Next Generation Safety Leadership.* CRC Press. Kindle Edition.
[4] Busch, C. (2018). *Brave New World: Can Positive Developments in Safety Science and Practice also have Negative Sides?* In: International Cross-Industry Safety Conference, [online] MATEC Web of Conferences, 273 (2019) 01003. https://doi.org/10.1051/matecconf/201927301003
[5] Gantt, R. (2016). *Speaking Truth to Power.* [online] safety differently.com. https://safetydifferently.com/speaking-truth-to-power/
[6] Conklin, T. (2019). *The 5 Principles of Human Performance: A contemporary update of the building blocks of Human Performance for the new view of safety.* Kindle Edition.
[7] Lloyd, C. F. (2020). *The New View* [online] safety differently.com. https://safetydifferently.com/the-new-view/
[8] Read, B. and Lloyd, C. F. (2020). Personal Correspondence.

[9] Read, B.R. (2020) *Sociotechnical Safety in Practice* [post] LinkedIn. https://www.linkedin.com/pulse/sociotechnical-safety-practice-brett-read

[10] Carrillo *op. cit.* p.68.

[11] Wikipedia (2020). *Sociotechnical system.* [online] https://en.wikipedia.org/wiki/Sociotechnical_system

[12] ABC.net.au, (2021). *Boeing ordered to pay $3.2 billion in compensation, penalties two years after deadly crashes.* [online] https://www.abc.net.au/news/2021-01-08/boeing-fined-by-justice-department-747-max-deadly-crashes/13041586?utm_medium=social&utm_content=sf241783421&utm_campaign=fb_abc_news&utm_source=m.facebook.com&sf241783421=1&fbclid=IwAR0HF59eesNiOpTaaAyBVRrmIC3RU6IXjn53mCKOic4Djk72b5Bw_cS9IIs

[13] Langewiesche, W. (2019). *What Really Brought Down the Boeing 737 Max?* [online] New York Times Magazine. https://www.nytimes.com/2019/09/18/magazine/boeing-737-max-crashes.html?utm_medium=10today.media.20190918.436.1&utm_source=email&utm_content=article&utm_campaign=10-for-today---4.0-styling

[14] Kitroeff, N., Gelles, D. and Nicas, J. (2019). *The Roots of Boeing's 737 Max Crisis: A Regulator Relaxes Its Oversight.* [online] New York Times. https://www.nytimes.com/2019/07/27/business/boeing-737-max-faa.html

[15] The House Committee on Transportation and Infrastructure. (2020). Final Committee Report on *The Design, Development & Certification of the Boeing 737 Max.* [pdf] https://transportation.house.gov/committee-activity/boeing-737-max-investigation

[16] ABC.net.au, (2021). *Boeing ordered to pay $3.2 billion in compensation, penalties two years after deadly crashes.* [online] https://www.abc.net.au/news/2021-01-08/boeing-fined-by-justice-department-747-max-deadly-crashes/13041586?utm_medium=social&utm_content=sf241783421&utm_campaign=fb_abc_news&utm_source=m.facebook.com&sf241783421=1&fbclid=IwAR0HF59eesNiOpTaaAyBVRrmIC3RU6IXjn53mCKOic4Djk72b5Bw_cS9IIs

[17] Dekker, S. (2015). *Safety Differently: Human Factors for a New Era.* 2nd ed. CRC Press. Kindle Edition. p.2

[18] Lloyd *op. cit.*

[19] Carrillo *op. cit.* p.68.

[20] Busch *op. cit.*

[21] Read, B. and Ritchie, R. (2015). *The 4th Dimension of Safety Performance* [post] LinkedIn. https://www.linkedin.com/pulse/4th-dimension-safety-performance-brett-read

[22] Little, D. (2008). *Safety as a social effect.* [blog] Understanding Society. https://understandingsociety.blogspot.com/2008/07/safety-as-social-effect.html

[23] Carrillo *op. cit.* p.68.

[24] Reason, J. (2000). *Beyond the limitations of safety systems.* [online] Australian Institute of Company Directors. http://www.companydirectors.com.au/director-resource-centre/publications/company-director-magazine/2000-to-2009-back-editions/2000/april/beyond-the-limitations-of-safety-systems

[25] Hopkins, A. (2005). *Safety, Culture and Risk: The Organisational Causes of Disasters.* CCH Australia Ltd. Print.

[26] Michaels, D. (2018). *7 Ways to Improve Operations Without Sacrificing Worker Safety.* [online] Harvard Business Review. https://hbr.org/2018/03/7-ways-to-improve-operations-without-sacrificing-worker-safety

[27] Smith, G. (2018). *Paper Safe: The triumph of bureaucracy in safety management.* Wayland Legal. Kindle Edition. p.3.

[28] International Association of Oil & Gas Producers. (n.d.). *Data Series.* [online] http://www.iogp.org/data-series identifies that 72% of fatalities and >90% of all incidents were caused by people not following rules and procedures correctly.

[29] Scott, A. and Balthrop, A. (2019). *Has Technology Made Highways Any Safer?* [online] EHSToday. https://www.ehstoday.com/safety-technology/has-technology-made-highways-any-safer?NL=OH-05&Issue=OH-05_20190514_OH-05_296&sfvc4enews=42&cl=article_5&utm_rid=CPG03000006316195&utm_campaign=34601&utm_medium=email&elq2=f09c18995b2d419bad421212ce9be1c2

[30] Clason, G. S. (1926). *The Richest Man in Babylon.* Penguin. Print.

[31] Conklin *op. cit.*

Schultz, James T. (2016) Leading People Safely: How to Win on the Business Battlefield. North Loop Books. Kindle Edition.

Hollnagel E., Wears R.L. and Braithwaite J. (2015). *From Safety-I to Safety-II: A White Paper.* The Resilient Health Care Net. Published Simultaneously by the University of Southern Denmark, University of Florida, USA, and Macquarie University, Australia. [pdf] https://resilienthealthcare.net/wp-content/uploads/2018/05/WhitePaperFinal.pdf

Dekker *op. cit.* p.2.

Carrillo *op. cit.* p.68.

Lloyd *op. cit.*

[32] Hopkins, A. (2009). *Failure to Learn: the BP Texas City refinery disaster.* CCH Australia Ltd. Print.

Chapter 5

Leadership that Creates 4-Dimensional Safety

The most effective leaders continually challenge themselves and ask: *"What else could I be doing to improve both my own and my team's performance?*

Leadership Vs Management

Most management roles require people to be able to be both managers and leaders. To be effective, it is important to understand the difference between leadership and management. Managers are first and foremost focused on maintaining function to sustain performance; improvement may or may not be part of their role.

Whereas the primary function of leadership is to create—but what do leaders create? In the most basic terms, leaders create something that didn't exist before them, before their involvement.

In our coaching work, people have asked *"Do I need to be a leader or a manager?"* The answer, as we said, is that in most roles you need to be both. The extent that you are required to lead or manage is determined by the nature of the role and how much autonomy you have. As an example, a manager of a gas plant is expected to operate the facility within its design parameters and to maintain it so that it can continue to operate as designed. It is of course desirable for a plant manager to also have good leadership ability, but this is invariably a second-tier attribute for selection. As a comparison, the role of a drilling rig manager in exploration in somewhere like the highlands in Papua New Guinea is much more dynamic and requires more day to day leadership skills.

In a business environment, leaders create performance, and they do that through their people. Leaders seek to understand and influence the subjective relationships and interconnectedness between people and technology. Managers are different, they seek to optimise the first 3 dimensions of performance. Leadership and management functions combine to guide the marriage of new technology, systems and processes intended to improve performance. The challenge of making sure that this is done well is what originally led to the development of sociotechnical systems theory. The failures that are represented by catastrophes such as Boeing 737 Max, the SAS Black Hawk Tragedy, and BP Macondo are all examples which serve to highlight the complexity of the challenge.

This quote from Albert Einstein captures the essence of what's missing:

"The intuitive mind is a sacred gift and the rational mind
is a faithful servant.
We have created a society that honours the servant and
has forgotten the gift."

The rational mind drives the science of management and has led to the oxymoron *"performance management"*. You cannot manage performance in people—you must lead your people to create the desired performance. Leadership requires the intuitive mind.

What is leadership?

Leadership always involves a relationship—no relationship, no leadership. Simon Sinek, in his book *Start with Why* says, *"There are only two ways to influence human behavior: you can manipulate it or you can inspire it."*[1] Manipulation, coercion, dominance or any of their associated forms are not leadership.

When you only manage your people, you reduce your relationship with them down to a purely transactional one. They will just do what they get paid for; you lose discretionary effort.

Effective leadership is the most powerful and ethical force multiplier available to organizations today. It is the most powerful because in nearly all circumstances it is under-utilized and yet it possesses the ability to leverage the entire human potential within the group. It is the most ethical because, at its core, leadership is about maximizing the growth and development of your people.

The fundamentals of good leadership have not changed for thousands of years. However, that doesn't mean that leadership is well understood, or that there is agreement about what constitutes a good leadership style or a good leader.

Stanley McChrystal in his book *Leaders: Myth and Reality* explores 13 historical leaders to understand what made them successful.

McChrystal's study of leadership is both very enlightening and simultaneously frustrating. His final analysis of what is leadership, leaves the student of leadership somewhat adrift,

"We lack the leadership equivalent to a general theory of relativity, a
theory that accurately and comprehensively predicts which leadership
qualities and strategies result in success. Such a model is still out of
reach, far beyond the scope of this book, but a step in its direction is
possible. That first step is learning where the mythology and reality
diverge."[2]

Leadership is a science and an art

The main reason that McChrystal was not able to identify an overall theory of leadership, akin to Einstein's general theory of relativity, is that leadership is not just science—it is both an art and a science.[3] Hughes et. al. in the first edition of their book *Leadership* (1993) describe leadership as an immature science which is still developing in fits and starts and where different researchers and authors lack consensus. The reason for this failure to develop precision in predicting human behaviour is due to people and their behaviour being highly complex.[4]

One of the biggest challenges in leadership is that people, those who you lead, are not all the same. They don't all think the same or act the same and they are not all motivated by the same things. They do things for their own reasons and as research into the psychology of leadership is increasingly identifying they are not as readily controlled or manipulated as the devotees of behavioural psychology believe.

Command and control leadership

The typical 3-D focused management approach has been to borrow from the military and adopt the conventional command and control style of leadership. This top-down hierarchical approach has been used in the military since the times of the Roman Legions, Alexander the Great and Sun Tzu. It was developed by the military as an expedient way of bringing large numbers of people together to perform their very specific role for a very specific purpose. That is, go into battle and fight an enemy. A colonel, a captain or a corporal all are trained and shaped by the military training system to perform specific but different functions. This approach is based on indoctrination and is designed to reduce the individual human qualities and to train people to behave in a predictable manner so that they perform their function as part of the system.

The command and control approach works (it is not ideal, but it is expedient) in situations which are predictable, where complexity is understood, and change is slow—such as the conventional battlefield. It is also effective for emergency response situations where individuals are expected to perform specific functions in a time sensitive, high consequence environment as part of a bigger team.

However, it is not a good approach for what the military originally termed VUCA environments—short for environments characterised by Volatility, Uncertainty, Complexity and Ambiguity. Conflicts like Iraq and Afghanistan where traditional military intervention has been problematic are very much VUCA environments. Increasingly sociotechnical business environments are becoming VUCA environments and organizations that are clinging to command and control, COP style leaderships practices are failing. The stagnating safety performance results that we are seeing in high risk industries are testament to the fact that this approach is not suited to creating proactive and sustainable safety performance.

Old school leaders, who cannot let go of the top down command and control leadership style do not perform well in the fast paced VUCA world that is typical of complex sociotechnical businesses.

There was a distinct difference in the leadership style that I experienced in the regular Army compared to Special Forces. Conventional Army units tended to cling to the command and control leadership model whereas Special Forces units and especially units like the SAS and SEALS use a very different leadership approach. In these units each team is made up of individuals with different but complementary skills. A different leadership style is needed by leaders working with inexperienced and less competent individuals or teams compared to a leader of a team of very seasoned, highly competent and committed people.

As a leader, your role is to create a team that has complementary skills, is committed to a common purpose and approach, and holds each other mutually accountable.

Safety leadership defined
How is safety leadership different to conventional leadership? The key difference is that safety leaders are not only focused on influencing others. Good safety leadership starts with yourself; it is a personal commitment. It involves having the courage and being personally committed to doing things well; even when no one is watching.

We define safety leadership as follows:

> *"Safety leadership is a process of self and social influence which maximises the efforts of yourself and others toward the achievement of safe outcomes."*

Leadership practices that create performance
Ten years ago, we published a paper that outlined the research we had done on the leadership practices that drive performance. Specifically, the leadership practices that, as Erik Hollnagel says makes things go well[5], and create high performance. We presented that paper at a Society of Petroleum Engineers (SPE), Asia Region HSE Conference.[6] The research we outlined in that SPE Paper had guided us in the development of our leadership driven approach to safety performance improvement.

Two months after that we published another SPE Paper and presented that at the 2010 International SPE HSE Conference. That paper outlined how we had implemented a leader driven safety performance improvement program in OMV Austria that saw OMV's Austrian operations, over a 3-year period, go from a poor safety performance to matching or exceeding industry best practice.

A month after that, on 20 April 2010, BP experienced a blow out on the Macondo Well in the Gulf of Mexico that killed 11 people and resulted in an oil spill of 4 to 5 million Bbl. (the biggest offshore oil spill in US history) and a cost BP in excess of US$60 billion. The Deepwater Horizon drilling rig owned by Transocean that was contracted by BP to drill the well burned and sank as a result of the blow out and explosion.

The April 2020 Society of Petroleum Engineers, Journal of Petroleum Technology (JPT) included an article titled *Post-Macondo Focus on Safety.*[7] In the article they provide a summary of lessons learned from Macondo:

SPE JPT Summary of Lessons Learned from Macondo

1. Inadequate equipment and contingency planning available to cap a deep-water spill.

2. Drilling crew confused about results of the pressure tests.

3. Failure to demonstrate the integrity of the cement job prior to temporary abandonment of an underbalanced well.

4. Inadequate design and operation of blowout preventers (BOPs).

5. Ineffective regulatory oversight.

6. Inadequate training of key personnel and decision makers for safe operations.

7. Inadequate management systems to ensure safety.

8. Need for a new approach to risk assessment and management.

9. Need for an improved system to collect and disseminate data and best practices on precursor incidents and lessons learned.

The above list highlights just how much the Oil & Gas industry is still firmly gripped in the clutches of the 3-Dimensional, Safety-I *"find and fix"* mindset. The above list is a perfect example of the *"management approach to a leadership issue"* that we referred to in the previous chapter. No doubt there were in 2010 and still are areas for improvement in the above list, but our concern is that this list misses the critical lesson to be learned if we are to create sustainable safety performance.

Nowhere in the article do the authors acknowledge that the blowout could have been prevented if the leaders responsible for making the technical and operational decisions about the well had ensured that they followed established best practice for well management. For readers not familiar with the Macondo Well blow out, here is a list of key points to understand about this catastrophe.

1. The blowout could have been prevented had they chosen the viable option to plug and abandon (P&A) the well. This would have meant writing off the US$120million sunk costs in drilling the well.

2. Instead of deciding to P&A the well the Well Management Team (WMT) decided to *"roll the dice"* on assumptions they made. They got it wrong and the blow out which cost BP US$60billion resulted. Mark Bly, the BP's head of safety and the leader of the investigation, admitted that BP onsite managers could have prevented the catastrophe had they acted on warning signs of a breach of the cement seal at the bottom of the well.

3. The WMT and BP well engineers had made decisions over the six weeks of drilling the well to not follow or carry out critical well design or well control practices. These decisions were intentionally intended to reduce costs on an already over budget well. The decisions meant that because they had deviated from best practice, they found themselves guessing about possible causes of results that should have provided a clear message to not proceed as they were. One example of this is that they chose to not conduct a cement bond log. This test would have confirmed that they did not have a seal and that the hydrocarbons were flowing into the well. Had the WMT known this they would have been certain that there were only two viable options.

    a. P&A the well and accept the loss of sunk drilling costs.

    b. Plug the existing well at a safe depth and rework the well.

4. Reports identify a level of dysfunctional relationships between the most-senior BP and Transocean managers on the Deepwater Horizon rig. There was not the level of shared meaning and commitment to a common purpose that you would expect to see on this type of drilling operation. This amounted to low levels of psychological safety and clearly poor decision making in the period leading up to the blow out.

It is now 5 years since Hollnagel and his co-authors published their white paper from Safety-I to Safety-II and Dekker published his 2nd edition of his book Safety Differently. It's concerning that the message that companies should not just focus on what went wrong but should primarily be focusing on capacity, is not getting through. The focus must shift to ensuring that things that should be done are done, to ensure that things go well.

It seems that an understanding of the fundamentals of the art and science of good safety leadership and the power they have to create performance outcomes are outside the frame of reference of managers that are stuck in the 3D Safety-I paradigm.

Leadership that makes things go well and creates performance

With Dr Keith Owen and research partners we conducted ethnographical research studies over a 3-year period with more than 1,000 work teams and 10,000 workers across two Petrochemical companies and a Utility company.[8]

We started out by asking three questions.

1. What leadership practices constitute superior leadership?

2. How do superior leaders influence the performance of their work units?

3. How can an organization improve its leadership strengths?

The key findings from the research we conducted were:

- Contrary to conventional management and safety thinking, improved team performance was not achieved through more management of the first 3 Dimensions of performance.

- >70% of team performance was driven by leadership (the 4th Dimension) and even more crucially it was the frontline leaders that created this.

- What the conventional approach to management and safety typically focuses on, through existing KPI's, does not measure any of this 70%.

- The same leadership practices that created safety performance also drove all other areas of team performance.

The Research Methodology

To create a benchmark, we used a balanced scorecard to create common measures of team performance. These performance metrics were used as outcome measures to determine if there was, in fact, a relationship between leadership competence, employee attitudes, and work unit performance. The results were very clear and very interesting — a small set of behaviours, when exhibited with superior competence (as judged by employees) were clearly linked to high levels of self and collective efficacy which in turn was linked to superior work unit performance.

Based on these findings we developed a set of measures of leadership practices which we compared using multiple regression analysis to compare leadership practices with team performance. Our findings in these studies helped us understand just how much, great performance is linked to and is dependent on great leadership, at all levels. These findings also made sense when we compared them to our experience from the organizations we had worked with. Whether it's the SAS and leadership that inspires and empowers individuals and teams to achieve incredible results against the odds or companies like

Schlumberger that continually innovate and think and act in ways that drive superior performance and technology; the leadership practices were the same.

The results of the study showed that a set of just four leadership practices were particularly important in influencing work team performance:

1. **Relationship focus**. A relationship focus, grounded in high levels of psychological safety including, trust, dialogue, respect, collaboration, and transparency. In other words, superior leaders focused on their teams: communicating, motivating, guiding/disciplining, managing conflict, and training subordinates.

2. **Self-Leadership.** High performing teams are made up of capable people who have the capacity and resilience to behave congruently with their values across diverse situations and demands. Self-leadership includes both the ability to regulate one's emotional and behavioural response to a situation as well as the strength of character and personal integrity to do so. This leadership practice can be considered as a sub-factor contributing to relationship focus.

3. **Achievement orientation.** An achievement orientation, which is based on mastery as compared to a performance orientation (discussed in more detail in Chapter 6). The best leaders maintained clarity on group purpose and provided team members the means to make daily progress towards realizing the team's purpose.

4. **Problem-solving/solution focus**. A problem-solving/solution focused approach, that was highly responsive and adaptive and consistently removed barriers in order to produce results. This leadership practice can be considered an enabler or supporting factor contributing to an achievement orientation.

The studies measured a range of performance indices including:

- Engagement Index (Level of Commitment and Motivated Effort),

- Total Recordable Injury Rate (TRIR),

- Sales Measures,

- Expense Control Measures,

- Productivity Measures,

- Long Term Value Added Projects, and

- Customer Satisfaction.

It was evident from the results of the research that specific leadership practices had a significant correlation with safety performance.

We found that in terms of safety the best performing teams outperformed other teams by a factor of three. When compared to the worst performing teams the difference was even greater. When we looked at the mediocre performing teams, we found that the leadership practices in those teams were neutral, that is they did not contribute to the performance of the team. In mediocre teams the leadership practices didn't particularly motivate people, they also didn't demotivate people.

It's said that *"success leaves clues"* and this was very much the case when we evaluated teams and their performance. The best performing teams had a set of shared characteristics and ways of operating. What was also not surprising was that the worst performing teams also shared common characteristics and flaws to their performance.

Our research showed there was a set of 20 leadership practices that predicted work unit performance. Six of the leadership practices were relationship factors and the remaining 14 were achievement orientation factors. Further, the work units of leaders rated as superior on these practices outperformed, by a significant margin, those who were rated as average or below. As it turned out, these practices were those that were later identified as strongly influencing the level of employee engagement and voluntary effort.[9]

Leadership that focuses on commitment not compliance

What we were measuring were the factors that create commitment. Conventional safety approaches fundamentally get this wrong, by focusing not on commitment but instead on compliance. Compliance is an outcome—it is created by individuals and teams that are committed to a set of standards and work practices for which they are willing to hold each other mutually accountable. Focusing on compliance leads to the Safety-I approach of tracking performance gaps. It focuses on all the times an error occurred as opposed to monitoring and ensuring that all 4 dimensions are being done well. When the management and leadership practices are in place to create a mastery orientation and ensure that things go well you get 4-Dimensional Performance.

Once we identified those superior leadership practices, we focused on how well leaders did those things with their team. We measured and tracked the desired leadership practices in the field. Where leaders were performing well, we acknowledged them for their success and supported them in their achievements. However, other leaders needed development; so we coached those leaders to develop their leadership practices. We measured their performance and continued to coach them where needed and were able to help those leaders and their teams create significantly better results. In Part 3 of this book we will look in more detail at what we have learned about HOW leaders create performance. Like most things in life, once we understand the paradigm and can see it for what it is, we can then practice and improve performance.

These studies formed the core of the research which led to the development of the Who CARES Wins Framework and the 4D Safety suite of online coaching and development tools.

Leadership is not for everyone

Typically, when working with leaders there are three groups that we can identify. The first group, which often makes up about half of the leaders, either have or will develop the required skills once they know what's expected. The second group, typically 30-35% of leaders, will need some coaching to help them in their development. The third group 15-20% of leaders seem to struggle with either the skill or the will to adopt the leadership practices that are required. When you make the expectation clear these leaders tend to leave the organization or in some cases will put their hand up for a non-leadership role. We discuss the process for developing leaders in more detail in Part 2.

Our findings are also consistent with the message of McChrystal in his book *Leaders*.

> *"Rather, it suggests that the training of leaders is still necessary and important, but how leaders are trained and developed should be revisited. In particular, leaders shouldn't be given a checklist of attributes. Rather, they should be equipped with an understanding of leadership as a system, see themselves as the enablers of that system, and learn how to adjust their approach based on the needs of that system."*[10]

The second part of this quote from McChrystal says *"understanding of leadership as a system"* and would seem to be somewhat contradictory of his view that it is not possible to come up with a general theory of leadership. If leadership did operate as a system it would be possible to define it and its components, so the use of the word system here seems to be a misnomer. However, when reading McChrystal's work as a whole he is clear that, leadership is complex, it is context related and it defies attempts to be broken into component parts, a la the standard systems approach. As stated earlier, leadership is both a science and an art.

If you want to improve your safety performance in a business or organizational context, we recommend focusing on the leadership practices that make things go well. Not surprisingly it's not achieved through the left side of the Integral Model and more systems and processes.

A Leadership Style that Motivates Millennials

We said earlier that a command and control leadership style does not work well in a VUCA[11] environment. These ineffective leadership practices are also increasingly being challenged and rejected by the typical millennial generation worker.

For many organizations, millennials are already the largest and most multicultural generation in their workforce; and this is only going to increase.[12] The challenge for organizations today is to be open and willing to understand and change to accommodate the Millennial mindset. [13]

Between the authors we have 7 children who fall into Gen Y, the Millennials, cohort. Each of our children are different, they have different wants and priorities. However, they are all different, in similar ways, to us and our generation. The differences to their grandparent's generation, who experienced the great depression, and the Second World War are even more stark. When thinking about generations we should keep in mind the words of Michael Dimock, President of the Pew Research Centre, who advises that: "… *generations are a **lens** through which to understand societal change, rather than a **label** with which to oversimplify differences between groups.*"[14]

The outgoing generation of leaders has, to their credit, overseen a massive positive change in safety expectations and performance globally. This change has been brought about in part by public reaction to projects like the Hoover Dam in Nevada, USA in the 1930's, which killed more than 150 people. It is worth noting here that the official figure at the time was reported as 96 deaths during construction. But in all 112 people were killed at site. Also, more than forty tunnelling workers died in hospital from respiratory issues related to carbon monoxide poisoning. However, to keep the reported fatalities down these deaths were officially reported as pneumonia. The change has also come about as a result of committed individuals like Paul O'Neill, CEO of Alcoa through the 1990's, who personally drove change in Alcoa and stressed safety as a core value and not a priority. Priorities are by definition, things that are managed. How much attention they are given goes up and down in line with perceived need. Values don't change.

The change achieved has been principally through engineering and management and has plateaued. In recent years, in many countries the workplace fatality rates have gone up. Fatality rates in the US were flat from 2011 to 2015 but have gone up each year from 2016 to 2018[15]. In Australia the 2018 fatality rates for the five worst performing industries were all up compared to their averages for the last five years. [16] More change has to happen, but this will only come about through changing leadership practices. On an encouraging note, the leadership changes that are needed are also the leadership changes that best connect with and engage millennial generation workers. There is no real surprise to this, what constitutes good leadership has not changed in thousands of years. It is more a factor of the current generation being less tolerant of the bad leadership practices that previous generations have endured.

Leaders need to understand these differences and must adjust how their organizations are managed and led.

In the coming decade millennials will make up the main group of decisions makers and key producers in organizations. The experts in the field provide some very useful guidance on what this group expects and wants.

Glenn San Luis in the article, *Motivating millennials in the workplace*, highlights that for millennials it's very much about passion and purpose. Hence it is critical to connect them to the bigger picture of the business. They need context, not just information but also interpretation. This creates engagement through answering their Why.[17] David Villa, advises that leaders should, take the time to acknowledge millennials strengths, weaknesses and personality traits and how they would mesh well with certain positions within your company.[18] Karen McCollough, says that millennials want to stand out and celebrate their uniqueness and pursue careers that align with their desire to make a difference. She also highlights, that they want to know how their performance will be measured.[19] Deidre Paknad in an article entitled, *Getting to the truth of what motivates millennials at work*, provides the insight that, there is no carrot and stick required, just clarity.[20]

We would suggest that this is good advice, but we would also add that these same leadership practices applied just as effectively to previous generations. The main difference was that previous generations put up with treatment that is not tolerated today.

CASE Study:
Justin Langer—and rebuilding the Australian Men's Cricket Team
In May 2018, in the aftermath of the ball-tampering scandal in South Africa, Justin Langer is appointed head coach of the Australian men's cricket team.

Prior to taking on the national role, Langer had been the head coach of the Western Australian team for 6 years. A job which he described as his dream job, but also one that he was prepared to give up for the noble ambition to rebuild the national team's culture and redeem their image in the eyes of the nation.[21]

The challenge of what Langer took on was immense and would not only require all his current leadership skills, it would also require him to push himself to develop further and to forge even greater skills. The previous coach, the captain, the vice-captain, and an opening batsman had all resigned or were suspended in the aftermath of the ball-tampering scandal.

The scale of the task that Langer had willingly taken on is testament to his character. In May 2018 Australia were ranked fifth in One Day International (ODI) cricket series and only third in test cricket. In 2019 the team would face their ODI World Cup defence and they would also play England in a test cricket series to attempt to retain The Ashes Trophy that they had won 4-0 in 2017. In his first outing as coach any comfort that Langer might have had about Australia's ability to rebound and return to being a top ranked team was crushed by the 5-0 defeat in their ODI series against England.

Moreover, as if the on-field sporting challenges were not enough, the team was also subject to unrelenting media commitments and scrutiny. In addition to two media contracts the team was also constantly shadowed by a film crew from Amazon Prime Video to produce an eight-part series documenting the fall and rise of Australia's men's cricket team. The series makes for an enthralling and often raw insight into Justin Langer's leadership journey.

Focusing on what's missing, not fixing what went wrong

At a press conference when Langer first stepped into the coaching role, he was asked, *"What would you like to change about Australia's cricket culture?"* In classic Langer form, his answer wasn't focused on all the things that were wrong, he focused on what was missing, *"One of the things that is really important is that we keep looking to earn respect. It's not just about how we play our cricket; it's about also being good citizens and being good Australians. Let's not underestimate how proud we should be of Australia's cricket history."* Langer replied.

From the start with his conversations with the team, Langer didn't focus on what went wrong in South Africa. He focused on what the team needed to do well to win and to earn the respect of their country and the cricketing world.

This sentiment was a guiding principle through much of Langer's leadership over the journey that he and the team took to gain redemption. Through the various interviews in the documentary series he shared his thoughts on being authentic and sticking to your principles—it is a fantastic journey into the mind of a great leader.

Building the foundation for performance

Like all great leaders Justin Langer knew the importance of dialogue and the power of creating shared meaning. In his first press conference and in many conversations that followed it, Langer focused on doing things well, creating standards and expectations, and building relationships. *"When you build a foundation, it takes work, it takes time, it takes patience."* he said.

As part of the process of setting up the team, Langer and Tim Paine, the captain, stepped the team through what would become the team's foundation. Langer had very successfully used this approach with the Western Australian Men's Team. He knew the power of creating a commitment to a set of expectations and standards that all team members chose to be responsible for creating and were committed to living by. The foundation was built on two concepts—Ethos and Expectations.

There were six Ethos statements:

- We respect the game
- We respect our opponent
- We love playing cricket
- We use common sense
- We keep things simple
- We play hard but fair

The team Ethos was supported by five clearly stated Expectations:

- ELITE HONESTY – *"It's the Australian Way as I know it, to look a person in the eye and tell them the truth. And to be brutally honest with yourself."*
- ELITE LEARNING – *"I get out of bed every morning looking to get better."*
- ELITE MATESHIP – *"We never leave a teammate behind and we always have each other's back."*
- ELITE HUMILITY – *"We leave our egos at home."*
- ELITE PROFESSIONALISM – *"I always stay ready, so I never have to get ready."*

Initially in his coaching with the team he focuses on building relationships in the team and being very supportive to help them to develop individually and collectively. However, following the 5-0 ODI defeat in England Langer confronts the team to focus on the basics and doing things well. He presses the players to focus where it is needed, *"Concentrate on your technique; concentrate on your next ball; concentrate on competing,"* he says.

In his book *Seeing the Sunrise* (2010) Justin Langer tells the story of how his grandfather, his "Pop" helped him cure his fear of heights. He shares the life lesson that he learned from his Pop, *"You must always look to where you want to go, rather than where you don't want to go."*[22]

It is important to note here that Langer is not talking about blind optimism and neglecting to do the *"hard yards"* to achieve what you want. To believe that, would be to miss the bigger picture and the point of the lesson. In our work with clients, we have talked about this concept with teams we have worked with. We have had people challenge this idea and say, *"Isn't that what NASA did with Challenger or BP and Transocean did on the Macondo Well in the Gulf of Mexico? ... They just focused on what they wanted—launching the space shuttle or finishing the drilling of the well."* The message to be learned from these examples is that every achievement must be built on a foundation of mastering the fundamentals and then doing them well. This is the key distinction between 4-Dimensional Safety and the conventional approach to safety.

Langer's focus on relationships was demonstrated on multiple levels. He set out to create a culture and a psychological contract with each team member, where cheating (like the ball-tampering incident) was unimaginable and had no place in the team. He constantly reinforced the need to talk and interact with teammates. He and his leadership team also focused the players on their connection with their values, teammates, family, and their country.

The power of A Why—and tapping into Autonomy, Mastery and Purpose

On their way to England for their UK tour and their debut with Langer as head coach, the team took a detour to Europe to visit the World War One battle fields of the Western Front. This was a very powerful and emotional time for team members—it was also one of many steps that Langer and his leadership team created to align everyone around their WHY and what commitment meant to them.

While they were at the Western Front every player and all the coaching staff including Langer, were each handed an envelope containing a message of support and inspiration from family members in Australia. The letters and messages had been arranged by Gavin Davey, the Team Manager. This was a complete surprise to all and the experience of reading the messages of love, pride and support left many in tears.

Langer referred to their experience of the Western Front at key times during the next 12 months journey. "*What I want you to keep thinking about, not just as you play this match but every time you represent Australia, you're not just representing us, you're representing the whole country,*" said Langer in his efforts to inspire the team to dig deep during the 2019 Ashes series in the UK.

During his first 12 months as head coach much of Langer's personal effort and energy was focused on instilling a passion and commitment to the team. He is widely recognised as having an incredible work ethic and approaches cricket with an intense level of commitment and passion. He also concedes that he struggles to accept defeat. As his first year wore on and defeats started to add up, Langer's intensity and drive was not hitting the mark for all team members. One team member offered feedback that some members of the team *"felt like they were walking on eggshells around him."*

It was a New Year message from former Australia women's captain Belinda Clark, acting in the role of Cricket Australia's High Performance Manager, that helped Langer see the need to fundamentally change. He vowed to "let go of stuff that I shouldn't be so stressed about."[23]

Other players voiced their concerns through captain Tim Paine and vice-captain Pat Cummins that regular negative assessments were starting to affect performance.

In the documentary series, Langer then shares in an interview that, what brought it all to a head for him was when he was sitting at breakfast in Sydney with his wife, Sue, and she started crying.

"She got really upset and said, 'I don't like what it's doing to you … you're not smiling'." Langer reveals. *"That was a massive wake-up call for me. It was really tough; it really got to me."* He added.

To his credit Langer took the feedback to heart and changed his approach. He allowed players to have more freedom to train and prepare as best met their individual needs.

The team responded positively to the change of approach and success in the ODI matches that followed changed the climate within the team. They had some reasons to celebrate and recognise player contributions. They also took the opportunity to acknowledge that their coach seemed to be absent and, in his place, a smiling version of the coach had appeared.

The team acknowledged that Langer had mellowed a bit, but at the same time they knew that he would never shy away from having the difficult conversations, confronting the moments of poor performance head on and laying open their thoughts and feelings.

This was never more evident when Langer lead the team in an uncomfortable review of their defeat in the Ashes third test which everyone knew that if left unaddressed the errors could cost them the Ashes Test series.

Following the team debrief of the match Paine shared with his coach, *"I found that very confronting to admit, in front of my team, that I made some mistakes."*

Langer advised, *"That's not a weakness, that's a strength, because we are all human and it's good to admit weakness or vulnerability in front of your mates."*

This statement sums up Langer's philosophy and his approach to leadership. When you create a commitment to a common purpose and when you give it your best and are giving it your all, it's OK to be human and be vulnerable in front of your mates. What Langer understands about teams is that when individuals in the team feel safe to do this, the team can pick up the slack, they can cover any gaps and create the best possible performance.

In 2017 the team was ranked 5th in ICC Test Team Rankings for world cricket. In 2020 Australia tops the Men's test team rankings making them arguably the best men's cricket team in the world.

That performance ethic and the culture that Justin Langer helped create, was at the heart of the turnaround of the Australian men's team.

Safety performance by design

The best leaders that we have worked with get it that they create the performance and they lead their teams this way. They create psychological safety, give their people a voice and make it safe for people to speak up and admit their errors. They understand that performance is not delivered by individuals who never make a mistake—those people don't exist. Performance is delivered by design, by leaders who create teams founded on relationships, mastery and a commitment to achieve outstanding performance.

Key Takeaways from this Chapter

1. Leaders are different to managers. Leaders create performance and achievement. Managers focus on maintaining function as a driver of performance.

2. You cannot *manage* performance in people—you must *lead* your people to create the desired performance.

3. Being able to define good leadership is a start; it tells you in broad terms what leaders do. To be a good leader, you also need to understand the leadership practices that drive performance.

4. >70% of team performance was driven by leadership (the 4th Dimension) and even more crucially it was the frontline leaders that created this.

5. Leadership is a process of social influence which maximizes the efforts of others toward the achievement of a greater good.

6. Safety leadership is a process of self and social influence which maximises the efforts of yourself and others toward the achievement of safe outcomes.

7. Leadership practices can be grouped into achievement oriented or relationship based practices.

8. Leaders focus on commitment not compliance. Commitment is the input and compliance is the outcome or the product of that commitment.

9. High achievement is driven by leaders who are aligned to a common purpose and an approach which will enable them to achieve that purpose.

10. Great leaders are willing to hold themselves and each other accountable for achieving the desired outcome.

Reflection Questions

1. Are we really tapped into the full potential of our people?

2. How good are the relationships in my organization? Do I care?

3. How well are we developing leaders in our organization? What is missing?

4. Is Safety performance a priority or a value in our organization?

Endnotes:

[1] Sinek, S. (2011). *Start With Why*. Penguin Books Ltd. Kindle Edition. p.17.
[2] McChrystal, S., Eggers, J. and Mangone, J. (2018). *Leaders: Myth and Reality*. 1st ed. Penguin. Kindle Edition.
[3] Hughes, R.L., Ginnet, R.C., and Curphy, G. J. (2018). *Leadership: Enhancing the Lessons of Experience*. 9th ed. McGraw Hill Education. Print.
[4] Hughes, R.L., Ginnet, R.C., and Curphy, G. J. (1993). *Leadership: Enhancing the Lessons of Experience*. 1st ed. Irwin. Print.
[5] Hollnagel E., Wears R.L. and Braithwaite J. (2015). *From Safety-I to Safety-II: A White Paper*. The Resilient Health Care Net. Published Simultaneously by the University of Southern Denmark, University of Florida, USA, and Macquarie University, Australia. [pdf] https://resilienthealthcare.net/wp-content/uploads/2018/05/WhitePaperFinal.pdf
[6] Winter, J., Owen, Dr. K., and Read, B. (2010). How Effective Leadership Practices Deliver Safety Performance AND Operational Excellence. In: *SPE Oil and Gas India Conference and Exhibition*. Mumbai, India, 20-22 Jan, 2010. SPE. https://onepetro.org/search-results?page=1&q=SPE-129035-MS
[7] Arscott, L. and Moreau, R. (2020) Post-Macondo Focus on Safety. *Journal of Petroleum Technology*, 72(4),
[8] Winter et. al. *op. cit.*

Owen, K., Culbertson, R. and Mink, O. (2011). *Winning Leadership Practices – Revisited.* Published in: http://trainingmag.com/training/reports_analysis/

[9] Winter et. al. *op. cit.*

[10] McChrystal et. al *op. cit.*

[11] VUCA environment—short for an environment characterised by Volatility, Uncertainty, Complexity and Ambiguity. See Chapter 5 for original discussion.

[12] Paknad, D. (2019). *Getting to the Truth of What Motivates Millennials at Work.* [online] WorkBoard. https://www.workboard.com/blog/motivating-millennials.php San Luis, G. (2018). *Motivating millennials in the workplace.* [online] Business Inquirer. https://business.inquirer.net/250365/motivating-millennials-workplace

[13] McCullough, K. (2018). *What motivates millennials in the workforce today.* [online] Karen McCullough. https://www.karenmccullough.com/millennials-today-new-workforce/

[14] Dimock, M. (2019). *Defining generations: Where Millennials end and Generation Z begins.* [online] Pew Research Center. https://www.pewresearch.org/fact-tank/2019/01/17/where-millennials-end-and-generation-z-begins/

[15] U.S. Bureau of Labor Statistics (2018). *Census of Fatal Occupational Injuries.* [online] https://data.bls.gov/timeseries/FWU00X00000080N00

[16] Safe Work Australia (2018). *Fatality Statistics by Industry.* [online] https://www.safeworkaustralia.gov.au/statistics-and-research/statistics/fatalities/fatality-statistics-industry#figure-1-worker-fatalities-proportion

[17] San Luis *op. cit.*

[18] Villa, D. (2018). *All you need to know to motivate millennials.* [online] Forbes. https://www.forbes.com/sites/forbesagencycouncil/2018/03/30/all-you-need-to-know-to-motivate-millennials/#3371914f60ae

[19] McCullough *op. cit.*

[20] Paknad *op. cit.*

[21] Ramsey, A. (2020). *Langer's coaching ride is doco's dramatic sub-plot.* [online] Cricket.com.au. https://www.cricket.com.au/news/feature/the-test-amazon-prime-doco-streaming-premiere-justin-langer-coaching-journey-ashes-world-cup/2020-03-10

[22] Langer, Justin. (2010). *Seeing the Sunrise.* Allen and Unwin. Kindle Edition. p.10.

[23] Ramsey *op. cit.*

Chapter 6

The CARES Framework—Leadership Driven Performance

In Chapter 5 we discussed leadership and we said that leadership is both a science and an art. The CARES framework which we introduce and discuss in the next several chapters maps the scientific part of leadership. As we researched what effective leaders did, we came to understand that WHAT they did could be mapped through the scientific method. In Part 3 of this book we will then add to the understanding by outlining the artistic part of leadership—HOW effective leaders do WHAT they do.

We refer to CARES as a framework because the relationships and achievement are connected. They both grow together in an incremental way. Additionally, endeavour is fuelled by strong levels of relationship and achievement.

It is essential that the leaders responsible for designing and creating the overall performance culture of the organization understand the concepts, including the terminology, outlined in Chapters 6 to 9 of this book. However, it is not necessary to teach all of these concepts or use this language with frontline leaders and teams. It is more effective for leaders to have conversations in straight forward language.

If we think back to the metaphor of mans' early attempts to fly that we discussed in Chapter 4, there is an insight to be learned from a continuation of this aviation metaphor. As a pilot you don't need to understand all the design and construction principles that went into building the aircraft you are piloting. But, as we said previously, it is important to understand the fundamental principles of aeronautics—lift, drag, pitch, roll and yaw. The flip side of this metaphor, as Boeing found out with the 737 Max, is that the designers of the aircraft need an expert understanding of the design principles and need the discipline and competence to apply them flawlessly.

Chapters 6 to 9 of this book explain and outline the key concepts and understanding that are prerequisite for the design and creation of sustainable safety performance. It is because senior leaders have not understood the dynamics of organizational development, including psychological safety and the psychology of motivation, that approaches like BBS have gained an audience.

Todd Conklin in his book, *The 5 Principles of Human Performance* said,

> *"I wish there were a model that we could use to describe this change from the traditional safety and reliability methodologies to the more enlightened 'safety differently' approach that is so foundational to Human Performance."* [1]

We have been working on answering that question through both ethnographic and applied research. Over time, we have come to understand the challenge as a sociotechnical one. Understanding sociotechnical leadership is at the heart of the 4-Dimensional Safety approach. As we said in Chapter 2, the change requires leaders who 'get it' and are capable of creating psychological safety.

As we studied effective leaders, we found it useful to develop a framework to help us understand the interconnectedness of the leadership practices that we were observing. This became the CARES framework. CARES outlines *WHAT* leaders do to create the trust, psychological safety, shared meaning and purpose which lead to sustainable performance.

A word of caution here. Conklin also made the point that a model would be useful because it would allow us to say to our organization's members, *"do these six things and we will be better, safer, and more reliable."* He added, *"Unfortunately, the world is not that simple."*[2] We do not disagree with him on this point. However, that is not what the CARES framework is. It is not a cure all, and it is for that reason that we refer to it as a framework. For things to be *"better, safer and more reliable"* there are many other things (see Chapters 3 and 4) that absolutely must also be done (within the framework) to create safe performance. The CARES Framework is about a 4-Dimensional approach. It is about the holistic leadership practices that create Sociotechnical Safety. What we will say here in as blunt a manner as needed—if you are not doing well in terms of CARES, don't bother with systems reviews, more procedures, more rules and controls. To do that would mean that you have fundamentally not understood the message of Safety-II, Safety Differently or 4-Dimensional Safety.

CARES—an Overview
CARES is about leadership practices; it outlines the key things that effective leaders do:

Creating an

Achievement oriented

Relationship based

Endeavour

Sustainably

Understanding CARES is a game changer
CARES is a framework for developing the capacity to make things go well. This point cannot be overstated—understanding the CARES framework and building these leadership practices in your organization is a game changer. Why is that? It's because

CARES in not focused on compliance and what went wrong, tracking failures and counting accidents; those things have been proven to not lead to sustainable safety performance. CARES is about a commitment to doing things well.

The good news is that the leadership practices that are outlined in CARES can be learned and are developed through training. Whereas the artistic part of leadership—which is based on HOW leaders do WHAT they do and is about values, character and courage—is developed via coaching and is discussed in more detail in Chapter 9.

> *"It is not because business is difficult that we do not CARE;*
> *it is because we do not CARE that business is difficult."*
> *– Brett Read*

The challenge that the above statement raises is: *"Who Dares to Care?"* The question that organizations should be concerned with and seeking to answer is—why is it necessary for our leaders (at all levels) to be daring in order to show care for their people? This question goes to the heart of the psychological safety in your organization. If people in your organization need courage and need to be daring to care and have regard for their co-worker's needs, feelings, or sense of belonging—then you are definitely running an organization that lacks psychological safety and most likely physical safety. Speaking up and caring does not require courage in organizations that embrace a 4D performance approach, where showing care and respect for people—is just *"how things are done around here."*

In our workshops we typically ask leaders a question, *"Do you, as leaders care about the people that you work with and who are in your team?"* The vast majority of hands go up, but then we ask people, *"Who feels well trained, well prepared, and well supported by a system that enables them to effectively care for their people?"* Almost all hands go down. And that's the dilemma for companies these days. Very few companies and very few people are well prepared to provide the care and the respect for people that is needed to create high performing teams. Amy Edmondson says this about the leadership challenge that most organization are struggling with,

> *"Today's leaders must be willing to take on the job of driving fear out of the organization to create the conditions for learning, innovation, and growth."*[3]

Our work has consistently proven that there are things that you can do that are not that difficult, as long as you understand the process—as long as you have a framework to work with and have people who are capable of building relationships and pursuing goals in an effective manner, then it's possible to create outstanding teams. If you look at the literature on teams, it's also well understood that to be an outstanding team you don't need to have a team of all A players. In fact, research has found that when you have a group of all A players it's very rare that they will become a strong team. It takes skillful leadership to get them to all gel and put their egos aside and focus on the team's requirements. Teams that are created with a majority of B performers, who just want to perform well but recognize that they need to do it through collaboration with their teammates are much better at delivering performance.

Creating

Creating means that you generate, produce, form, build, construct, invent, originate, initiate, conceive, or establish something. Great leaders are not just about ideas, they are not just dreamers, they live in the world of action and achievement. There are three things that all great leaders do in common, they:

1. Create **shared meaning,**

2. They **focus** on what's important and guide their people to focus on their role, and

3. They take **action.**

Leaders create shared meaning and purpose, which tells their people what to focus on. Shared meaning and a common purpose guides people in their choices and decision making. Thirdly, when your team has shared meaning and share a common purpose this serves to call them into action. Job design and clarity on work practices are an essential part of creating a sustainable high performance environment.

When leaders do these three things, they create psychological safety and a climate where people are willing to innovate, to try something new or untried. In this regard, the best Leaders could also be called Pathfinders. Being a pathfinder means that you have the courage to step into unexplored territory; a willingness to confront chaos. But, as we said previously, leaders walk the fine line between order and chaos. The best leaders have a reasoned, risk managed approach as opposed to a reckless, devil may care, "*let's just roll the dice*" approach.

Achievement Oriented

By Achievement Oriented, we mean that there is an objective in mind – a goal we deeply wish to attain. That goal is foremost in our thinking, our doing, and in particular in our Being—it is something that we are committed to. That commitment to achieve is based on our WHY and our relationship to our purpose; why is it important and what drives it?

As mentioned in Chapter 4 our research into the leadership practices that create high performing teams identified that more than 70% of a team's performance is driven by leadership practices.[4] From measuring more than 1,000 different work teams we were able to identify the top 20 leadership practices that were common to the best performing teams. Those leadership practices can be split into two distinct sets of practices that influence and drive sustainable performance. Some examples of the identified leadership practices are shown in Table 6.1.

Factor	Sample Item
Relationship Focus	Actively seeks my opinion and input about how to create a safer work environment.
	Respects me as a person.
	Shows through actions that he/she is committed to safety.
Achievement Orientation	Helps the team solve problems to remove barriers to safety performance.
	Applies performance standards fairly and consistently.
	Empowers us to take action to improve the quality and safety of our work.
	Walks the talk – provides me the support that I need to address safety issues.

Table 1. Some of the Factors Measured by the Safety Leadership Profile

We have been teaching and coaching on these leadership practices for the last two decades. Over that time, we have refined how we work with them and track them in teams. Today they are a key part of our 4D Safety software and 4D Dashboard and Tracker. The power of these as educational tools to help leaders and teams be able to make things go well is literally quite astounding.

As already stated in Chapter 2, the best performing teams have an achievement orientation which is based on mastery as compared to a performance orientation.

A mastery orientation is focused on continually developing and improving our personal ability to achieve. It should not be confused with the pursuit of perfection. Perfection is unattainable and people who purely focus on perfection are continually frustrated by their inability to achieve it. Mastery is different. Mastery is focused on doing things well and getting better over time. People are capable of developing and growing in ability— both mentally and physically. They achieve this by training and positively stressing their body and mind to develop robustness and resilience. Over time this leads to increased levels of ability to perform and withstand stress.

Martial arts grading systems, which are typically signified with the award of different coloured belts, are based on the concept of mastery. This approach recognises that the martial artist achieves a level of mastery of a defined skill set and mind set and then progresses to a new more challenging level. In this regard martial arts shares much in common with the Continuous Improvement (CI) philosophy which is another example of a mastery orientation.

Mastery is internally focused and is characterized by the belief that success is the result of effort and the use of appropriate strategies. Mastery is achieved through leadership and development, and a focus on self-leadership. It creates positive psychological motivation because the focus is on being better than we were yesterday, and the recognition that there is always opportunity for improvement. A mastery orientation leads to innovation, persistence, resilience, self-efficacy and sustainability and it embraces the concepts of Safety Differently, Safety-II and 4-Dimensional Performance.

In comparison, a performance orientation is characterized by the belief that success is the result of superior ability or of surpassing one's peers.[5] Performance oriented individuals are highly competitive and desire to outperform others and demonstrate (validate) their ability. Unlike a mastery orientation, which is internally focused on increasing one's own ability, the motivation in a performance orientation is externally focused and has been linked to inconsistent results and lacking sustainability. It embraces a scarcity mindset and typically relies on management concepts like, competing for limited resources, doing more with less and creating lean and agile organizations.

The Australian Cricket team's ball-tampering scandal came about through a myopic performance orientation. Justin Langer's leadership-driven rebuilding of the team was built on a foundation of mastery.

A performance orientation leads to a Safety-I approach with its focus on control and order. It typically also prescribes what human behaviour will lead to performance and seeks to control this behaviour through the use of carrot and stick behaviour-based safety approaches. Teams or individuals that are motivated by a performance orientation are motivated to work hard when they are being observed or are being outperformed by a competitor.

Elite military units, sporting teams and individual sportspersons are able to combine mastery with the drive to perform at the highest level. Success in competitive environments and even more so combative environments, where the outcomes are life and death, requires an achievement orientation that includes both mastery and elite performance. But even in this realm, a performance orientation is not the answer. Those individuals who focus on outperforming the competition invariable come up short. The focus is external and is on beating the competition—this mindset is reactive and has also been linked to the motivation to cheat or act illegally, as in the previously mentioned ball tampering case and the Australian men's cricket team. The best performers are the ones who focus not on what others are doing; instead, they are focused on what they need to do to be their best. First, they understand themselves and their needs. Then they focus on doing those things as well as they can. This focus is what Hollnagel identified as the mindset required for Safety-II. In his book Safety-II in Practice he describes it this way:

> "In relation to safety, the established wisdom is to learn from accidents. Accidents are unwanted occurrences, and it makes obvious sense to try to avoid these as far as possible. According to the causality credo, accidents have causes that can be found and—in principle—eliminated. In order to prevent accidents from happening again it is therefore necessary to learn from them, QED. To this conventional view of safety, a Safety-II perspective offers an alternative. If something that goes wrong has a cause, then something that goes well must have one too. Since many more things go well than go badly, it makes sense to try to learn something from them. Learning from failures alone is limiting, in addition to being rather expensive. An organisation should learn from everything that happens, from what goes well and from what goes badly – and from everything in between."[6]

When leaders are focused on mastery, they have a fundamentally different relationship with their people. They focus on what's needed for things to go well, which leads to the need to develop their people, to guide and support them to be their best.

Relationship Based

By Relationship Based, we mean that effective leadership—the ability to increase the efforts of others in pursuit of a common goal, is based in the strength and depth of our relationships. In other words, our ability to relate establishes what we are capable of.

Our research identified that Relationship is the foundation that Achievement is built on, so in this regard relationship comes first. However, in your role as a leader you are expected to achieve specific outcomes. This can leave some people feeling torn between the two options. In terms of safety and more broadly performance, how you achieve those outcomes is determined by several relationships that you are constantly making decisions about. These relationships are:

1. Your relationship with yourself,

2. Your relationship with others,

3. Your relationship to your environment and purpose.

The best leaders we have worked with understand that how much they can achieve is determined by the relationships they create. They *"get it"* that relationships form the foundation that achievement is built on. Creating relationships based on shared meaning, trust and purpose—a commitment to a common goal is a leader's prime role.

The social philosopher, Eric Hoffer understood the power our relationship with ourselves has on our ability to build and maintain relationships with others.

"The remarkable thing is that we really love our neighbor as ourselves: we do unto others as we do unto ourselves. We hate others when we hate ourselves. We are tolerant toward others when we tolerate ourselves. We forgive others when we forgive ourselves. We are prone to sacrifice others when we are ready to sacrifice ourselves."7
— Eric Hoffer

In terms of safety performance, the depth of our relationship is defined by our *"Being"*—not by our *"Doing"* alone. It is the understanding that: it is what we value, what is important and what we will fight for, that defines who we are—our *"Being"*. It's the strength of our relationships, our commitment, that gives us the strength of conviction to prevail. Do you shrug your shoulders and make the excuse that we've followed the procedure, or do you have the values based mindset that injuries are unacceptable and moreover, the courage to intervene when you are not comfortable with the risk?

Endeavour
Endeavour is to strive for an outcome, even though its achievement is not certain. It is defined as a *"purposeful or industrious undertaking (especially one that requires effort or boldness)"* or an *"earnest and conscientious activity intended to do or accomplish something"*. It is a journey toward accomplishment. Endeavour is most simply: *"Committed Action."* That commitment to act should also embrace resilience and the ability to persevere or pivot and adapt as needed. How a leader creates endeavour, what meaning they create, what they focus on and what they act on is a huge determinant of the level of endeavour they get from their team. The key factors that influenced endeavour in teams were relationships and creating autonomy, mastery and purpose.

Sustainably
Sustainably refers to the capacity to maintain, over the long term, the integral performance culture that the leader creates. A culture of sustainable performance seeks both resilience and robustness. We discussed resilience and robustness in Chapter 1, but it is helpful to revisit the nature of these concepts again as both resilience and robustness are qualities which are inherently necessary in a sustainable organization. Resilience is fundamentally a skill or capacity which is developed and maintained and may well be perishable when not exercised, drilled, or practiced. Resilience is emergent—whereas robustness is a capacity or quality that exists. The opposite of robust is fragile, while the opposite of resilient is brittle. In terms of objective things think of holding or maintaining its shape—robustness. Returning to or regaining its shape—resilience. In terms of people think of strength or ability to take a knock, suffer setbacks and not give up or give in—robustness. Ability to adapt and survive—resilience.

Sustainable high performance is the objective and only an integral culture can sustain performance during changing times and over time as people and technology changes. Sustainable safety performance is values-based, as opposed to rules based. In such a culture, the focus is not on compliance with rules, what people do, but on values that determine what behaviours are acceptable, who they are Being. This point became obvious as we studied team performance. The best performing teams achieved and sustained their performance by creating a foundation of relationships.

Leadership Practices need to suit the context

So, the CARES framework outlines WHAT leaders do, that's always the same regardless of the context. However, to get the most out of the CARES framework it is important to understand that leadership is context related; HOW a leader does what they do is critically important. How a leader relates, communicates and what they expect and focus on varies with context and even from situation to situation. Here's an example, training in the SAS is, as you would imagine, extremely focused, very physical and total commitment is expected. As an SAS leader you can set the bar for your team at an incredibly high level. Can you imagine how it might work out if I brought the same leadership expectations and approach to coaching my kids under 12 football team. It would be like the Arnold Schwarzenegger movie, Kindergarten Cop. It wouldn't work.

HOW leaders do what they do is the focus of Part 3 of this book, but it is worth noting that how a leader builds relationships, how they create achievement oriented teams depends on many things, such as:

- The societal values and culture they are operating within.

- The organizational culture.

- The level of development, especially the skills and competence of team members.

- The level of commitment of team members.

- The environment they are operating in, including for example, the marketplace, competition, and access to resources.

How leaders bring the 4 Dimensions of performance together to create sustainable performance, is where the art of leadership comes to the fore. This is related to the leader's ability to walk the fine line between order, which is achieved in the first 3 Dimensions, and chaos, which is orchestrated in the 4th Dimension.

The power of CARES is that it provides a straightforward framework that:

- Enables safety leaders to be more effective by focusing on the key leadership practices that have been proven to really drive safety performance.

- Provides a structured way for organizations to measure, monitor and develop the safety leadership capability of their leaders and teams.

- Enables organizations to focus on and track the 4th Dimension of safety performance—safety leadership.

When an organization applies a CARES approach you get a very different level of engagement and ownership. The outcome is self-governing work teams who work safely.

When motivated by shared values and a common purpose, teams become self-governing and are alert to the possibility of human error. As a result, team members watch out for themselves and each other. Andrew Hopkins has written extensively on this subject and the concept of *"Collective Mindfulness."*[8] As a safety leader, the end state we should be striving towards, is one of mastery where safety and performance excellence is expected and supported by all, and people hold each other mutually accountable for achieving this. When fully developed and ingrained, a values-based, self-governing culture is like a heavy flywheel that sustains momentum and keeps the organization moving in the desired direction.

Good Safety Leadership meets all aspects of CARES, it requires a complete appreciation of the subject and the people, a clear understanding of the objective, and values-based committed action. Anything else will fail to deliver. When leaders truly understand this, walking the talk is not an issue, nor is *"practicing what we preach"* an issue, because we know who we are. That knowledge of who we are (our Being) means we can only act (our Doing) in accordance with who we are. We are consistently guided by our courage and strength of character, by our virtue and integrity, by the depth of our Being.

Key Takeaways from this Chapter

1. CARES is a framework that outlines WHAT leaders do to ensure that things go well. What they do is always the same regardless of the context.

2. HOW a leader does what they do is critically important, it will vary with context.

3. Creating shared meaning and purpose, a commitment to a common goal is a leader's prime role.

4. Our commitment to achieve is based on our WHY and our relationship to our goals and purpose; why is it important and what drives it?

5. Leaders create Action. They are willing to try something new and untried; they are Pathfinders.

6. There are 3 relationships that we must work on:

    a. Your relationship with yourself,

    b. Your relationship with others, and

    c. Your relationship to your environment and purpose.

7. In terms of safety performance, the depth of our relationship is defined by our values—our *"Being"*; not by our *"Doing"* alone.

8. How a leader creates endeavour, what meaning they create, what they focus on and what they act on is a huge determinant of the level of endeavour you will get from your team.

9. Endeavour is most simply: *"Committed Action."*

10. A mastery orientation leads to innovation, persistence, resilience and sustainability.

11. Sustainable safety performance is values-based, as opposed to rules based.

12. How leaders bring the 4 dimensions of performance together to create sustainable performance, is where the art of leadership comes to the fore.

13. The outcome of a CARES approach is self-governing work teams who work safely.

Reflection Questions

- We use frameworks for other parts of our business why not leadership?

- What leadership framework do we use today?

- What would it take to initiate a 4-Dimensional framework?

Endnotes:

[1] Conklin, T. (2019). *The 5 Principles of Human Performance: A contemporary update of the building blocks of Human Performance for the new view of safety.* Todd Conklin. Kindle Edition.
[2] *Ibid.*

[3] Edmondson, A. C. (2019*). The Fearless Organization: Creating Psychological Safety in the Workplace for Learning, Innovation, and Growth.* John Wiley & Sons, Inc. Kindle Edition.

[4] Winter, J., Owen, Dr. K., and Read, B. (2010). How Effective Leadership Practices Deliver Safety Performance AND Operational Excellence. *SPE Oil and Gas India Conference and Exhibition.* Mumbai, India, 20-22 Jan, 2010. SPE. https://onepetro.org/search-results?page=1&q=SPE-129035-MS

[5] Senko, C. and Harackiewicz, J. M. (2002). Performance goals: The moderating roles of context and achievement orientation. *Journal of Experimental Social Psychology,* 38 (6), pp.603–610.

[6] Hollnagel, E. (2018). *Safety-II in Practice.* CRC Press. Kindle Edition. p. 62.

[7] Hoffer, E. (n.d.). *Eric Hoffer>Quotes>Quotable Quote.* [online] goodreads. https://www.goodreads.com/quotes/91031-the-remarkable-thing-is-that-we-really-love-our-neighbor

[8] Hopkins, A. (2005). *Safety, Culture and Risk: The Organisational Causes of Disasters.* CCH Australia Ltd. Print.

Chapter 7

Creating Performance

Creating is the first element of the CARES framework. Everything we achieve in life is created twice—first in our minds and then in the physical world.

There are three decisions that we are continuously making in our lives:

1. what we make things **mean,**

2. what we choose to **focus** on, and

3. what **actions** we take.

We can be steering a path and designing our destiny based on conscious answers to these 3 decisions or we can be drifting along as a victim of our past or present and unconscious forces that are driving us.

To create an effective vision, we must truly understand what we want and why we want it and then have clarity about how we can achieve that purpose. it is vitally important to understand this concept—it's the choices we make about what something means to us, what we focus on and what action we take, that determines how things turn out and what we achieve. If we are not clear about our Why, if we lack clarity, if we are not consciously making these decisions with a plan and a clear intent in mind then we will never end up achieving our goals.

This was 100% true for me when I decided to attempt selection for the SAS Regiment. For a couple of years before I made the decision to try for selection, I was reading stories about the origins of the SAS. Their exploits in North Africa in World War Two and the achievements of the Australian SAS in Borneo and Vietnam. I was on a posting as a staff officer in Sydney and working for LTCOL Bill Hindson MC, MG who had been awarded the Military Cross for his exploits as an SAS officer in Vietnam.

Bill was a marathon runner when I met him, and over the time we worked together, I had the good fortune to join him for lunchtime 15km runs. On those runs we talked about the SAS and the idea started to form in my mind that I might be able to do the selection course. Bill was instrumental in helping me understand that there was only one mindset that got you through the selection course, and that was a commitment to never giving up. He helped me understand that the course was designed to push the body into all kinds of hell. *"It was not your body that got you through the course; it was your mind. How badly you wanted it!"* was Bill's sage advice. Of course, you needed to be able to complete the gruelling physical demands of the course, but ultimately it was your mindset, your Why, that got you to the end of the course.

This is just as true for safety performance. We said earlier, safety performance gets created by design or by default. If you as the leader, aren't steering the performance based on a commitment to how you believe it should be, then it is like a ship without a rudder—it will go whichever way other forces, the wind and currents, take it.

Creating Shared Meaning

Leaders create three distinct things through their leadership practices:

1. They create shared meaning and purpose which provides clarity,

2. They focus on their purpose to ensure team members understand what's expected,

3. They take action and call their people into action.

The best leaders do this most effectively not by barking orders as per the very limiting command and control approach. Instead, they share their intent with their team and meet their team members' need for meaning and understanding of the purpose behind what they are doing. Understanding and connecting with the leader's intent creates shared meaning which then guides the team's ability to focus on what's important. It enables them to avoid distractions and to apply their skills, experience and wisdom to ensure that their actions are aligned toward achieving the intent that they are committed to.

The leader's role is to answer three questions to guide and enable their team to perform. Those questions are: WHY, HOW and WHAT. How well a leader does this determines the performance of their team. What sits behind each of those answers (that a leader provides) is outlined in Figure 5.

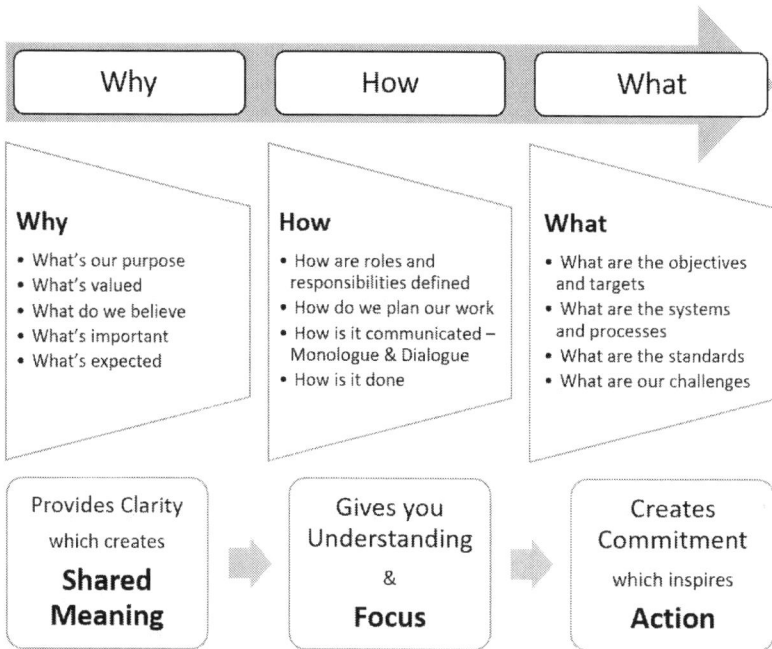

Why	How	What

Why
- What's our purpose
- What's valued
- What do we believe
- What's important
- What's expected

How
- How are roles and responsibilities defined
- How do we plan our work
- How is it communicated – Monologue & Dialogue
- How is it done

What
- What are the objectives and targets
- What are the systems and processes
- What are the standards
- What are our challenges

Provides Clarity
which creates
Shared Meaning

Gives you
Understanding
&
Focus

Creates
Commitment
which inspires
Action

Figure 5. Your WHY for Safety

How well leaders *"walk the talk"* and act with integrity and congruence in living up to the agreed standards, determines how well they meet their teams need for meaning and purpose in the work they do. When leaders do this well, they earn trust, a sense of belonging and purpose, which are major contributing factors in psychological safety.

Good leaders create psychological safety—the ability to speak openly without fear of negative consequences. Poor leaders who use coercion and manipulation or those who rigidly follow a command and control style fail to create psychological safety.

A sense of belonging, which is typically experienced as feelings of inclusion and being valued are essential elements of every high performing team. Our need for belonging is so strong that people will adopt common attitudes, and expectations to belong.[1] When people feel a really strong sense of belonging to a particular group, they will often conform to group norms of dress and patterns of behaviour—of course this can be a positive or negative outcome e.g., outlaw gangs. Belonging is created and influenced through relationships, it can't be mandated, coerced, or legislated.

The Janitor at NASA

A great example is captured in the famous apocryphal story of the janitor at NASA. As the story goes, in 1962, when President John F. Kennedy visited NASA, he saw a man carrying a broom and asked, *"What do you do here?"* to which the man answered, *"I'm putting a man on the moon."* The janitor's answer was testament to how well NASA had in the early days of the Apollo space program created a common purpose and sense of teamwork.

Shared meaning creates performance

The big difference between the best leaders that we have worked with and the not so good was their ability to align their team to a shared meaning and purpose. A McKinsey Consulting article titled *Increasing the meaning quotient of work* quoted research that showed, workers who feel that they have purpose and are connected and aligned with that purpose report that they are as much as 5 times more engaged and effective in their roles.[2] This is consistent with our findings in our research, which showed that leaders who effectively create shared meaning and commitment to a common purpose, create the foundation for high performing teams. These teams that are 3 – 8 times more effective and productive on measures such as safety, productivity, cost control, wastage and staff turnover.

When leaders fail to create shared meaning and common purpose people invariably become more self-oriented and are increasingly motivated by self-interest. As things deteriorate, trust and psychological safety are severely eroded and gradually self-interest becomes self-preservation. There are a virtually endless number of negative effects and consequences that flow from a lack of shared meaning and common purpose. This is why you don't see teams in highly competitive, high consequence endeavours such as the SAS or Formula One racing focusing and dwelling on all the things that have and could go wrong. Instead, they focus on building performance capacity and making sure that things go well. They do this by firstly, understanding what's needed to make things go well, then creating those conditions through all 4 Dimensions of performance—what we call a mastery focus. High performing teams focus on training, practicing, and doing drills to ensure that the sociotechnical system functions as expected.

When this approach to building performance is adopted it creates a very different mindset to performance. This change happens in the minds of individuals and also at the team level. At an individual level people stop worrying about *"missing the shot"*, getting it wrong or making a mistake. Instead, they trust themselves and they *"trust the process"* — their focus shifts to doing what they have practiced and done well so many times before. At a team level they know that everyone is committed to the process and focused on doing their bit and performing their role as and when needed.

This process is familiar to anybody who has played team sport at a high level or trained in special forces units like the SAS or the US Navy SEALS. The skills and the performance required are broken down into learnable chunks and practiced.

Creating performance is not an academic exercise. It requires practice, making mistakes, trial and error that leads to learning. As the saying goes: *You can't teach a kid to ride a bike in a seminar.* The trick is to create an environment where it is safe to fail. Which is quite different from the idea that: *If at first you don't succeed, perhaps skydiving is not for you!*

A good example of this is the process used for helicopter underwater escape training. The oil and gas industry recognised that one of the most dangerous aspects of working offshore was the helicopter transit to the offshore facility. When helicopters crash or ditch into water, they have historically been a major cause of fatalities. However, it was typically not the impact of the crash that killed people; it was drowning. Getting people out of a capsized chopper that can quickly fill with water was the problem. These days offshore operators are trained and drilled to be able to perform this escape. How this training is done is a good example of building capacity. They are not just loaded into a simulator and immersed in water while rotating 180 degrees to end up hanging upside down in their seat belts in freezing cold water in the dark. The training is incremental, each of the stages in the process is learned and practiced, creating the competence to perform that task. First in their own time and then with practice at an effective speed. Once each stage is mastered the complete process is drilled, first on land, then with the chopper floating on water, then capsized and sinking, until eventually they can perform the full process as part of a crew. When trained and drilled in this manner a very high percentage of people are capable of effectively extracting themselves quickly and orderly from the chopper.

This same process is what has enabled Formula One teams to reduce their pit stops from minutes a few decades ago to under 2 seconds today. The solution relies on shared meaning and understanding of systems and processes that lead to a common purpose and approach.

The typical descriptors of frustrations or disconnects that workers identify in teams that lack shared meaning and common purpose include:

- Not being clear what the goals and values of the work group are.

- Not clear about their roles and responsibilities relative to the goals.

- Perceived conflicts between performance and safety goals.

- People not being provided the resources and support needed to complete assigned tasks.

- People not consistently held accountable for safety performance.

- Workers seeing leaders not accepting responsibility for safety issues.

Leaders create and challenge paradigms

Having implemented successful cultural change and performance improvement programs in different countries we have become very clear about the significant impact that different paradigms can have on the success of the program and the time it takes to create the change.

Early in my career I was introduced to the concept of paradigms. A paradigm is simply a mental model, a way of thinking which filters your view of the world. Each of us perceives new ideas, things, or phenomenon through our existing paradigms. To be effective a leader needs to understand how our mental models get created.

The most influential leaders constantly challenge accepted paradigms and thereby create new ones. The title of this book is based on the need to change our paradigm of safety and to reimagine safety with a new and more enlightened view—a new paradigm.

Paradigms can be held by an individual, or they can be shared amongst a group, a community or a society. There are four things that combine to form our Paradigms and they can be remembered by the acronym KERB.

KERB

- Knowledge

- Experience

- References

- Beliefs and Values

Knowledge

Knowledge can be defined as acquaintance with facts, truths, or principles. But we should be wary of viewing knowledge this way. Knowledge is not the same as fact. Knowledge is the facts as we understand them at a particular time or level of evolution. Knowledge is temporal and does not always match what actually exists. Prior to 1492 the knowledge of that time was that the world was flat. Everyone 'knew' the world was flat. The accepted facts of the time were that sailing west from Europe would result in the voyagers eventually sailing off the edge of the world. In 1492 Christopher Columbus proved that accepted fact wrong when he sailed west and *"discovered"* the Americas. It was not until 1521 that the Magellan expedition circumnavigated the world and confirmed that it is round.

History is full of moments when new discoveries and new knowledge resulted in paradigms being turned upside down. We can all recall times when we have learned something new that completely changed our way of thinking about a topic or thing.

Updating your paradigms and learning new things is enlightening and can also be a source of entertainment for others. In 1989 I was working and living in Mendi in the Southern Highlands Province of Papua New Guinea (PNG).

It was very different to the world of SAS operations that I had been working in the year before. The first explorers arrived in the PNG Highlands in 1947. Prior to that time the people in the PNG Highlands were still living a tribal stone age lifestyle.

I was part of a team of 23 Australian Army managers and supervisors that was integrated into the PNG Government Department of Works.

A few years before my time there, our predecessors had established a Boy Scouts Troop in the town of Mendi and a couple of Army team members were the Scout Masters. They had been fund raising and now had enough money to sponsor two local scouts to attend the pacific-rim Scouts Jamboree which was to be held in Japan.

This was a huge experience for the young scouts who both lived in tribal villages in grass huts with no mains electricity or running water. There were so many firsts for them on this trip that continually confronted their paradigms of what they knew of the world. One of those was initially very upsetting for one of the scouts but later he revelled in retelling the story to his mates when he arrived back home.

The two scouts and two scout masters flew from the PNG Highlands to Tokyo where they overnighted at a city hotel before travelling to the jamboree location. Both scouts had been wide eyed and constantly pointing out new and amazing sights to each other from the moment they arrived at the airport in Tokyo. The hotel in Tokyo was a very big multi-story complex. As the second scout stood in front of the lift, he was not really sure what they were waiting for. He had never seen a lift and didn't know what they were. All he knew was that he had seen his friend and the other scout master enter this little room with strange doors that looked something like a sideways turned mouth (the lift).

The second scout had been watching this little room since his friend had entered it. To his horror the lift doors opened again, and the lift was empty. He was freaked out by this and was sure that the room had swallowed his friend. No amount of reassurance that it was safe would get him to step into the lift. They had to get one of the hotel staff to go up and get his friend to come down before he would believe what he was told about the lift. When they got back home to PNG, they told all their friends and family about the buildings in Tokyo that had rooms that magically jumped around inside the building and would take you where you wanted to go. New paradigms can—take some getting your head around.

The British science fiction writer Arthur C. Clarke formulated three adages that are known as Clarke's three laws, of which the third law is the best known and most widely cited. The third law states:

"Any sufficiently advanced technology is indistinguishable from magic."[3]

Experience
Experience is as Confucius said, often the bitterest way of learning wisdom. In the military they teach a concept called revolution in military affairs (RMA). RMA is a way of understanding how new tactics and technology rewrites paradigms of how conflict is managed, and wars are waged. Some of the RMA events in history include the invention of the bow and arrow, the use of gun powder in cannons, the air war in the First World War, and the tactics of Blitzkrieg in the Second World War.

Just imagine the paradigm shift of the first naval captain whose ship was torpedoed by a submarine. You're standing there on the bridge, feeling safe, no other ships in sight, and you see this white streak in the water making a bee line for your ship. You would be curious but not concerned right? But moments later you have a whole new level of experience. However, it's still a while before you complete the paradigm when you debrief your experience with naval intelligence and a new RMA has begun.

References
References are anything that you learn about but have not experienced yourself. References can be informative and useful, but they can also be wrong. We have all had times when we have been pleasantly surprised or disappointed when something that we were expecting based on other people's experiences or something we had read turns out to be quite the opposite.

In February 2018, we travelled to Kurdistan, Northern Iraq to kick off a safety leadership development program for a Norwegian client that was conducting operations there. ISIS was still being cleared out of Mosul which was only 80km west of Erbil where our client maintained their headquarters. We were both amused by the range of responses we got from family and friends based on their level of understanding of the conflict and ethnopolitical circumstances on the ground. Some thought we were going into an active war zone, others who understood more about the conflict and knew more about the Kurdish people and the Peshmerga forces, knew that they had routed all attempts from

ISIS to extend their forces in Kurdistan. The Kurds were extremely anti-ISIS and constantly vigilant for anybody that looked like they could be an ISIS supporter. At the time we felt safer in Erbil than we would have in some of the major capital cities in Europe.

Beliefs and Values

Beliefs and Values are subjective views that we hold. They are formed and bonded over time through the influences of family, friends, society, and life experiences. By the time you are an adult, you can hold very definite views on just about everything. Rosa Antonia Carrillo in her book *The Relationship Factor in Safety Leadership* very succinctly explains the difference between a belief and a value. *"A belief is not a passive thing like a value. Values can be espoused, but not practiced. Beliefs are so deep that you sometimes don't even know they are influencing your decisions."* .[4]

Beliefs and values can be a guiding force that helps us navigate and make sense of the world. However, when they are misguided and not based in reality, they can be very harmful for us.

In PNG we were regularly supported by Royal Australian Air Force and Australian Army Aviation aircraft to help us move stores and equipment to remote locations. On one occasion we had several Army helicopters helping us to move equipment. We also had some PNG Defence Force soldiers working with us. One of whom was from the Highlands. He had arranged for leave at the end of the work with us, and as we were flying over his village whilst moving equipment, he asked if we could drop him off to save him the 2-day walk through the rain forest from the closest road. Expecting it to be just a slight deviation in the flight and a routine stop, my boss approved the request.

In general, the villagers understanding of the outside world was at that time still very limited. When the first white people arrived in the Highlands after the Second World War, they organised the locals to build airstrips and they started flying in materials. The tribal people had no understanding of modern technology. Their paradigms did not begin to allow them to understand planes—with these strange looking white people inside them, who arrived and gave them axes, knives, and metal cooking pots. This led to the creation of the *"Cargo Cult"* which was based on the idea that the white people were a form of god who controlled these strange types of birds (planes and helicopters) that would carry the gods and the cargo in their bellies and then supply it to the people in the Highlands—just like a parent bird feeding its young. Many of the tribal elders in the young soldier's village still held the belief that the planes and helicopters were birds. In Tok Pisin (Pidgin English) the word for plane and bird were originally the same word—balus. Helicopters which were typically not seen until years later, and after missionaries had arrived in the Highlands, got a different name. In Tok Pisin the names of things are often a description of the thing. So, helicopter is *"mix masta bilong jesus christ"*, literally meaning, *"mix master from the heavens"*.

The chopper with two pilots, the load master and the young soldier who was heading home, landed on some flat ground at his village. Many of the people from the village had been sitting out over the past two days watching the helicopters ferrying loads overhead. When they landed a crowd quickly gathered to see the chopper. The young local soldier tried to keep people back while the crewman unloaded his pack. But before he could stop him, an old man moved forward and tried to touch the spinning tail rotor which to him looked like the glistening feathers of a bird of paradise—he was sadly, killed instantly.

The soldier immediately realised that the crew of the helicopter were now in danger because the villagers were likely to carry out *"pay back"* and kill one of the air crew. The pilot made a quick radio call to us and then grabbed a handheld radio as they exited the chopper and took off down the mountain. It took them half a day to get across the valley and up to the top of another mountain where we picked them up just before last light.

The next day we returned to the village with a police escort to begin the negotiation process to pay compensation in respect of the sad loss of one of their tribe and to recover the stricken helicopter, which they had tied to a tree so that it could not fly away.

Some years later I read a passage in George Clason's book *The Richest Man in Babylon* which based on experiences like those in PNG had very real meaning for me.

> *"Our acts can be no wiser than our thoughts, our thinking can be no wiser than out understanding."*[5]

Reimagining the Paradigm of Safety

Currently the field of safety is being reimagined by many under the *"New View"*. As always, we need to be wary of flawed thinking and flat out charlatans who proclaim wisdom, that when critically reviewed does not hold up. Encouragingly there are some very clever thought leaders who are sharing their understanding of the flaws in the established paradigms of safety and are offering further ways of understanding the current gaps and offering insights to help move us forward. As an introduction, we suggest that an understanding of the works of Dekker (2015[6], 2019[7]), Hollnagel (2018)[8], Conklin (2018)[9], Carrillo (2020)[10], and Lloyd (2021)[11] is essential reading. These authors all advocate a shift which is closely aligned with our 4-Dimensional approach to safety. Their writing and their works along with this book all contribute to broadening the knowledge base to understand a more holistic sociotechnical approach to safety.

Changing how we relate to safety – the Complexity and Complicatedness Paradigm

One of the frustrations that we have with the conventional approach to safety is that it makes safety and performance significantly more complicated than it needs to be. The paradigm of sociotechnical safety enables an understanding of both complexity and complicatedness, and how leaders effectively work with both.

Complicated systems and technology can be simplified by understanding their individual components. They are linear and therefore predictable. Complex systems are nonlinear and are hard to predict. As we discussed in Chapter 2, they can't be managed by the same COP—Control, Order, Prescribe linear processes and control mechanisms that work with complicated systems.

The solution requires an integral approach as previously outlined in the discussion of the Integral Model. Leaders need to be able to understand and operate from an integral 4-Dimensional paradigm. The first 3 dimensions—which are about systems, organizations, and technology—require an understanding of their complicatedness. Whereas the 4th Dimension—which is about people and socio or human factors—requires leaders to understand and deal with complexity.

The issue with the conventional safety approach is that it tries to manage complex nonlinear sociotechnical systems with complicated linear approaches. As we have said they are not the same thing and therefore cannot be managed this way.

The complex responses of people need to be influenced through leadership—they cannot be managed. Some people mistake coercion, manipulation, bullying and other ways of *"managing"* people as leadership—but they are not—none of these approaches work out well in the long term. Managing people in an attempt to get them to perform is problematic on multiple levels. It also doesn't develop people so they can learn and bring their talents and smarts to work. It doesn't work in a dynamic VUCA[12] environment because as the manager you can't be there 24 hours a day. If you want your people to think you need to lead differently.

Behaviour Based Safety (BBS) is a good example of a linear approach to a nonlinear complex system. It is a management approach to a leadership issue. We will discuss the limitations of the BBS approach in more detail in Chapter 8.

Creating mindfulness and ownership

Human nature is such that if we do or have something for long enough, we can start to take it a little bit for granted. If we are undertaking high risk activities and nothing bad happens, if we take shortcuts and break the rules without negative consequences, we can start to believe that our actions don't matter, and that safe performance is the default outcome.

Parachuting became different for me after my very low opening. After that jump I was clear that every jump would end in a predictable outcome unless I prepared for and performed properly during the jump. From that jump onwards, I owned the outcome and focused on doing things well and creating the outcome I wanted on every jump. This simple shift in mindset and sense of mindfulness every time I jumped changed my entire outlook on the activity.

Summarising the Safety Leaders role in creating performance

It is the Safety Leader's role to create and maintain a sense of mindfulness; it is critical that we operate not with a feeling of chronic unease but one of constant vigilance. Constant vigilance that we are doing everything that we know we should be doing to the best of our ability—mastery. Then we should be asking those that are doing the work, are on the tools, are operating the equipment—what else is needed? What's missing, what's not meeting the need or could be done better—not what's wrong or who's doing wrong.

Safety Leaders create their workplace climate and ultimately culture (safe or otherwise) by their purpose and what they focus on.

Key Takeaways from this Chapter

1. The leader's role is to answer three questions to guide and enable their team to perform. Those questions are: WHY, HOW and WHAT.

2. Leaders create three distinct things through their leadership practices: They create <u>shared meaning</u> and purpose which provides clarity, they <u>focus</u> on their purpose to ensure team members understand what's expected, they take <u>action</u> and call their people into <u>action</u>.

3. Leaders Create and challenge paradigms.

4. KERB is a good acronym to help remember where our paradigms come from.

   - Knowledge

   - Experience

   - References

   - Beliefs and Values

5. Beliefs and values can be guiding force that helps us navigate and make sense of the world. However, when they are misguided and not based in reality, they can be very harmful for us.

6. Values can be espoused, but not practiced. Beliefs are so deep that you sometimes don't even know they are influencing your decisions.

Reflection Questions

1. Have I written down my Why for Safety?

2. As a leader do I create clarity and shared meaning?

3. Do I focus on the things that are important I.e., a 4-Dimensional View of Performance and Safety?

4. Are we leading, or are we using a management approach to a leadership issue?

5. Am I consciously creating and shaping my paradigms? Or do my unconscious paradigms shape me?

Endnotes:

[1] Carrillo, R. A. (2020). *The Relationship Factor in Safety Leadership: Achieving Success through Employee Engagement.* Routledge. Kindle Edition. p.1.

[2] Cranston, S., and Keller, S. (2013). Increasing the Meaning Quotient of Work. [online] *McKinsey Quarterly*, January. https://www.mckinsey.com/business-functions/organization/our-insights/increasing-the-meaning-quotient-of-work#signin/download/%2F~%2Fmedia%2FMcKinsey%2FBusiness%20Functions%2FOrganization%2FOur%20Insights%2FIncreasing%20the%20meaning%20quotient%20of%20work%2FIncreasing%20the%20meaning%20quotient%20of%20work.pdf%3FshouldIndex%3Dfalse/1

[3] Wikipedia (2021). *Clarke's three laws.* [online] https://en.wikipedia.org/wiki/Clarke%27s_three_laws

[4] Carrillo *op. cit.* p.1.

[5] Clason, G. S. (1926). *The Richest Man in Babylon.* Penguin. Print.

[6] Dekker, S. (2015). *Safety Differently: Human Factors for a New Era.* 2nd ed. CRC Press. Kindle Edition.

[7] Dekker, S. (2019). *Foundations of Safety Science: A Century of Understanding Accidents and Disasters.* CRC Press. Kindle Edition.

[8] Hollnagel, E. (2018). *Safety-II in Practice.* CRC Press. Kindle Edition.

[9] Conklin, T. (2019). *The 5 Principles of Human Performance: A contemporary update of the building blocks of Human Performance for the new view of safety.* Todd Conklin. Kindle Edition.

[10] Carrillo *op. cit.* p.1

[11] Lloyd, C. F. (2020). *Next Generation Safety Leadership.* CRC Press. Kindle Edition.

[12] VUCA environment—short for an environment characterised by Volatility, Uncertainty, Complexity and Ambiguity. See Chapter 5 for original discussion.

Chapter 8

Endeavour – understanding human behaviour and motivation

Our research into the leadership practices that create high performing teams highlighted that the best leaders inspired their team to strive for a common purpose and were instrumental in creating significantly higher levels of commitment and self-determined effort. To help us organize our thinking we grouped these ideas in our CARES framework under the heading of Endeavour.

What characteristics of leadership and culture provide the necessary ingredients, that cause employees to choose to apply discretionary effort and exhibit self-governance around a set of core values? Our search to understand this issue has been guided by the work of Rotter,[1] Bandura,[2] and Seligman,[3] regarding the determinants of self-motivated effort. The work forms what is called efficacy theory and is a part of cognitive psychology.

A basic premise of efficacy theory is that people work in order to meet their needs[4]. There are three primary sets of goals of all people at work: equity, achievement and belonging. Efficacy Theory asserts that employees seek to meet these three needs in any employment situation. It further asserts that, when all three needs are met, the result is high levels of commitment and motivated effort directed toward accomplishing organizational goals. This commitment and motivated effort is often referred to as engagement.

A large body of research shows that employee commitment and effort translate into stronger business performance. Jeffrey Pfeffer[5] in his comprehensive review of the research, concludes that companies with engaged employees are 30 to 40 percent more productive. Research also shows that companies with highly engaged employees performed consistently better than their industry comparison group[6,7] Research has shown that the more engaged an employee is the more committed he is to the organization and his work, both rationally (as shown through effort expended) and emotionally (as shown through enthusiasm for the work). Whereas fully engaged employees are both enthusiastic and willing to work hard, less engaged employees show signs of apathy and expend only enough effort to get by.[8]

Creating Endeavour

How do you create an engaged, self-governing work force? In the world of safety, there are two basic approaches to achieving improvements in safety performance. The first of these approaches are those referred to as Behavioural Based Safety (BBS) Programs. These programs are based on behavioural psychology and are grounded in the operant learning principles that were first articulated by B. F. Skinner and promulgated by his student Aubrey Daniels. The second approach is based on cognitive psychology and recognises the need to deal with the sociotechnical, 4-Dimensional nature of safety performance. It is values and relationship based. This approach draws on research and theories rooted in expectancy, efficacy, and attribution theories, first developed by Julian Rotter and then extended by Albert Bandura and Martin Seligman.[9]

More recently Carrillo, Lloyd, Owen, Read and Ritchie have been writing about their work and successes in creating leadership driven relationship based safety performance improvement.

We want to briefly discuss BBS with the view to helping you form a better understanding as to why the assumptions underlying BBS programs are erroneous and do not lead to a culture that supports sustainable safety.

Research shows that as much as 95% of incidents and injuries result from human behaviour. This is why so many of the efforts to improve safety performance focus on the issue of controlling human behaviour. To achieve this aim and driven by conventional, Safety-I thinking, organizations typically introduced a BBS program. Such programs are based on the principles of operant conditioning, which theorize that behaviour is controlled by its consequences. This is illustrated in the ABC Model shown in Figure 6.

What the ABC Model is missing

The ABC Model was developed by Skinner and when applied to safety at work, theorises that a circumstance at work serves as an antecedent, stimulus, or cue to perform a specific safety-related behaviour. This behaviour operates on the environment to eliminate the risk and if successful, it produces a consequence, the nature of which is determined by the quality of the behaviour. A 'correct' behaviour produces a positive consequence while an 'incorrect' behaviour produces a negative consequence. In either case, the relationship between the cue and the behaviour is strengthened by the nature of the consequence it produces. In other words, there is a feedback loop linking consequences and antecedents.

Skinner further proposed that a stronger consequence increases the frequency with which the correct behaviour occurs and decreases the frequency with which an incorrect behaviour occurs.

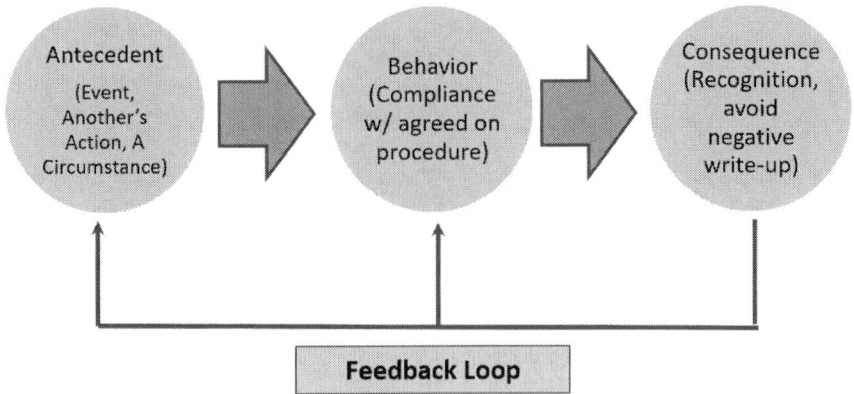

Figure 6. The ABC Model of Behaviour

Engaging individuals and working to create and encourage safe behaviours are essential parts of any approach to safety, unfortunately BBS programs often fail to do this. The reasons for this stem from a fundamental flaw in the ABC model about the nature of human behaviour.

The first reason such programs fail is that human behaviour is not controlled by consequences but by the individual's expectations, which is a belief that something will (or will not) occur. In other words, behaviour is not externally controlled by consequences but is internally controlled by a person's beliefs about the antecedent. If the person believes that something will happen when she encounters a given antecedent, then she will act in accordance with that belief, regardless of the consequence. This is why people regularly do things that, to an observer, are clearly self-defeating. Programs based on external control create compliance but not commitment and as soon as the external control is relaxed, so too is the level of compliance. These programs are not sustainable.

A second reason has to do with the impact that our values can have on our behaviour. Contrary to the 'logic' of the ABC Model and Maslow's Hierarchy of Needs people will endure pain and suffering and even death to act in accordance with a strongly held value. Being true to our values explains why some people will turn and run towards the fire instead of running away from it. This behaviour cannot be explained by the ABC Model.

A third reason has to do with the way people respond to external rules. The average person in a carrot and stick environment is, after a while, very likely to break safety rules because this is the way our minds work—people seek to improve something or make it easier. This is why systems built on the premise of enforced compliance to a set of rules don't consistently deliver the expected results. The flaw here is on focusing on compliance instead of commitment. Behaviourist approaches, of offering rewards or metering out punishments, do not create commitment—it only creates resentment—and the only relationship it creates is negative. People resent being punished, end of story. If you are dealing out punishments, especially against standards that workers have not committed to, they will resent you.

A fourth reason behavioural based programs don't work as expected is that they are based on an inherently flawed assumption of the operant approach that safety improvement can be managed. The systems management perspective is that safety can be engineered into the design and operations of any system. But in terms of sociotechnical systems, this turns out not to be the case. As we have pointed out, behaviour cannot be externally controlled. Wise managers understand that having an inherently safe design and procedures to enable the safe operation of the equipment is just the start. Leaders need to engage people so that they consistently operate the equipment within its design envelope and as per established procedures.

The message here is that people are not robots, nor are they pigeons or dogs and one size does not fit all. The problem invariably is that managers implementing a typical behaviour based program think that the ABC Model allows you to predict behaviour, e.g., if a particular antecedent is present you will get a particular behaviour—if you do this, then you will get that thinking.

If you understand the model as it is shown in Figure 6 you will see that, yes, an antecedent will lead to behaviour, but the behaviour may be different from one individual to the next. Every individual in a sense chooses how they react to an antecedent. Their choice may be to act in a particular way or to do nothing; not reacting or not taking any action is still a behaviour. The individual controls this, not the manager.

So, while the primary concept of BBS i.e., influencing individual behaviour is very sound and is an essential part of creating a culture of performance the use of the ABC Model in creating that culture is flawed.

This aspect of human nature has been confirmed in numerous studies where they attempted to understand what motivates us. The studies highlighted that we are not as endlessly manipulatable as the ABC Model would have us believe.[10]

Behavioural scientists when researching work typically divide what we do on the job into two categories: algorithmic and heuristic. Algorithmic work is linear and predictable, which is why it can be reduced to an algorithmic success formula. i.e., If you do this, then you will get that. Heuristic work is the opposite—the VUCA[11] concept that we discussed in Chapter 5 seeks to provide some understanding of heuristic work.

BBS is an approach that was designed by behavioural psychologists in the 1980's who believed that people also think and act in an algorithmic way. But this is just not true. Clive Lloyd in his book, *Next Generation Safety Leadership*[12] expressed it this way,

> *"I don't know anyone in my large network of psychologists who would use behaviorism as a modality of choice (unless they are training their dogs of course). Yet, despite the fact that the approach fell out of favor decades ago, BBS (which is based on the underlying principles of behaviorism) is still distressingly commonplace in the mining, oil, and gas and construction sectors today."*

Managers who don't understand the flaws in a behavioural approach, can easily fall into the trap of treating people like human resources and get excited by the idea of a silver bullet that will have people behave in the *"right way"*. An oil & gas company did exactly this when they tried to expand the application of a BBS program that had been successfully implemented on one of their offshore platforms. The BBS program had been developed by the workers on the facility after they had been given a budget to create it. It included guides and training videos (many home grown), observer checklists for work practices that were repeatedly performed on the facility and numerous initiatives developed by the people involved in the program to help people understand what it was about, why it was being done and the part each person could play in helping each other be safe. In effect the workers on the facility had created a BBS system and a values based system interwoven in it.

Senior executives liked the results and were keen to see the program *"rolled out"* in other parts of the company. They attempted to unbolt the program from the one facility and bolt it on to another offshore rig operated nearby. It failed but the worst of it was that it took time to fail and, in that time, created resentment, frustration and mistrust among the very people whose support was crucial to its success. While this attempt was short lived, the negative experience of behaviour based safety programs lingered and stalled further attempts to get any program that focused on behaviours off the ground. The reason it failed is that the values based part of what the workers had created, on the first rig, existed on the right side of the integral model (it existed in the subjective world) and therefore could not be unbolted and installed on the other rig. It was therefore incomplete and did not make sense to, nor have ownership by, the people who had been 'given' it.

The key issue to be understood with BBS is that the way it is typically practiced by many companies relies on the carrot and stick approach to influencing behaviour (See Figure 6). This approach works to a degree for simple, straight forward tasks where there is little complexity, and the outcomes of the behaviour are relatively certain. Factory production lines are a good example. However, even in this environment the outcome is not certain—people make mistakes, they overlook things, they act inconsistently.

Interviews we have conducted with employees reinforce their concerns and have highlighted some of the problems with BBS programs. The feedback we got is that these programs are often perceived in a negative way. They can be seen as focusing on failures, or catching people doing something wrong, or seen as a *"dobbing on your mate"*. They can focus on blaming the worker involved as being the root cause of the problem.

Calling it for what it is

It's not just the workers who are calling 'BS' on BBS programs and the conventional approach to safety. Many safety professionals are also extremely frustrated and disillusioned with the way safety is being done. Of course, there are some safety professionals, who just don't see the problem. They are typically very low on emotional intelligence. They actually like their role, they like being able to play COP and to *"catch the negligent workers doing stuff wrong."* These safety people don't build relationships with the people doing the work and usually have very little real understanding of what it's like in the workplace that they are supposed to be serving and supporting. But some safety professionals are speaking out and trying to make a difference.

Sam Goodman is a safety professional in Phoenix, Arizona. He wrote a book called *Safety Sucks*[13] that pulls no punches in identifying and calling 'BS' on many of the issues that are common in the conventional/Safety-I approach that is still rife in many industries and countries.

We have had several conversations with Sam and it's clear he understands great leadership and is strongly driven by values and doing the best job he can. In 2019 Sam started a Podcast called *The HOP Nerd*. Through his Podcast, his writing and his consulting Sam is a role model for the change that is needed within the Safety profession. Here's how Sam described his purpose in his book, *"… my 'why' is to inspire people to join me in challenging and changing the not-so-great things that are a part of this profession. We deserve better and so do future safety professionals."*[14]

Sam has experienced what many safety professionals experience as they work in companies that are following a 3D Conventional Safety approach. In his words,

> *"Within my first few years as a safety professional, I was looking for a way out. I was done! … At the time I was tired, I was worn out, and I craved a life outside of work. I was burned-out, I was done with the beatings and I was tired of being the scapegoat for company failings. I was exhausted from constantly fighting to make things better in a broken system and from being placed in a position of being at odds with management and frontline employees."*[15]

If you want an insight into just how badly flawed safety is in some industries and companies, you don't have to read too far in *Safety Sucks* to get the picture,

> *"A lot of companies hold safety practitioners culpable for the failings of the organization, the failings of flawed safety management systems and approaches, and the failings of poor leaders. Post-accident, everyone knows the most logical question is to ask, 'where was safety at when this happened' or to demand that they manage down the classification of an injury."*[16]

What motivates us and why it does

If we are to reimagine how safety leadership might be, we need to understand the different drivers of motivation and how the brain processes them.

Advances in neuroscience have helped us understand how the brain processes different stimuli and how they motivate us.[17] Increasingly, neuroscientists are identifying the intricate functionality of the various areas of the brain. Figure 7 outlines three main areas of the brain. Different stimuli trigger responses from different parts of the brain.

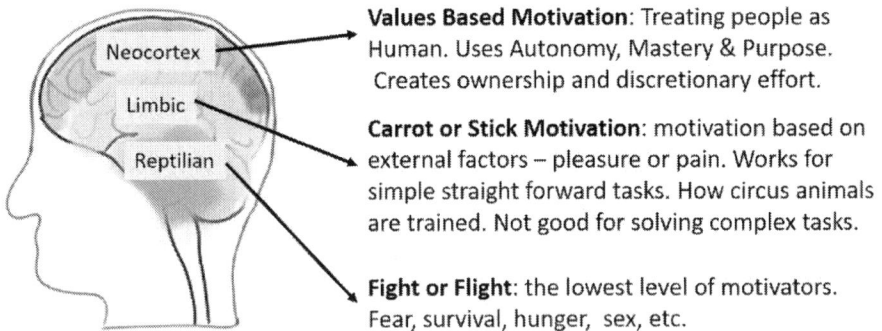

Values Based Motivation: Treating people as Human. Uses Autonomy, Mastery & Purpose. Creates ownership and discretionary effort.

Carrot or Stick Motivation: motivation based on external factors – pleasure or pain. Works for simple straight forward tasks. How circus animals are trained. Not good for solving complex tasks.

Fight or Flight: the lowest level of motivators. Fear, survival, hunger, sex, etc.

Figure 7. Levels of Motivation

At the base of our spine is what is often referred to as our reptilian brain. It is made up of cell types that are like those found in reptiles' brains. This part of the brain doesn't do much thinking or reasoning, it responds in conditioned ways to certain stimuli—especially danger. The emotional response to danger, especially unfamiliar danger, is fear. Fear typically triggers the reptilian brain which reacts instinctively in a *"hard wired"* manner called the fight or flight response. There is a third response possible, and that is to freeze. We see this response from some people when they are out of their comfort zone or they experience a particular danger for the first time. They will get overwhelmed and just freeze up, which can make the situation more dangerous for them and others.

When we perform competently in dangerous situations, we develop a feeling of self-efficacy and our brain learns to respond to the danger in a more reasoned and thoughtful way. Instead of our reptilian brain hijacking our thought processes and readying us for a fight, flight or freeze response, we are able to be more resilient, varied and potent in our actions and responses. This is why drills are so important. But as we have said already, we need to approach drills not with a mindset of chronic unease, we need constant vigilance to ensure that what we expect to happen is in place and is happening.

The mid level of the brain is the limbic or mammalian brain. It performs the same function in all mammals and is more highly developed in animals who live in packs or social hierarchies. Animals communicate with each other through nuances and body language, so the mammalian brain is highly attuned to social nuances, body language and norms. This part of the brain responds to pleasure or pain, or what is often referred to as the carrot and stick approach. This is why carrot and stick motivation is so effective for training animals. The mammalian brain is also where emotions are felt and processed. It triggers our need for:

- relationships,

- to belong and be accepted, and

- our fear of being rejected.

The outer layer of the human brain is the neocortex. It is involved in higher functions such as sensory perception, generation of motor commands, spatial reasoning, conscious thought and reasoning, and language. In terms of motivation, Daniel Pink in his book *Drive* comprehensively reviews the research that shows there are three essential elements that all leaders should focus on:

1. Autonomy—the desire to be self-directed and in charge of our own lives,

2. Mastery—the desire to get better and better at something that matters, and

3. Purpose—the yearning to do what we do in the service of something larger than ourselves.[18]

In our research into the leadership practices that motivated high performing teams we identified 14 Achievement Oriented leadership practices that were highly correlated with outstanding team performance. What was really informative was that all 14 leadership practices were about autonomy, mastery and purpose. The best teams had no aspect of fear motivation or carrot and stick motivation.

DIPI—Dangerous, Important, Pleasurable, Interesting

As leaders it is important to understand why fear and carrot and stick motivation are not the most effective ways to create performance. As our brain takes in stimuli from our senses it processes these stimuli through a part of the brain called the amygdala. It scans the stimuli from our senses and prioritises them for meaning against a scale called DIPI, which stands for Dangerous, Important, Pleasurable, and Interesting.

When we experience a dangerous situation that triggers fear, the brain immediately starts to prepare the body for action by releasing adrenaline, raising the heart rate, increasing blood flow to muscles and firing up the nervous system. But how individuals respond to their fear varies significantly.

Having been a free fall skydiving instructor and taken hundreds of students on their first freefall jump I can confirm that people react in a wide variety of different ways to the fear of their first skydive. The majority just get nervous, but they are very attentive and focused on performing. Some go really quiet and some talk a lot. Those who can't control their fear find it difficult to learn and to put what they learn into practice. The most definitive examples of this are the students who go blank in free fall and stop responding to the instructor's signals and fail to even pull their rip cord at the required opening height.

It is always an interesting moment to observe the cognitive process when you hand someone their ripcord which you pulled for them. Very few people need you to ask the question, *"What was the most important (the second part of DIPI) thing you needed to do up there?"*

When the student lands their parachute on their first jump they experience a sense of elation. The adrenaline that was flooding their system and making them feel ready for action is blended with dopamine, the body's natural *"pleasure drug"*, which helps them feel alive and has them walking around *"on cloud nine"*.

Being part of a high performance team is very much like this. You don't need to be throwing yourself out of a plane to experience this sense of elation. Pikes Fish Place in Seattle is a great example of this.[19] This story is a brilliant example that,

- being an intrinsic part of a team creates a sense of belonging,

- finding excitement in your work, stimulates functional amounts of adrenaline and dopamine,

- if the same work allows you to be yourself and make a difference, it will meet your needs for autonomy,

- doing a good job in your role meets the need for <u>mastery</u>, and

- making people happy and feeling connected meets the need for <u>purpose</u>.

HOW we motivate people is critically important

The sociotechnical nature of work and the advances in technology means that workplaces are increasingly becoming knowledge workplaces. Increasingly the linear algorithmic work of process or production line workers is being done by robots. Humans are increasingly working on heuristic work where the solution is not known, and people need to collaborate to achieve the desired outcomes. Research has shown that workers today spend 50% more time collaborating than they did 20 years ago.[20] Outdated command and control or behaviour based leadership approaches are proven to be totally inadequate for modern workplaces.

In a VUCA[21] environment, how we motivate people is a critical factor in determining success or failure. One of the things that brought us (Brett and Rod) together and made working together enjoyable was our inherent understanding that, when you motivate people with fear—bad things happen. We had both seen enough of this fear based leadership early in our careers to understand the downside. We knew from experience that when people are fearful, they won't admit mistakes, they hide things, underreport problems and errors, and in the worst cases will be outright deceitful and fraudulent.

VW's Dieselgate Emissions Scandal, Boeing's 737 Max crashes, BP's Texas City and Macondo explosions, NASA's loss of both the Challenger and Columbia space shuttles are just a few examples of the bad things that can happen when people fear speaking up and identifying problems. Poor leadership stifles collaboration and the creation of shared meaning and a common purpose.

On a positive note, this understanding is becoming more common and researchers such as Harvard Business School's Amy Edmondson and Teresa Amabile are providing the evidence to show what needs to change.

Edmondson in her book *The Fearless Organization* says that,

> *"When people have psychological safety at work, they feel comfortable sharing concerns and mistakes without fear of embarrassment or retribution. They are confident that they can speak up and won't be humiliated, ignored, or blamed. They know they can ask questions when they are unsure about something. They tend to trust and respect their colleagues. When a work environment has reasonably high psychological safety, good things happen: mistakes are reported quickly so that prompt corrective action can be taken; seamless coordination across groups or departments is enabled, and potentially game-changing ideas for*

innovation are shared. In short, psychological safety is a crucial source of value creation in organizations operating in a complex, changing environment."[22]

Edmondson further highlights the negative effect of fear based leadership and advises that it's hard for people to do their best work when they are fearful. How psychologically safe a person feels impacts the propensity to engage in learning behaviours, especially information sharing, asking for help, or experimenting.[23] Edmondson adds a further insight into the downside of fear based motivation,

"What many people do not realize is that motivation by fear is indeed highly effective – effective at creating the illusion that goals are being achieved. It is not effective in ensuring that people bring the creativity, good process, and passion needed to accomplish challenging goals in knowledge-intensive workplaces."[24]

Amabile found that while external motivation—the carrot and stick approach—can work for algorithmic work, it has a devastatingly negative impact on heuristic work.[25] Our own research found that both algorithmic and heuristic work performance was significantly improved by leaders who treated people as humans and created relationships, autonomy, mastery and purpose.[26] This led to us coining the term RAMP, which identifies the things leaders need to create to RAMP up performance.

How could rewards possibly backfire?

But what about rewards? Surely people won't resent you for giving out rewards. Well no, not initially, but it's an unsustainable, no win game.

Let us look at the experience of Oil & Gas drilling operations. For more than two decades, the process of offering rewards for safety performance has been commonplace in companies that have followed a BBS type approach. But as many have discovered trying to choose who gets the prize is fraught with peril. There are always differing opinions about who was more worthy of the prize. Especially when misreporting and covering up known events becomes part of the game. Those that miss out come to resent the farcical system and the managers that created it. Those that game the system, lose respect for managers when they don't win.

As people become more accustomed to getting big rewards for just doing their job, they resent the company and the managers in charge for being stingy with the BBS rewards and prizes. On one offshore rig that we worked with to change the culture, one very influential crew member expressed the crew sentiment as follows. *"The boys are not happy, we know that they have the budget to offer more prizes, but the boss is just being tight—on Rig XX they're all getting iPads."* he said.

Values Based Safety

Creating a sustainable high performance culture that operates within a sociotechnical system requires a different approach—it is inherently about values and creating an alignment to a set of values that motivate behaviour. This requires a 4-Dimensional leadership driven approach.

A 4-Dimensional approach focuses on commitment not compliance. It recognises that commitment is an enabler; compliance is an outcome to be achieved.

Compliance	Commitment
Control	Acknowledgement
Order	Commitment
Prescribe	Empower
Rules	Values
Management	Leadership
External motivation	Internal motivation
Extrinsic rewards	Intrinsic satisfaction/ownership
Compliance	Self-governance

Table. 2. Rules Based compared to Values Based Safety

Table 2 highlights the fundamental difference between rules based and values based safety. Leaders who *"get it"* understand that people are capable of and freely choose self-governance when they are empowered and committed to shared values. It is important here to not be under any misconception about values based safety compared to behaviour based safety and what they are focused on. They are both focused on creating safe workplaces and both involve the need to address the unsafe behaviours that put people at risk and lead to accidents. The difference is that BBS is based on the ABC model which is incomplete and is why BBS programs do not of themselves lead to the elimination of injuries. This is because behaviour cannot be directly controlled; behaviour is in fact a by-product. Anybody who understands how teamwork is created will intuitively understand this point.

Take the example of the boss who wanted to create high performance teams and organized teambuilding days where people ran around chanting team, team, team while thrusting their fists in the air and patting each other on the back. Meanwhile their competitor set about ensuring that leaders in their company knew the business plan and understood how to get there. Those leaders then worked with their people on mastery and made sure that they had the necessary skills, (not the same but complementary skills) and that they were aligned and committed to a common purpose, shared performance goals and a shared approach for which they held themselves mutually accountable.

The competitor knew that teamwork wasn't an input to be focused on, it wasn't even the output. The output for functional teams is performance and the best teams get big amounts of that. Teamwork for those that really understand it, is a by-product of doing all the other things well. It is subjective and it is created not managed.

Developing a culture that values safety is exactly the same. Contrary to traditional thought, it is not developed by focusing on compliance with management systems. It actually requires a paradigm shift to a leadership commitment to safety as a <u>way of doing business</u>.

Another dynamic to be aware of is that rules-based organizations (and cultures) contain an inherent tension between outside-the-box thinking and inside-the-box compliance. Sustainable safety performance requires each individual to step up and lead, to take responsibility both for their own work and for the performance of others and this cannot be achieved by trying to manage antecedents and consequences; this can only be accomplished through values based self-governance. One of the values that is essential for working safely in any company is a commitment to follow the rules and procedures of the organization. People will only do that when they created the procedures and know that they own them and can update them as needed when they no longer meet the need for work as done (WAD).

Key Takeaways from this Chapter

1. The sociotechnical nature of work and the advances in technology means that workplaces are increasingly becoming knowledge workplaces.

2. Increasingly the linear algorithmic work of process or production line workers is being done by robots.

3. Humans are increasingly working on heuristic work where the solution is not known, and people need to collaborate to achieve the desired outcomes.

4. In a VUCA[27] environment, how we motivate people is a critical factor in determining success or failure.

5. When you motivate people with fear—bad things happen.

   - People have an inherent need for <u>autonomy</u>, <u>mastery</u>, and <u>purpose</u>.

   - A 4-Dimensional approach focuses on commitment not compliance. Commitment is an enabler; compliance is an outcome to be achieved.

6. Teamwork is a by-product of doing all the other things well. It is subjective and it is created not managed.

Reflection Questions

- How successfully have we moved on from linear, algorithmic workflows?

- How are we motivating our people?

- Are we still using a command and control leadership style?

- Are we ramping up our performance through, Relationships, Autonomy, Mastery, and Purpose (RAMP)?

- Do we use a values based approach that creates self-directing teams?

Endnotes:

[1] Reference to Rotter, J. 1973. Internal locus of control scale. In: Robinson, J. P., Shaver, R. F. and Wrightsman, L. (1991). *Measures of Social Psychology* Attitudes: Volume 1. Academic Press. Print. p.53. https://www.elsevier.com/books/measures-of-personality-and-social-psychological-attitudes/robinson/978-0-08-057110-2

[2] Bandura, A., Barling, J., Loughlin, C., and Kelloway, E.K. (2002). Development and Test of a Model Linking Safety-Specific Transformational Leadership and Occupational Safety. *Journal of Applied Psychology,* 87 (3), pp.488-496.

[3] Seligman, M. (1975). *Helplessness: On Depression, Development, and Death.* W.H. Freeman. Print.
Seligman, M. (2006). *Learned Optimism: How to Change Your Mind and Your Life.* Vintage Books. Print.
Seligman, M. (2002). *Authentic Happiness: Using the New Positive Psychology to Realize Your Potential for Lasting Fulfillment.* Free Press. Print.

[4] Sirota, D., Mischkind, L. A. and Meltzer, M. I. (2005). *The Enthusiastic Employee: How Companies Profit by Giving Workers What They Want.* FT Press. Print.

[5] Pfeffer, J. (1998). *The Human Equation.* Harvard Business School Press. Print.

[6] Sirota et al. *op cit.*

[7] Winter, J., Owen, Dr. K., and Read, B. (2010). How Effective Leadership Practices Deliver Safety Performance AND Operational Excellence. *SPE Oil and Gas India Conference and Exhibition.* Mumbai, India, 20-22 Jan, 2010. SPE. https://onepetro.org/search-results?page=1&q=SPE-129035-MS

[8] Corporate Leadership Council (2004). *Engaging the Workforce: Focusing on Critical Leverage Points to Drive Employee Engagement.* [online] Corporate Executive Board.

https://www.scribd.com/document/56150887/CLC-Engaging-the-Workforce-Focusing-on-Critical-Leverage-Points-to-Drive-Employee-Engagement

[9] Winter et al. *op. cit.*

[10] Pink, D. H. (2009*). Drive: The Surprising Truth About What Motivates Us.* Riverhead Books. Print.

[11] VUCA environment—short for an environment characterised by Volatility, Uncertainty, Complexity and Ambiguity. See Chapter 5 for original discussion.

[12] Lloyd, C. F. (2020). *Next Generation Safety Leadership.* CRC Press. Kindle Edition. p.23.

[13] Goodman, S. U. (2020). Safety Sucks!: *The Bull $H!# in the Safety Profession They Don't Tell You About.* Hominum, LLC. Kindle Edition.

[14] *Ibid.*

[15] *Ibid.*

[16] *Ibid.*

[17] Stangor, C. and Walinga, J. (n.d.). Introduction to Psychology: Chapter 4: Brains Bodies and Behaviour – 4.2 Our Brains Control our Thoughts, Feelings and Behaviour. 1st Canadian edition. [online] BCCampus Open Education. https://opentextbc.ca/introductiontopsychology/chapter/3-2-our-brains-control-our-thoughts-feelings-and-behavior/

[18] Pink *op. cit.*

[19]The FISH! Philosophy (2012). *Best Leadership Training to improve Development Programs with FISH! For Leaders Series.* [video] https://www.youtube.com/watch?v=j3kQujxU2Bw&list=PL5SV2LUfJflIIbjOEwYLcucFJcQ nNEeCF&ab_channel=TheFISH%21Philosophy

[20] Cross, R., Rebele, R., and Grant, A. (2016). Collaborative Overload. *Harvard Business Review*, [online] Jan, 2016. https://hbr.org/2016/01/collaborative-overload

[21] VUCA environment—short for an environment characterised by Volatility, Uncertainty, Complexity and Ambiguity. See Chapter 5 for original discussion.

[22] Edmondson, A. C. (2019*). The Fearless Organization: Creating Psychological Safety in the Workplace for Learning, Innovation, and Growth.* John Wiley & Sons, Inc. Kindle Edition.

[23] *Ibid.* p.14.

[24] *Ibid.* p. 57.

[25] Amabile, T.M. (1996). *Creativity in Context.* Westview Press. Print.

[26] Winter et al. *op. cit.*

[27] VUCA environment—short for an environment characterised by Volatility, Uncertainty, Complexity and Ambiguity. See Chapter 5 for original discussion.

Part Three

The Six Factors that Create Relationships, Achievement and Sustainable Performance

Chapter 9

HOW Leaders Create an Achievement Orientation

Based on the many successes we have had improving safety performance in many different countries and environments, we can confidently say that developing the leadership practices that creates high performing teams remains the biggest competitive advantage of any organization.

The leadership practices and approach that creates sustainable self-directed work teams can be readily understood. There are two parts, the first is captured in the CARES framework—WHAT leaders do (which we discussed in Chapter 6). The second thing to understand is HOW leaders create relationships and achievement.

As we studied the leadership practices of effective leaders, we observed Six Factors that were linked to the CARES Framework and were consistently present in every case of sustainable high performance.

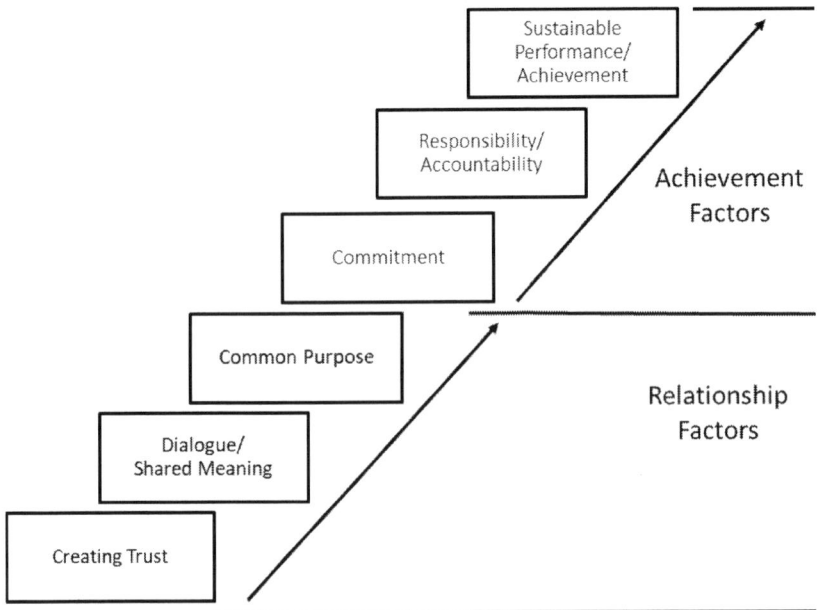

Figure 8. The 6 Factors that Create Relationships and Achievement

These Six Factors are shown in Figure 8 and are listed below:

1. Creating Trust

2. Dialogue/Shared Meaning

3. Common Purpose

4. Commitment

5. Responsibility/Accountability

6. Achievement/Sustainable Performance

An overview of the Six Factors

The Six Factors are like building blocks. As we build and strengthen each block it supports the development of the next one. Over time, each block, each level, is strengthened and developed so that more and more people are at the same level. As people achieve higher levels of trust, they feel comfortable disclosing more about their needs, their desires, and preferences, and also their weaknesses/areas for development. They feel comfortable being vulnerable with each other. Trust grows when they can do this and not be hurt or suffer. Their positive experience of the other person serves to create greater levels of trust and shared meaning and where their interests align this becomes a common purpose. Trust, dialogue and common purpose are the three factors of the Relationship Base that Achievement is built on.

Achievement also has three building blocks. Sustainable performance always starts with commitment. When people are committed to something, they are willing to step up and take responsibility for it and hold themselves accountable for achieving the change or the performance they want.

When leaders do this effectively, they create strong teams and great teamwork, where people feel a sense of connection, belonging and purpose. It creates high levels of psychological safety and self-efficacy, which also makes them better friends, parents, and neighbours.

Ed Catmull, the co-founder of Pixar, believes that his *"job as a manager is to create a fertile environment, keep it healthy, and watch for the things that undermine it."*[1] Catmull is talking about psychological safety—creating a safe environment, where trust becomes an inherent factor that enables and accelerates innovation.

As Catmull says, you don't have to tell people to be creative or to aim higher; they feel inspired on their own. Catmull adds, *"We start from the presumption that our people are talented and want to contribute."* When people feel safe, they will strive to achieve.

Understanding this, allows you to see how ludicrous the BBS approach of offering trinkets and prizes for safety performance is. People don't need external and extrinsic motivation to be safe—it's in their best interest. They just need leaders to do the things that create the operating climate needed to enable them to be safe.

The CARES Framework and the Six Factors
We outlined in Chapter 5 that our research has shown that there are 20 leadership practices that are at the heart of a caring approach. These form the CARES Framework, 6 Relationship practices and 14 Achievement Oriented practices that are common to the leaders of high performance teams. When leaders do these things well, sustainable safety performance is the result.

The Six Factors are different to the CARES framework, because the elements in the CARES framework always exist in some fashion. For example, in a poor performing organization relationships are still there, they just aren't very positive and supporting. They are invariably characterised by hostility, militant industrial relations, control and coercion. Achievement orientation will exist, but again it is flawed. In poor performing teams, achievement is typically focused on a performance orientation (see Chapter 6), outperforming the competition, doing more with less, stretch targets, and other management "*innovations*" that create high stress, not fun workplaces that burn people out and usually have high attrition rates. Endeavour will also be there, but it won't be focused on mastery and doing the best job possible, instead it will be focused on self-orientation and self-preservation. These workplaces are not fun, they are not productive, are not sustainable and generally don't have a good safety performance. If you can understand and embrace the approach outlined in the Six Factors you will create an entirely different workplace culture.

Understanding the Six Factors
The Six Factors are linear in nature because each factor enables the next one to happen and exist. The best way to understand these is by understanding the absence of them, and the downward spiral this creates. For example, without trust there won't be meaningful dialogue. Just think about that from a personal perspective—are you interested in having an open, honest, and meaningful conversation with someone you don't trust? Why would you? Conflict could be just around the corner. Why would you want to share stuff that could make you more vulnerable? The less the other person knows about you the better. The downward spiral continues, without meaningful dialogue shared meaning and common purpose don't get created. Without a common purpose there is no committed team. There's just a bunch of people trying to survive and find a way that they can be safe. Without commitment, people will avoid accountability and will convince themselves that they are not responsible.

Developing Leadership Competencies

As leaders work with the Six Factors they can start with the basics and as they gain skill and experience, they can add to their approach. However, it is important to understand that the approach never changes; the Six Factors always apply.

Think of the development of the Six Factors as being similar to the development of any skill or ability. If you want to be highly proficient in your chosen endeavour you will firstly need to study and understand it. Secondly, you will need to practice and train to build a level of proficiency. Weightlifting is a good example. When you first start you can't lift much or do many reps. Over time as you develop you can achieve more; you can lift more, and you can sustain it for longer.

As a leader, your ability to work with the six factors initially starts out like a novice in the gym, lacking in both robustness and resilience. Over time with continued practice and development you can create a highly robust and resilient team, capable of exceptional levels of achievement and sustainable performance. Also, as with going to the gym and building condition once you stop going and working out you will lose condition and capability. The same applies to the six factors you must stay with it.

Key Takeaways from this Chapter
1. The CARES framework—outlines WHAT leaders do.

2. The Six Factors outlines HOW leaders create relationships and achievement.

3. People don't need external and extrinsic motivation to be safe—it's in their best interest.

4. They just need leaders to do the things that create the operating climate needed to enable them to be safe.

Reflection Questions
- Do you as a leader make the distinction between what people do and how they do it?

- Do you ever use the expression, *"I don't care how you do it, just – do it."*?

Endnotes:

[1] Catmull, E. (2014). *Creativity, Inc.: Overcoming the Unseen Forces that Stand in the Way of True Inspiration.* Transworld Digital. Kindle Edition.

Chapter 10

Leadership that creates Relationships

We said at the start of Chapter 6 that, it is essential that the senior leaders who are designing and creating the overall performance culture of the organization understand the concepts outlined in Chapters 6 to 9.

However, this detailed understanding of the concepts underpinning performance is not needed for front line operational leaders to be effective. The power of the Six Factors is that they outline the steps that leaders need to take to create performance. Senior leaders in organizations certainly need to ensure that their approach is aligned to the principles and practices that we have outlined in this book. Think back to the recipe metaphor that we used in Chapter 1. If you follow the recipe, you'll create what's described. If you leave things out, get the quantities wrong, don't prepare well or mismanage the execution, the outcome won't be good.

So our message for senior leaders is—understand the recipe, prepare well, engage your frontline leaders in the delivery and you'll create the outcome you seek.

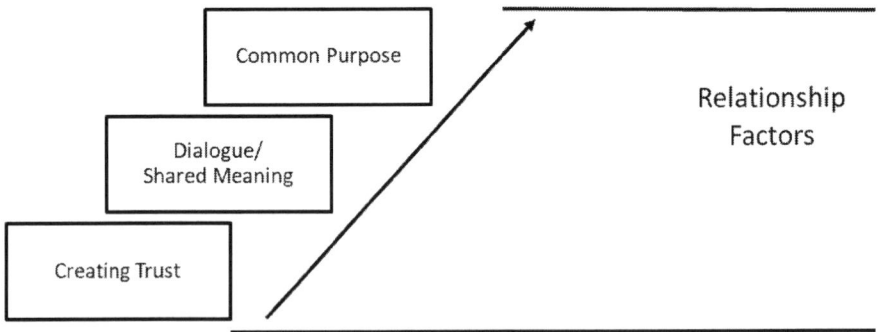

Figure 9. The 3 Relationship Factors

Relationships start with trust

As discussed in Chapter 6 Relationships are the foundation that all Achievement is built on. Without solid relationships achievement will be significantly less than optimum, inconsistent and ultimately unsustainable.

As we previously said, leadership is about relationships—no relationship, no leadership. When you create the relationship foundation to safety as a value and people understand each other, trust each other, and are aligned around a common purpose, people will commit to working safely.

The first step in the Relationship base is trust. Based on our experience of building and leading teams operating in inhospitable environments and carrying out high risk activities we are clear that no quality or characteristic is more important than trust. It is the foundation that both relationship and achievement are built on.

The Integral Model helps us understand that leaders earn trust by being in dialogue with their team. Great leaders have real conversations that address the real issues that their people are dealing with. Leaders need to have the skills to earn the trust to be able to have difficult conversations about topics that don't have an easy answer or maybe the issue is a dilemma that doesn't have a perfect answer and the only effective solution requires a compromise where both parties must give something for a successful, or at least functional outcome. When they can do this effectively, they create psychological safety.

The importance of trust and how it is developed is not very well understood by many leaders and especially in the field of safety. This point was made by Gunningham and Sinclair in a study focused on the Australian coal mining industry. They found that *"unless the mistrust of the workforce can be overcome then even the most well-intentioned and sophisticated management initiatives will be treated with cynicism and undermined."*[1]

It is worthy of note that the authors in the above quote discuss overcoming mistrust compared to earning or having the trust of the workforce. Studies of trust have found that trust and distrust do not sit on the same continuum.[2] An absence of trust does not automatically lead to mistrust and that's because when trust is absent the default position for the average person is neutral. For example, when you meet someone for the first time and don't know anything about them, there is no reason to mistrust them, however you also don't have any history with that person, any context that helps you decide how and to what extent you can trust them.

Mistrust is different, it is negative and includes an expectation of actions and outcomes that may be harmful of hurtful for you. Trust and mistrust are earned.

Leaders need to be able to earn the trust of those they work with and also need to be able to create psychological safety in their team and organization. There is a difference between the two concepts. A key difference is that psychological safety is experienced at a group level.[3] Team members working together will have shared perceptions of whether or not the climate is psychologically safe. Trust, by comparison, refers to interactions between two individuals or parties; trust exists in the mind of an individual and pertains to a specific target individual or organization.[4]

Rachel Botsman is a Trust Fellow at Oxford University's Saïd Business School and a leading expert on trust in the modern world. She has a good way to understand trust by comparing it to how we use money. She explains, we assign a value to money and use it to conduct transactions. Money is tangible and it has an agreed value. She further explains,

> *"Trust is different, trust essentially is a human feeling, we know when we feel trust, but it's not something that we can easily measure or agree on what it is. So the way I think about it is that if money is the currency of transactions, trust is the currency of interactions. And when you start to see it like that you start to see why it's so fragile and why it's so valuable in our personal and professional lives."[5]*

How leaders earn trust

We have had clients say to us, *"I want you to teach my managers and supervisors how they can build trust."* Statements like this highlight one of the most misunderstood things about trust. Leaders often think of trust as something that they can control; they don't. They can earn trust, it is given, and the person giving it controls when it is given and to what extent.

In their book *The Trusted Advisor,* Maister, Green and Galford introduce a very useful way to understand how trust can be earned and how it can be lost. They call it the Trust Formula.[6]

$$\text{Trust} = \frac{C + R + I}{S}$$

Where:

T = Trust

C = Credibility

R = Reliability

I = Intimacy

S = Self Orientation

Figure 10. The Trust Formula

Maister et. al. explain that there are four distinct realms that we are tuned into and assess to help us make decisions about how much we should trust someone. [7]

Component	Realm	Example
Credibility	Words	I can trust what she says about ...
Reliability	Actions	I can trust him to ...
Intimacy	Emotions	I feel comfortable discussing this ...
Self Orientation	Motives	I can trust that she cares about ...

Table 3. Trust Realms

Understanding the four realms helps us do the things that earn trust and most importantly avoid mistrust.

Credibility

> *"**To be** persuasive, We must be believable,*
> ***To be** believable, We must be credible,*
> ***To be** credible, We must be **truthful**."*
> — *Edward R. Murrow*

Most leaders understand the need for credibility and work at achieving this. It's about expertise, it's why people seek qualifications. But credibility is more than just having knowledge, it is also about experience and competency which is why credibility takes time to establish.

There are both rational and emotional components of credibility and both are needed to create an integral approach. The concept of credibility includes notions of both competency/accuracy and completeness/integrity. These align with the objective and subjective realms of the integral model.

Leaders need to be competent in terms of objective things—systems and processes, data, goals and measurement. They also need to be credible in terms of subjective things such as intentions and aspirations.

When someone is perceived to be accurate, we use the word *"believable"* to describe them. When we are talking about their completeness, on the other hand, we say they are *"honest."*[8]

Reliability
Reliability for a leader is fairly straight forward. It is a measure of whether you do or don't deliver on things that you are accountable for or that you have chosen to be responsible for. It is especially about things that you have committed to others to be responsible for.

A quick way to destroy trust is to make a commitment to others and then not deliver. We can probably all remember that person that puts their hand up and says, *"Leave that to me, I can do that."* and then they don't deliver.

Intimacy

Intimacy refers to the safety or security that we feel when entrusting someone with something. We might say, *"I can trust her with that information; she's never violated my confidentiality before, and she would never embarrass me."*

Intimacy in a work setting is not about sharing our private lives. It is about being comfortable sharing personal thoughts, preferences and needs with those you work with. Ultimately it is about feeling you can be authentic at work. Authenticity highlights the interwoven nature of trust and psychological safety. The greater the level of psychological safety the more people will trust and feel they can safely be vulnerable, being more intimate and less self-oriented. That trust then creates a virtuous cycle and generates greater levels of psychological safety and authenticity.

Be careful though, intimacy can be a double-edged sword when it is not adequately tempered with balanced self-orientation. BP CEO, Tony Hayward, experienced this in the Macondo well blowout and Gulf of Mexico oil spill. Hayward focused on his own discomfort rather than that of those harmed by the catastrophe. In response to a media question, he said, *"There is no one who wants this over more than I do. I'd like my life back."* The media and others drew the direct comparison to the 11 who died and the people whose lives would never be the same again. Hayward's moment of self-disclosure certainly didn't do him any good.

When there is intimacy people will speak candidly but also with feeling and empathy. It is important to be able to disagree without being disagreeable.

Self-Orientation (Putting your people first)

Self-Orientation refers to a person's focus. In particular, whether the person's focus is primarily on him or herself, or on the other person. We might say, *"I can't trust him on this deal—I don't think he cares enough about me, he's focused on what he gets out of it."* Or more commonly, *"I don't trust him—I think he's too concerned about how he's appearing, so he's not really paying attention."*

Once a leader understands the importance of the self-orientation dimension of trust it can change their entire perception of their role as a leader. It shifts their vision of who they want to be as a leader.

A simple way for a leader to earn trust with their team is to always have their back. When the boss arrives to share their displeasure about a result, make sure that you stand up and be accountable, your team—your result. But when there is praise to be given always encourage your boss to speak directly to your team and to acknowledge them for their hard work. This is about servant leadership—remember true leaders always eat last.

The trust formula above is very useful for understanding how we manage interactions at the individual level. Who the leader is being in their interactions has a significant impact on their perceived trustworthiness. Are they being credible, are they reliable? Are they capable of an effective level of intimacy—having meaningful conversations of what is real, what's needed, what's causing concern? Are they capable of being a servant leader and putting the team's needs first or are they just self-oriented?

When working with groups leaders need to be able to earn trust—but also create psychological safety.[9] To do this effectively leaders need to understand group dynamics. A good way to think of the difference is that trust influences a person's decisions about how vulnerable they are willing to be when interacting with another person or group. Psychological safety is created by what leaders say and do in their team and the group; it influences how someone feels in a given situation. As we discussed in Chapter 7, leaders provide clarity by answering their team's questions regarding Why—How—What as outlined in Figure 11 below.

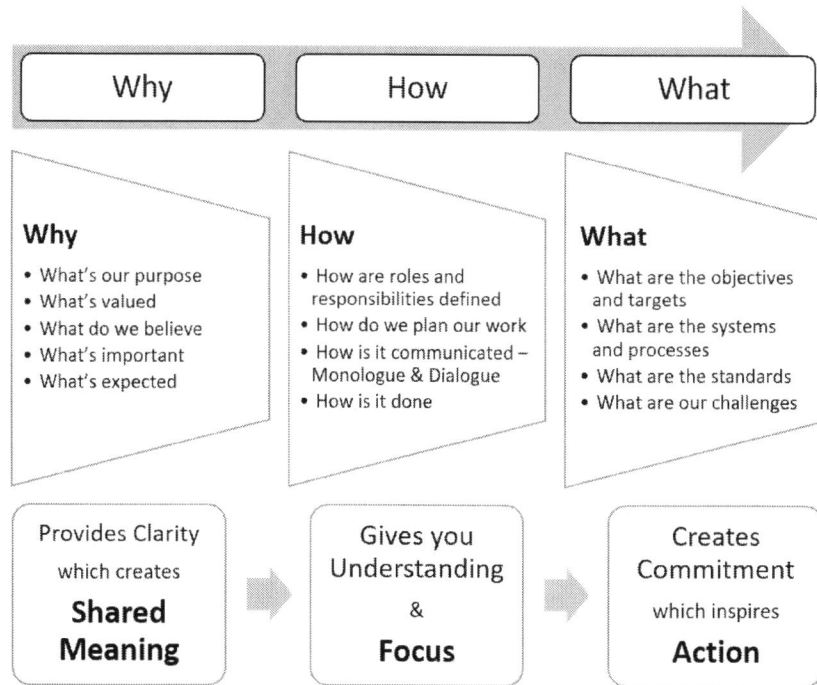

Why	How	What
• What's our purpose • What's valued • What do we believe • What's important • What's expected	• How are roles and responsibilities defined • How do we plan our work • How is it communicated – Monologue & Dialogue • How is it done	• What are the objectives and targets • What are the systems and processes • What are the standards • What are our challenges
Provides Clarity which creates **Shared Meaning**	Gives you Understanding & **Focus**	Creates Commitment which inspires **Action**

Figure 11. The Why, How, What of Sustainable Safety

Defining trust

Rachel Botsman explains that trust is a mixture of vulnerability and expectations and based on this understanding she offers a simple yet very useful definition of trust:

"Trust is a confident relationship with the unknown."[10]

As someone who has done many high risk activities for both work and sports, this definition resonates with me and is very meaningful. Understanding trust this way allows you to see that it is relationship based and is something that develops. As Botsman explains, *"it enables us to navigate uncertainty, to place our faith in strangers, to cope with unknown people and unknown things. The greater the uncertainty, the greater the unknown, the more trust that is required."*[11]

When high levels of trust exist among members of a work team, there is a confidence that their peers' intentions are good, and that there is no reason to be protective or careful around the group.

In essence, to create high performance teams which are characterized by trust and psychological safety, teammates must get comfortable being vulnerable with one another.

Trust and healthy conflict

When it comes to relationships, trust is all about vulnerability. As you build a relationship with someone you become more willing to be open, to be exposed, and to share things about yourself. You are more willing to rely on that person in various ways, trusting that they have your best interests at heart. Vulnerability-based trust is a powerful factor in team performance. Team members who feel comfortable being vulnerable with one another don't waste time and energy hiding things. They are willing to admit error or weaknesses and be open about their fears or concerns. They are willing to speak about their needs and voice their concerns knowing that there may be a lack of alignment about goals and purpose. They have faith that teams members will act *"above the line"* and not put operational objectives above relationships and team unity. They don't fear having healthy conflict.

Trust is contextual and subjective but real

Think of some people in your life that you really trust. They could be a family member, a friend, someone you work with. Typically, the nature of the trust you have in the person will vary depending on your relationship with them and the context.

You trust family, friends and work colleagues in different ways and for different things. You decide how and in what ways you will trust them based on a range of feelings and emotions. Trust is highly contextual and highly subjective.[12]

In our work, it is not unusual to hear the question, *"Do you trust 'So and So'?"* The answer to that question should always be, *"To do What?"* Trust is not an umbrella term; it is related to a specific thing. I trust my family in ways that are unique to family members.

I trust myself to drive on the racetrack in motorsport events at speeds well over 200 KPH. I co-drive/navigate for a mate in tarmac rally events on closed country roads at similar very high speeds. Being a passenger in a car under these conditions is a very calculated decision and not something that I would trust just anybody with.

In many high risk work activities, there is a need to trust work colleagues that they will do their job and perform their role, knowing that if they fail someone could be hurt or killed.

Trust and self-determined effort

The most effective teams that we have observed and worked with have high levels of self-efficacy as defined by Albert Bandura.[13] Bandura identified that such feelings develop when people, through their own self-determined actions, are successful at achieving their goals and meeting their needs.

The emphasis here is on self-determined, for the literature is clear on this point—feelings of efficacy do not emerge when there is no correlation between intention, effort, and outcome. When this correlation is lacking, the causes of outcomes are attributed to outside forces like compliance with rules, or fear of punishment. However, when this correlation is present, the causes of outcomes are attributed to self-determined effort.

Self-determined effort combined with positive outcomes creates increased confidence in one's ability to have an impact and make a difference. Over time this increases the degree to which people believe that they, as opposed to external forces (beyond their influence), have control over the outcome of events in their lives. This is why giving people autonomy is so important.

Self-determined effort and dialogue

Understanding the link between self-determined effort and dialogue is a really important point for improving performance. A number of researchers have found that how much a worker believes they can influence their workplace has a significant impact on how much they are willing to trust and share information with others. This becomes a virtuous cycle, dialogue creates shared meaning and over time increases trust. Increased mutual trust leads to higher levels of confidence and self-determination which in turn drives more meaningful dialogue. The origins of the word itself—dialogue, comes from the Greek words dia and logos which translates as *"flow of meaning."*[14]

This concept has been recognised for a long time and is captured in the aphorism:

"Where attention and focus goes, energy flows,
Where energy goes, achievement grows."

Creating shared meaning through trust

In our leadership development programs we have found that when leaders are introduced to these simple concepts and are able to apply them the benefits in terms of improved performance are quite profound.[15]

The Trust Triangle model shown in Figure 12 outlines the process for developing the trust and psychological safety that underpins performance. If a leader can do these things well, they create the second step in the relationship foundation—shared meaning based on a shared understanding. Through dialogue both parties arrive at a position of shared reality and shared values. This approach needs to be *"whole brained"*, engaging both the left brain with its focus on rational, logical fact based things as well as the right brain focus on creativity, integration, emotions, and interpersonal factors. Over time as our understanding of each other develops and deepens, that understanding develops into greater levels of trust which creates a feeling of psychological safety.

When leaders fail to create shared meaning and a common purpose, people invariably become more self-oriented and are increasingly motived by self-interest. As things deteriorate trust and psychological safety are severely eroded and gradually self-interest becomes self-preservation. You only need to look at any industry that has historically bad industrial relations issues to see this playing out.

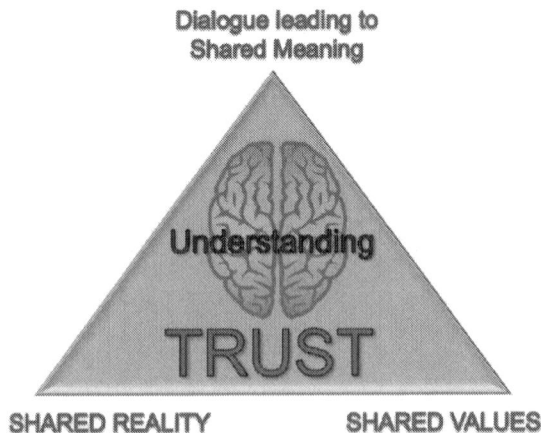

Figure 12. The Trust Triangle –Understanding and Trust

A good place to start the dialogue that creates shared meaning is to go through the Why—How—What flow diagram that we discussed earlier (See Figure 11). Firstly, do a check on whether you have provided information on each of the points to create both clarity and understanding. How have you done that? Too many companies do that as a monologue—directives, developed on high and then handed down to the organization as a monologue that people are expected to adopt.

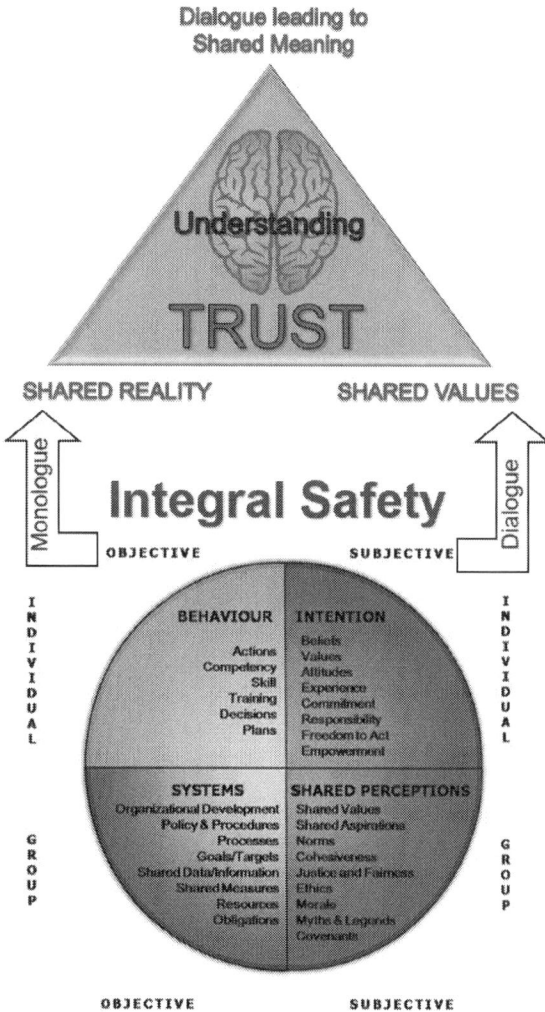

Figure 13. Leadership that Creates a Common Purpose

Figure 13 shows the process that effective leaders use to create the third step in the relationship foundation—a commitment to a common purpose. When leaders adopt an integral approach and engage their people in effective dialogue they build mutual understanding, and as we said, this creates shared meaning, shared reality and values. These factors create a culture where psychological safety and trust are drivers of high performance.

A horrible environment to work in

Unfortunately, too many businesses only operate through the left side of the integral model. They focus on systems and behaviour; they communicate primarily through monologue—volumes of procedures and rules. There is no positive relationship between management and workers in this approach. The command and control leadership model is favoured by these organizations. It is not about relationships that are based on engagement and commitment. Instead, it is about authority and compliance. In its most ineffective form this approach creates distrust and hostility. Leaders don't trust workers and seek to keep them in line through behaviour based, carrot and stick or even worse fear based leadership practices, founded on arbitrary rules for dismissal. Workers resent this leadership approach and rebel in ways that they can. They don't communicate and they withdraw discretionary effort and only comply with rules and processes when being policed to do so by a controlling and dominating chain of command. This type of leadership creates a horrible work environment.

Understanding why procedures aren't followed

When we start working with an organization, we recommend that they conduct a review of their incidents over the last 24 months and calculate the percentage of incidents where individuals did not follow existing procedures or an established work practice. Typically, the percentage is greater than 80 percent and, in some cases, more than 90 percent of their incidents fall into this category[16]. We then analyse these incidents against the concept of 4D Safety and the Integral Model to identify where the gaps exist.

Questions to be considered to identify the cause of these failures include, for example:

- Is this an engagement/commitment issue, if so, then the issue sits in the Intention Quadrant of the Integral Model? It is therefore a leadership issue, and any solution needs to focus on the 4th Dimension of performance – Human Factors and Leadership.

- Is this an individual competency and skill issue? If it is, then it's a Behaviour Quadrant issue and requires a management approach focused on the 3rd Dimension – Systems and Procedures focused on individual and group training.

- Or is the cause linked to other factors such as stretch targets and trying to push production levels above design parameters, which sit in the Systems Quadrant. Or it may be related to plant and equipment which has design flaws or is not fit for purpose? This requires a management approach focused on Dimension 1 – Schedule and Production and will have implications for Dimension 2 – Costs (possibly both CAPEX and OPEX) and appropriate resources.

The solution to each of these issues starts with working through the six factors. First establish trust, which will enable you to have conversations and dialogue that creates shared meaning. As team members start to trust you, they will share their challenges, their frustrations, and their needs. You create deeper levels of understanding and trust. You can start to have conversations about their reality and what they value and will commit to. Having discussions about their frustrations such as gaps between how they actually work compared to how the procedure is written is a good place to start. This is often called work as imagined (WAI) versus work as done (WAD). Aligning WAI and WAD all of a sudden becomes simple when workers and managers want the same thing and are committed to working together to achieve it. When leaders create this environment, workers feel that they own the procedures and are more likely to follow them. But there is another step required which is part of the achievement orientation and is discussed in Chapter 11.

Ask the right questions – don't tell

The best companies develop shared meaning through an iterative process of dialogue with front line operators. Constantly asking questions and being in meaningful dialogue to mutually confirm and ensure, firstly, what is needed and secondly, that what's needed and expected is being done. See Chapter 9, and the discussion of dialogue that creates shared meaning, for some examples of questions to ask. But please, always keep in mind that you don't create shared meaning and you certainly don't shift peoples' thinking by telling them or talking at them.

I learned this in a sales program I attended some years back. The guy running the program was a brilliant salesperson he could sell anything. His advice was that if he wanted to influence someone, he had to get them to tell him what they needed.

The way he put it was, "*People typically believe less than 10% of what they are being told but believe 95% or more of what they say.*" If you want someone to act on something or to commit to something, you need to get them to tell you why they want it or why it's important. Of course, he was talking about people talking to someone that they don't know well or trust. But as a leader, starting out with your team, needing to build relationships, isn't that where you are? You haven't earned their trust yet. As we discussed earlier, at the start trust is usually neutral, and depending on the actions of your predecessor and other leaders in your company you might be dealing will levels of mistrust.

As trust increases all parties are less fearful about engaging in passionate dialogue about issues. Increasingly, they can engage in constructive conflict debating contentious issues confidently secure in the trust that all parties are committed to a common purpose.

The impact of fear on psychological and physical safety

Timothy Clark in his book, *The 4 Stages of Psychological Safety* identifies leadership practices that eradicate fear as a key principle in creating psychological safety.

> *"The presence of fear in an organization is the first sign of weak leadership. If you can banish fear, install true performance-based accountability, and create a nurturing environment that allows people to be vulnerable as they learn and grow, they will perform beyond your expectations and theirs."*[17]

Unfortunately, as we have seen in many of the examples in this book, too few organizations effectively focus on creating the relationship base that supports psychological safety. However, what is even worse is when you have individuals who have the courage to voice concerns and report problems, but the organization's leadership either, can't see the issue and doesn't trust them enough to act on their advice or doesn't have the skills and competency to be able to create the solution. In the latter case these leaders typically resent the people who speak up and raise a concern. As the saying goes:

> *Those who Identify the problem, become the problem.*

Trust must flow both ways

In high risk operations and industries, it is a matter of life and death, that we need to be able to trust the chain of command to do their job and manage things well.

In 1986, seven Astronauts trusted NASA's leaders to properly manage the systems and procedures as they strapped themselves into the Challenger space shuttle. Less than 2-minutes after launch the space shuttle exploded in a fireball which resulted in the deaths of all 7 astronauts. An identified problem with the O rings on the solid rocket boosters caused the explosion. NASA managers had known since 1977 that contractor Morton-Thiokol's design of the SRBs contained a potentially catastrophic flaw in the O-rings, but they had failed to address this problem properly.[18] On the day of the launch, the engineers and the contractor responsible for the solid rocket boosters were not confident that the O rings would perform as required in the unseasonal cold temperatures experienced— they recommended not to launch. NASA management did not trust their advice and bullied and coerced them to change the recommendation. Initially, NASA management denied any knowledge that forewarned of the possible catastrophe. The flaws in NASA's management of the space shuttle program eventually came out in the Rogers Commission Report.[19]

Ten years later in 1996, 20 Australian SAS operators were passengers on Blackhawk helicopters which they trusted the Chief of the Army and his executive to manage and ensure the Blackhawks and those who flew them were up to the job. That trust was misplaced. As mentioned in Chapter 1 the Army had reviewed the problems with the management of the Blackhawk fleet and recommended that the challenging Special Forces support tasks not be carried out. But the Chief of the Army did not trust the advice and recommendations of his 2 Star General in Operational Command of the Blackhawks. Orders that tasked the SAS to be able to mount airborne assaults from Blackhawks were not changed—3 Aviators and 15 SAS soldiers died as a result. The Chief of the Army denied any responsibility for the tragedy and instigated court martial proceedings against five operational level officers.

We have had people say to us that these incidents involving Special Forces operations, or NASA and Astronauts are so far removed from "*normal business operations*" that they are not that relevant, but to say that is to miss the point. In the cases we have discussed, the people closest to the operation recognised the dangers and spoke up. They reported their concerns to their managers who failed to act and keep the individuals involved safe.

But the same is happening on a daily basis in workplaces around the world. In her book *The Fearless Organization* Amy Edmondson had this warning that is worth heeding:

> "*Remaining silent due to fear of interpersonal risk can make the difference between life and death. Airplanes have crashed, financial institutions have fallen, and hospital patients have died unnecessarily because individuals were, for reasons having to do with the climate in which they worked, afraid to speak up.*"[20]

The role of trust in Sociotechnical Safety

The increasingly complicated nature of technological systems and the growing complexity inherent in sociotechnical systems means that old school command and control leadership doesn't work. The changing nature of work means it is rapidly becoming impossible for senior managers to make effective risk management decisions regarding changes or drift in systems and processes in their span of operations.

What is needed is leaders who are capable of earning trust and who trust their people. This is a fundamental difference that we have observed between the way high performing teams operate and most businesses operate. In high performing teams, like the best

Formula One teams, the SAS or the US Navy Seals, it is clearly understood that trust is a critical factor in team performance. If mutual trust does not exist, the communication and interaction necessary for the successful execution of the complicated and complex tasks that Special Forces units undertake is not possible.

The difference can be understood by looking at the importance placed on competency and trust in selecting people and can be understood from the matrix shown at Figure 14.

In high performing teams the primary focus is on trustworthiness. The perfect team member is a person who is a Nine—highly trustworthy and highly competent. Of course, every company wants to employ people who are highly trustworthy and highly competent. The difference becomes clear when you recognise which box is the second choice. In high performing teams the selection process focuses on understanding both dimensions—trust and competency, and the second choice is to go for a Six.

Many businesses don't have any effective measures of trustworthiness. The typical measures used for selection focus on qualifications, certifications, past results, and achievements are measures of competency and performance not trustworthiness. So, they end up employing Nines, Eights and Sevens. High performing organizations select Nines, then Sixes and then Three's. The difference this has on the culture of the organization and the way people interact is profound, both in leadership roles and as team members.

7 HC/LT	8 HC/MT	9 HC/HT
4 MC/LT	5 MC/MT	6 MC/HT
1 LC/LT	2 LC/MT	3 LC/HT

Competency (vertical axis label)

Trust

Figure 14. The Trust – Competency Matrix

Leaders who are a seven are toxic. They are not trustworthy and also don't trust their people. They are not honest in their reporting and cannot be relied upon to do the things that are expected of them. They will become deceitful and deceptive rather than admit to not knowing something, not performing, or making a mistake. BP and the Macondo Well blowout, VW and the Dieselgate scandal, the collapse of Barings Bank through Nick

Leeson's trading in Singapore, and the Enron scandal all come to mind here. The impact of this type of leader can be far reaching, they can:

- shut down employee communication and feedback,
- stifle productivity,
- hinder growth and development, and
- hinder new initiatives.

They also do not make good team members as they are not able to maintain strong and long lasting relationships. They claim credit for other people's work and seek to undermine team members they feel are a threat. They will not speak up or stop the job when they see a problem. They typically, cut corners, hide quality issues, and generally can't be relied on.

A person who is a Three is a very different prospect. They generally don't make it to leadership roles unless nepotism is involved and then the results can vary widely based on a range of factors. For example, if they are capable of learning they may develop quite quickly when teamed up with a mentor or supportive team members. You see this quite often in privately owned and operated companies where a family member is given preferential development.

As a team member, in an environment where there is psychological safety, they can be relied upon to stop the job and ask questions if they are unsure of something. If they are not confident in their ability to take on a particular task, they will say so and ask for support.

Schlumberger had a culture expecting high performance and would in managerial roles sack the bottom 10 per cent of managers each year based on performance reports. They also promoted very much on performance but paid a lot of attention to team work to avoid the pitfalls mentioned above.

A mistake that I saw more than once with this approach is that highly competent technical people would get promoted but they lacked the 4th Dimension leadership skills and would underperform as a leader. They would not last in that role; the company would lose a highly competent technical person and the individual's career would be damaged in the process.

The challenge is for organizations to create the psychological safety where people can have a voice and are trusted to raise concerns and flag when things are not going well. The good news is that as a result of modern technology, getting this feedback from the coal face all the way to the executive leadership team is becoming increasingly easier to achieve.

As we worked with clients, we developed a range of online feedback tools that are designed to monitor and track leading performance measures of competency and safety leadership.[21] We believe that in modern sociotechnical operations, organizations must make use of technology and track sound 4-Dimensional leading indicators in real time, in order to avoid any unnecessary risk for their people and organization.

Trust and Psychological Safety are not the same thing

"We now know that psychological safety emerges as a property of a group, and that groups in organizations tend to have very interpersonal climates. Even in a company with a strong corporate culture, you will find pockets of both high and low psychological safety."[22]

— Amy Edmondson

Edmondson says that trust and psychological have much in common, but she highlights that they are not the same thing. Psychological safety is experienced within a group, whereas trust is about the interactions between two individuals or groups.[23]

We need to be able to trust our boss and feel psychologically safe within our team. Without both, people become fearful, with the result that:

- People do not speak up and don't ask questions.
- Clarity, shared meaning, and common purpose are missing.
- Team engagement is low and a sense of helplessness is pervasive.
- Reports and metrics are unreliable.
- Ideas are not shared, problems go unaddressed, innovation and change efforts faulter.
- Systems and processes don't get challenged and bureaucracy reigns.

Our research that we discussed in Chapter 4 also supports these findings and led to the development of the Leadership Efficacy Chain (see Figure 15).[24]

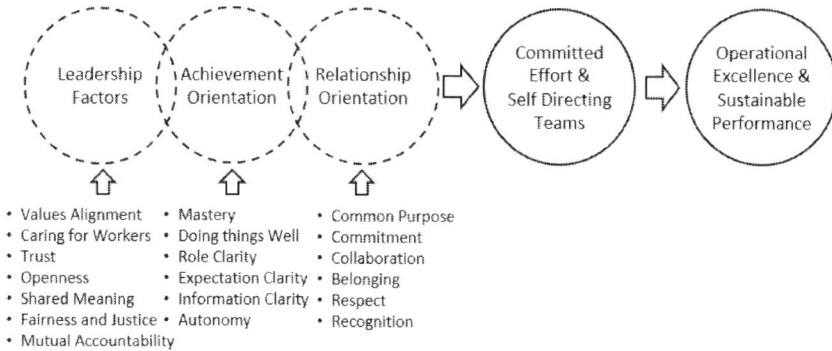

Figure 15. The Leadership Efficacy Chain

It is the job of leaders to create a climate which is based on psychological safety, where people are willing to speak up and speak about problems.

Our work sometimes sees us being engaged to work with companies that have a long history of poor performance. In every one of these engagements, we have found that trust is low and in the worst cases mistrust is high. No significant improvement and certainly no sustainable performance is possible until leaders can earn the trust of their workers. For trust to develop leaders need to be seen to be credible and reliable. If workers raise concerns and nothing changes, they will soon stop raising their concerns. Dialogue reduces or stops altogether, and a vicious cycle begins.

Dialogue that creates Shared Meaning and Common Purpose

4D Safety is not about focusing on what's wrong or fixing things. We need to focus on making things go well, and we do that by focusing on mastery and making things better. Here are some questions that we recommend to shift the thinking and focus to a 4D Approach:

1. What do we need to do more of or do differently to create an environment of care and respect in our workplace?

2. What do we currently not do well? What's missing in our current approach?

3. How could we improve?

Clive Lloyd makes the point that, *"leaders of more mature cultures don't merely keep their employees well informed—rather they are also well informed by their employees—indicating genuine two-way communication."*[25]

157

The understanding and shared meaning that develops from genuine dialogue is a game changer. It allows organizations to move from a carrot and stick, motivation style to a relationship and values based approach. It changes the dialogue from a—"*if you do this, then you'll get that*" transactional approach, to one of—because we are committed to the same things and have a common purpose, this is what we are prepared, willing and able to do.

In our 4-Dimensional Safety approach the above questions are a part of our online tools that are available to operators and their supervisors. Having this information from the frontline gives managers and supervisors the opportunity to have meaningful conversations with their teams. From this process, they can focus on and act on what's not going well. When they do this, they create credibility and quickly earn trust. This creates psychological safety and a sense that *"we all want the same thing"*—we are committed to a common purpose.

Key Takeaways from this Chapter

1. Leadership is fundamentally about relationships—no relationship, no leadership.

2. Great leaders have real conversations and act to address the real issues that their people are dealing with—and in doing so they earn trust.

3. Trust and distrust do not sit on the same continuum.

4. Trust and mistrust are earned.

5. There are four areas that leaders should focus on to earn trust, Credibility, Reliability, Intimacy, and Self-orientation.

6. Trust is a mixture of vulnerability and expectations, a useful definition of trust: *Trust is a confident relationship with the unknown.*

7. A positive expectation of the future leads to feelings of self-efficacy—feelings of efficacy do not emerge when there is no correlation between intention, effort, and outcome. Leaders need to pay attention to this correlation.

8. Trust and psychological safety are not the same thing. Psychological safety is experienced within a group, whereas trust is about the interactions between two individuals or groups.

9. Remember the No D!(kheads rule. The Trust-Competency Matrix helps us understand this.

10. Great leaders build relationships, shared meaning and commitment to a common purpose.

Reflection Questions

- Do I recognize and reward those who bring issues forward that need addressing?

- How well do I do the things that earn trust?

- Do I make sure that what I say is always credible?

- Am I reliable? Can people trust me for my word?

- Am I willing to have discussions with my team members about how things really are, or do I avoid having difficult conversations? Creating intimacy requires courage and a willingness to confront the truth no matter how unpleasant or inconvenient it may be.

- Do I put my people first? This is about servant leadership—not being self-oriented. Remember true leaders always eat last.

Endnotes:

[1] Gunningham, N., & Sinclair, D. (2012). *Working Paper 85 – Building Trust: OHS Management in the Mining Industry.* [pdf] National Research Centre for OHS Regulation. http://regnet.anu.edu.au/sites/default/files/publications/attachments/2015-05/WorkingPaper_85_0.pdf

[2] Botsman, R. (2020). *The importance of trust.* [video] https://www.linkedin.com/learning/why-trust-matters-with-rachel-botsman/the-importance-of-trust

[3] Edmondson, A. C. (2019*). The Fearless Organization: Creating Psychological Safety in the Workplace for Learning, Innovation, and Growth.* John Wiley & Sons, Inc. Kindle Edition. pp.16-17.

[4] Edmondson *op. cit.* pp.16-17.

[5] Botsman *op. cit.*

[6] Maister, D. H., Green, C. H. and Galford, R. M. (2002). *The Trusted Advisor.* Simon & Schuster. Print.

[7] *Ibid.*

[8] *Ibid.*

[9] Edmondson *op. cit.* pp.16-17.

[10]Botsman, R. (2020). *The real meaning of trust.* [video] https://www.linkedin.com/learning/why-trust-matters-with-rachel-botsman/the-real-meaning-of-trust

[11] *Ibid.*

[12] Botsman, R. (2020). *Challenging assumptions about trust.* [video] https://www.linkedin.com/learning/why-trust-matters-with-rachel-botsman/challenging-assumptions-about-trust

[13] Bandura, A. 1997. *Self-Efficacy: The Exercise of Control.* Freeman. Print.

[14] Senge, P. M. (1990) *The Fifth Discipline: The Art and Practice of the Learning Organisation.* DoubleDay. Print.

[15] Read, B., Zartl-Klik, A., Veit, C., Zamhaber, R., and Zepic, H. (2010). Safety Leadership that Engages the Workforce to Create Sustainable HSE Performance. In: *SPE International Conference on Health Safety and Environment in Oil and Gas Exploration and Production.* Rio de Janeiro, Brazil, 12-14 April, 2010. SPE. https://onepetro.org/search-results?page=1&q=SPE-126901-MS

[16] International Association Oil & Gas Producers. (2019). *Data Series.* [online] identifies that 72% of fatalities and >90% of all incidents were caused by people not following rules and procedures correctly. https://data.iogp.org/

[17] Clark, Timothy R. (2020). *The 4 Stages of Psychological Safety.* Berrett-Koehler Publishers. Kindle Edition.

[18] Presidential Commission (1986). *Report to the President on the Space Shuttle Challenger Accident.* [online] NASA. https://history.nasa.gov/rogersrep/genindex.htm

[19] *ibid.*

[20] Edmondson *op. cit.* p.8.

[21] Read, B., Ritchie, R. and Butler, C. (2015). *It's Time for a Global Rethink on Safety Performance.* [post] LinkedIn. https://www.linkedin.com/pulse/its-time-global-rethink-safety-performance-brett-read/

[22] Edmondson *op. cit.* p.8.

[23] *Ibid.*

[24] Winter, J., Owen, Dr. K., and Read, B. (2010). How Effective Leadership Practices Deliver Safety Performance AND Operational Excellence. *SPE Oil and Gas India Conference and Exhibition.* Mumbai, India, 20-22 Jan, 2010. SPE. https://onepetro.org/search-results?page=1&q=SPE-129035-MS

[25] Lloyd, C. F. (2020). *Next Generation Safety Leadership.* CRC Press. Kindle Edition. p.5.

Chapter 11

Achievement Factors

Figure 16. The Three Achievement Factors

As we said in Chapter 3, It is essential to ensure the first 3 Dimensions of performance—production and schedule, costs and resources, and systems and processes are done well. They are the enablers of performance. If any of these Dimensions are not adequately planned or managed, then performance will suffer or possibly fail all together.

However, doing these 3 Dimensions well is not enough, these 3 Dimensions create compliance with a system not commitment to a value. We need to achieve compliance, but hopefully by now you are clear that compliance and sustainable high performance are outcomes that come out of our commitment to doing things as well as possible.

When you get the 4th Dimension working in harmony with the other 3 Dimensions you get great operational performance.

Commitment
The most critical step in creating sustainable performance is commitment. The first thing to understand about commitment is that it is an absolute term. Safety allows us to understand this clearly—you can't be reasonably committed, or very committed to safety. You are either committed to operating safely or you are not. If you as a leader don't understand this, you should, because your team certainly does, and they will form an either/or judgement about whether or not you are committed to safety.

When you create the relationship foundation to safety as a value and people understand each other, trust each other, and are aligned around a common purpose, people will commit to working safely. This commitment shows up as choosing to be responsible for yourself, for others and for the task. Team members who are committed are *"all in"* they choose to be responsible, are good for their word and are willing to be held accountable by others for what they do and the results achieved. This is the foundation that sustainable performance and achievement are built on.

Responsibility and Accountability

These two words have become so overused and misused in the management monologue of organizations. This is made even more confusing by the lack of clarity re what is actually meant by either word. Dictionary.com defines <u>accountable</u> as: *"subject to the obligation to report, explain, or justify something; <u>responsible</u>; answerable."* And the definition of <u>responsible</u> says: *"1. answerable or <u>accountable</u>, as for something within one's power, control, or management. 2. involving accountability or responsibility."*[1]

So, in the English language the two words are often used interchangeably. But in the world of leadership and people's behaviour the two words have very different meanings. From a leadership perspective, accountability is an obligation that you owe to another person or group; it's external. Choosing to be responsible for something or someone is a decision, it is a choice that people make; it is internal to the individual.

Why is this distinction important? Because from a safety and performance perspective it creates self-determined effort verses the Safety-I external Control, Order, Prescribe approach to compliance focused safety. In the typical 3D Safety-I approach you may get compliance but not commitment.

You can't change someone's behaviour or mindset by holding them accountable for something that they don't believe they are responsible for. You need their buy-in, you need them to choose to be responsible for the outcome.

Achievement and Sustainable Performance

The ultimate goal of building greater trust, dialogue and healthy conflict, commitment, and accountability is the achievement of results.

Creating Sustainable Performance

Many years ago, I presented at a safety conference in Abu Dhabi on the success we were having changing the safety performance in OMV Austria.[2] At the conference I sat in on a panel session that was chaired by another Australian who ran a large consulting company. His company had also done a lot of work with clients in Oil & Gas, Mining and Construction, so I expected the session to be very informative. Early in the session, panel members were discussing culture and climate and using the terms interchangeably. A member of the audience raised his hand and asked, "*What is the difference between culture and climate?*" The panel chair didn't have a succinct answer, he replied "*Well they are slightly different, but the differences are complex and there isn't time in this session to go into the detail.*" He finished with "*For the purposes of this discussion treat them as the same.*"

I could not believe what I had just heard and was very disappointed that a supposed "*expert*" could give such poor advice. Albert Einstein once said, "*If you can't explain something simply, you don't understand it well enough.*" In the same way that a pilot should understand the basic principles of sustained flight: lift, drag, pitch, roll and yaw—which we discussed in Chapter 1, every leader should understand the difference between climate and culture.

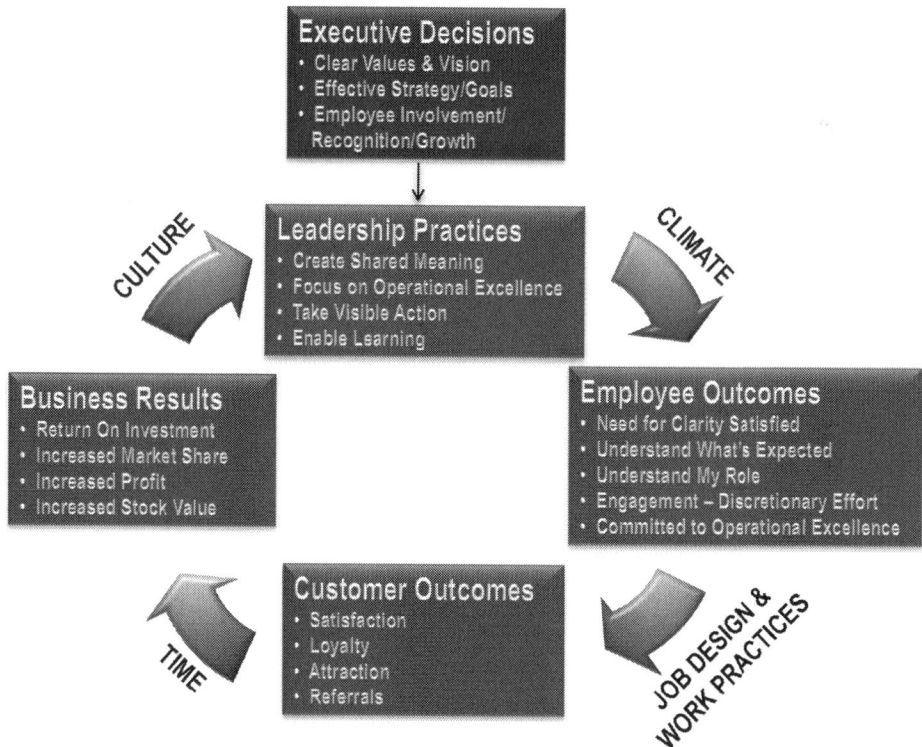

Figure 17. The Sustainable Performance Model

As we studied high performing teams and the leadership practices that create cultural change, we mapped what we were observing in what we now call the Sustainable Performance Model, see Figure 17.

Focus on Climate to influence Culture

This model allows a leader to understand the key aspects of why they do what they do. Simply put:

> *Leadership practices directly influence and create the climate, while culture is a by-product of multiple different forces that influence the organization.*

The important point to note here is the difference between climate and culture. We can steer and create the climate through leadership practices. Culture, on the other hand, is a product of many different factors interacting over time. In this regard leadership is an essential but nuanced factor in creating a culture—it is important to understand that leaders don't directly create the culture; they create the right climate for the culture to develop.

The model captures the most important messages from our research and applied practice in creating sustainable safety performance. These are that:

1. Sustainable performance is first and foremost driven by executive decisions regarding their people and how they interconnect with organizational systems and technology. In other words, health and safety excellence starts with executive leadership.

2. The focus of that senior leadership needs to be on the establishment of and commitment to collective practices, i.e. both leadership practices and work practices that creates safety as a value.

3. Leadership practices throughout the organization must then ensure that people are committed to and supported to do what is needed to ensure that things go well.

The Sustainable Performance Model is based on two streams of thought. The first is empirical. The arrows connecting the boxes represent a path of cause and effect starting with the box on the top (Executive Decisions) and then moving to Leadership Practices and then moving clockwise. The second is a view of leadership as a process of influence. Executive decisions set the stage for the evolution of the organization's shared assumptions that shape and then reinforce the organization's collective practices.

The Sustainable Performance Model is neutral—it describes the variables. It is up to the organization to determine what kinds of outputs are created (consciously or unconsciously).

This model is iterative, and the components interact. By this we mean that performance is influenced and determined by each of these elements and factors listed in the model. For example, Leadership Practices must fit the current Climate, but Leadership Practices also influence the Climate, so over time they also steer or create aspects of the Climate.

An example of this is the different leadership styles adopted by leaders working with inexperienced and less competent individuals or teams compared to a leader of a team of very seasoned, highly competent people.

Leaders of inexperienced and less competent people should expect individuals to be learning and making mistakes. The climate needs to be one of instructing and supporting people in their role while they are gaining experience.

Whereas leaders of people who are experienced and able to perform their role with confidence need to create a different climate. Individuals should be delegated full responsibility and autonomy and should not need to be supported and coached. Highly experienced and committed individuals can be expected not to make serious mistakes and should understand when to seek additional input and advice.

Development is the focus, Leadership Practices and Climate will drive or influence Employee Outcomes. As Employee Outcomes (Processes, behaviours, levels of commitment, etc) become shared these create shared work practices. Work practices are supported or constrained by organizational factors that are captured on the model as Job Design. Within job design, there are three factors that relate to clarity:

1. Role Clarity—where they fit in the organizational structure,

2. Expectation Clarity—What they are expected to do and how they are expected to do it, and

3. Information Clarity—That they get the information they need to perform as well as they can.

As we work with leaders to help them increase their effectiveness and improve their team's performance, we always focus on how they create clarity and shared meaning and how they answer three questions—the WHY, the HOW and the WHAT. These three questions and the role they play in trust and psychological safety were discussed in Chapter 9.

As we researched leaders, a key factor that distinguished the best leaders from the others was their focus on creating clarity. Good leaders understand that when clarity is missing, shared meaning and common purpose cannot exist. The worst leaders in our studies treated information as power. They weaponised it and used it to their advantage, they withheld it from some and shared it with others to create power groups.

As we move around the model, we see that work practices serve to create Customer Outcomes (both internal or external customers) and over time these work practices drive Business Results.

Culture appears at this point in the model because we are recognising that an organization's culture develops over time and is driven by all the previous elements of the model.

As teams develop, they cycle around the Sustainable Performance Model. Understanding this allows us to see the integral nature of organizational performance. For example, does culture drive performance or does performance drive culture? Well, clearly culture is a big determinant of performance—it can be a driver of high performance or reinforce poor performance. However, performance also has an effect on culture—high performance and sustained success create a different culture. This is also referred to as a virtuous cycle or vicious cycle.

Executive decisions strongly reflect and reinforce values—especially in terms of creating psychological safety by promoting and supporting employee wellbeing and safety. These executive decisions flow through the organization and inform leadership practices and the creation of norms and work practices that support safety excellence. The research data suggests that when these decisions are aligned with action, then leadership practices will reflect the overriding commitment of the organization to create a climate of operational excellence and sustainable safety performance.

Climate, engagement and discretionary effort

When leaders meet their workers needs for meaning, purpose and psychological safety, they create employee engagement[3]. Workers will volunteer to be part of safety performance improvement and will apply considerable discretionary effort to achieving these improvements. In this environment employees choose to do what is needed, especially in terms of adapting and supporting change. With good leadership practices you get a strong and positive climate for safety performance. This creates an environment for proactive and focused achievement oriented behaviours. Understanding the Sustainable Performance Model provides clarity about how the organization's collective practices are shaped and sustained and how these are linked to sustainable performance.

Leadership and Culture

The way culture works is that it shapes what people perceive, what they believe to be important and critically what is possible within that environment. This means that all cultures are self-fulfilling. Culture, in effect, is like the organization's DNA. Over time the members of a culture come to act in a manner that is consistent with the shared view of reality, values, and possibility.

Lou Gerstner who as CEO of IBM steered the turnaround of that company in the 1990's, described the importance of culture this way:

> "Until I came to IBM, I probably would have told you that culture was just one among several important elements in any organization's makeup and success - along with vision, strategy, marketing, financials, and the like... I came to see, in my time at IBM, that culture isn't just one aspect of the game, it is the game. In the end, an organization is nothing more than the collective capacity of its people to create value."[4]

In our leadership workshops we often ask the question. *"Who knows that they would be healthier and possibly live longer if they lost 5 kilos or more in weight, please raise your hand?"* Most hands go up.

We then ask people to put their hands down if they are effectively doing something about it right now. Most people keep their hands up. That's how much difference knowing something makes.

We used to conduct culture surveys for our clients around the world. The work that we had done with Dr Keith Owen meant that we had a very sophisticated model of culture and performance and could pinpoint with a high degree of accuracy what the cultural gaps were. What we found though—was that knowing what their culture was and where the gaps were did not create the change needed. Even having individual managers develop action plans to make changes didn't achieve much. Furthermore, what was achieved was often temporary in nature.

Conducting a culture survey can be a bit like taking your car to a mechanic who connects it to a diagnostic machine, he creates a printout and tells you that your engine is running too rich and the timing is too far advanced. Unless you know how to retune your engine that information is basically useless to you. Unlike a car engine where a couple of onetime adjustments will correct the tune and have it running well, changing your organizational culture is much more involved and takes time.

This begs the question—is there any value in understanding what your organizational culture is, and specifically what your culture of safety is? We believe there is, but we need to make sure we measure the right things and take action that makes a difference. Just knowing what your culture is doesn't achieve much.

Creating a 4D Performance Culture that includes Safety

While the concept of a culture is subjective by nature, it is well established that culture both influences behaviour and drives objective outcomes; it has a very real effect on performance.[5]

We said previously that culture gets created by design or by default. There is a tendency for people to think that all organizations have a safety culture. We prefer to not use the term safety culture. All organizations have a culture, safety may or may not be part of it. An organization can have a culture that supports and enables safe operations, or it can have a culture of no safety or anywhere in between.

A second assumption is that culture is about shared values as opposed to shared practices. A value is a belief that guides behaviour; however, most studies show there is a very low association between what a person says he or she values and what he/she does.[6] Definitions that revolve around just shared values suffer from the fact that values are not good predictors of behaviour. This is why we follow the lead of Hopkins[7] who defines culture in terms of the shared collective practices of the organization i.e. *"the way we do things around here"*. This logic follows that of Schein[8] who defined culture as *"A pattern of shared basic assumptions learned by a group as it solved its problems of external adaptation and internal integration."*

A culture is more than the aggregate of all the individual intentions and commitments to safety or operational performance; just as a team is more than the sum of its individual players. Culture is like a habit. First, we create the climate which supports the development of the culture (habit) and then we become part of the culture (habit) and it unconsciously guides our decisions and actions. When leaders create a culture which has a mastery orientation that includes safety, it acts like an invisible set of guiding principles that informs people how to manage risks and do the job. These invisible principles and the thinking they create, guide, and become our safety practices.

In any organization, culture defines what is:
- Reality (what is perceived)
- Important (what is of value), and
- Possible (Freedom of choice)

To guide us in the leadership work we do we define a culture of safety as:

The set of shared understandings, beliefs, assumptions, perceptions and values that inspire, influence and drive safe behaviour and work practices in the organization.

Reimagining Safety Key Performance Indicators

When you understand the CARES framework, particularly the importance of relationships and having an achievement orientation that is grounded in mastery, then you can start to see your organization's performance in a completely different light. Looking at organizations from this perspective we have been able to reimagine what performance looks like and to come up with a set of key performance indicators which are significantly different to those used in conventional safety. These are not backward looking KPI's that seek to measure what has gone wrong, and all the areas where people have failed or not performed as expected. Instead, they are forward looking, leading indicators that seek to measure how well people are doing all the things that they need to do to create the capacity for things to go well.

The interesting outcome of this journey to develop the tools and measures of performance was that we were able to optimise and shorten the leadership development and training programs that companies typically put their people through. Previously we would conduct 3 to 5-day Supervisor Leadership or Safety Leadership Courses aimed at teaching the skills needed to be an effective leader. As we started to track and measure leadership practices, we found that a good percentage of leaders already understood the fundamental principles. Sending these leaders on multi-day safety leadership courses, that they didn't need, was a waste of their time and the company's resources. It became clear that when you provide a framework that spells out what is wanted from leaders and give them feedback on how well they are doing it, many leaders can work it out themselves and improve their leadership effectiveness on the job. This is consistent with the principle of:

"What gets expected gets respected."

Key Takeaways from this Chapter

1. Achievement and sustainable performance starts with commitment.

2. You can't change someone's behaviour or mindset by holding them accountable for something that they don't believe they are responsible for.

3. Leadership practices directly influence and create team and organizational climate, while culture is a by-product of multiple different forces that influence the organization.

4. Culture is like a habit. First, we create the climate which supports the development of the culture (habit) and then we become part of the culture (habit) and it unconsciously guides our decisions and actions.

5. Culture defines what is: Reality (what is perceived), Important (what is of value), and Possible (Freedom of choice).

6. When leaders create a culture which has a mastery orientation that includes safety it acts like an invisible set of guiding principles that informs people how to manage risks and do the job.

Reflection Questions

- Are our leaders committed to safety? It's a yes or no question.

- Do we focus on leadership practices and climate?

- What is our culture like and what is steering it?

Endnotes:

[1] Reference (n.d.) *Responsible.* Dictionary.com [online] https://www.dictionary.com/browse/responsible?s=t

[2] Zartl-Klik, A., Read, B. and Samhaber, R. (2006). Step Change in HSEQ Performance through Leadership Initiative. In: *SPE International Health, Safety & Environment Conference.* Abu Dhabi, U.A.E., 2-4 Apr, 2006. SPE. https://onepetro.org/search-results?page=1&q=SPE-98584-MS

[3] Pink, D.H. (2009). *Drive: The Surprising Truth About What Motivates Us.* Riverhead Books. Print.

[4] Gerstner, L. V. Jr. (2003). *Who Says Elephants Can't Dance: Leading a Great Enterprise through Dramatic Change.* HarperBusiness. Print.

[5] Winter, J., Owen, Dr. K., and Read, B. (2010). How Effective Leadership Practices Deliver Safety Performance AND Operational Excellence. *SPE Oil and Gas India Conference and Exhibition.* Mumbai, India, 20-22 Jan, 2010. SPE. https://onepetro.org/search-results?page=1&q=SPE-129035-MS

[6] Aronson, E., Wilson, T. D., Akert, R. M. and Sommers, S. R. (2017). *Social Psychology.* 9th ed. Pearson. Kindle Edition

[7] Hopkins, A. (2005). *Safety, Culture and Risk: The Organisational Causes of Disasters.* CCH Australia Ltd. Print.

[8] Schein, E. H. and Schein, P. A. (2016). *Organisational Culture and Leadership.* 5th ed. Wiley. Print.

Chapter 12

Bringing it all together to create Sustainable 4D Performance

We hope that you will join us in our commitment to making the changes needed to create sustainable safety performance. If we are to achieve that goal, we need to do two things. Firstly, we need to be able to understand and align on what it takes to make these changes. Secondly, we need to recognise that there are some people who oppose the change, for reasons that we have already outlined in this book. They believe the conventional management driven approach which is rooted in behavioural psychology is enough. To answer the first need, we will share with you some of our lessons and successes achieved on this journey. To respond to the second need, we will speak plainly and openly about the issues that we believe are holding safety back.

So far in this book we have covered the theory that leaders must understand in order to create sustainable 4-Dimensional Safety performance. In Part 1, we have answered the question of why we need to rethink our approach to safety and what's required to shift our focus from a limiting 3D, Safety-I approach, which tracks problems and what's gone wrong, to a 4-Dimensional sociotechnical approach that focuses on mastery and what leaders and teams do to make things go well.

In Part 2 of the book, we outlined what the most effective leaders do to create a Safety Differently, 4-Dimensional approach which sees people as the solution and not the problem. We have mapped out the CARES framework which, when applied effectively, enables leaders to create a climate to support the change from a Safety-I to a Safety-II paradigm.

We have discussed, that to apply a 4-Dimensional approach we need to understand the complicated nature of technical systems and complexities of dynamic sociotechnical systems. To effectively work in this space, we need to be able to understand and reason through the range of factors that impact the sociotechnical environment that we operate within.

We need to effectively manage the complicated, linear, technical systems and apply leadership to influence the complex nonlinear nature of our social systems. Furthermore, to effectively implement change in a VUCA[1] environment we need to move beyond the limitations of a command and control leadership style to a relationship based, 4-Dimensional integral approach. This approach is multi-faceted. It is not limited by the short-sighted achievement orientation of outperforming the competition. Instead, it actively seeks to engage our people and to create self-directing teams which are committed to a mastery orientation. It seeks to ensure that we have the discipline to do what's needed to build robust sociotechnical systems that also have the resilience and adaptive capacity to ensure things go well.

We also need to be able to understand the nature of limiting paradigms that stop us from seeing the whole picture. If we can understand the temporal nature of our knowledge, experience, references, beliefs, and values we can provide the leadership to challenge existing paradigms and create the paradigm shifts required to learn and to reimagine safety performance.

In Chapter 8 we proposed that if we are to be successful in creating sustainable safe operations, we need to apply our understanding of the science of what truly motivates people. In Chapter 10 we explored how the best leaders earned trust and created psychological safety which promotes learning, endeavour and the discretionary effort that is the hallmark of self-directing teams.

The challenge is to be able to bring all of this understanding together to enable our leaders and teams to create sustainable safety performance.

What does it take to make a change?
The change and performance improvement that we have helped organizations create has always required several things within the organization.

1. An understanding and acknowledgement that there is a need for change.

2. The courage to make it happen. A values-based commitment—an intent to make that change happen. To simply know at an intellectual level that "*we should*" change isn't enough. This is about engaging the right side of the Integral Model to start to create an integral approach.

3. The need to take a mastery view to identify and understand where the gaps exist—in all quadrants of the Integral Model. What are we not doing well?

4. Next a framework based on a 4-Dimensional approach is needed to help guide and influence decision making and identify the necessary actions to achieve the desired change.

5. Finally, monitoring, measurement and tracking of 4-Dimensional results are an essential requirement to create a sustainable change.

The Person in the mirror
Recently we have noted one of the latest gimmicks from what we call the "*poster brigade*" that serves as a perfect example of failing to understand what is needed to create sociotechnical safety (ST-Safety) that functions across all four dimensions of performance.

It was a sticker on a mirror that said, *"You are looking at the person who is responsible for your safety."* The trouble with this message is that it is incomplete.

When you work in a high-risk environment, you know that the work you do is dangerous, but it is common to think *"it won't happen to me."* Or, to think that the training and the hard work you've done to develop and maintain competency and proficiency is enough. You think you've got the risks covered. We do need to ensure that people look out for themselves and look out for their mate's safety. The sticker on the mirror can be an effective part of creating awareness of personal or individual safety at the sharp end, but it doesn't address the process safety issues or the organizational issues that create catastrophes—Major Accident Events. The SAS Black Hawk Tragedy, NASA Challenger Disaster, BP Macondo, Boeing 737 Max are just some examples of sociotechnical safety failures.

Perhaps we could also add a mirror in the Executive Team's bathroom or the boardroom that says, "*you're looking at the person who is responsible for the safety of the 15,000 people that work for your company.*"

Perhaps if Boeing had such a mirror then they might have acted differently and told the airline owners and pilots of the new 737 Max aircraft that the designers had installed a system (MCAS) that could control the pitch of the plane and send it into an unrecoverable dive if they did not react quickly and hit the manual override.

It is imperative that leaders at all levels, but especially Directors on Boards and senior leaders, who are making the decisions about the quality and integrity of the operations, maintain situational awareness and a realistic risk orientation.

When leaders can effectively apply the Six Factors, we have outlined in Chapter 9 they meet the organizational needs of:

1. Giving leaders at all levels the tools and understanding to properly evaluate and manage the risks,

2. Ensuring that the KPI's and feedback mechanisms, based on leading indicators, keeps leaders at all levels accurately informed as to what is happening at the job site, and

3. Creating the psychological safety where leaders at all levels are supported to make hard decisions.

Work practices, values and beliefs
In the previous chapter we defined a culture of safety as:

The set of shared understandings, beliefs, assumptions, perceptions and values that inspire, influence and drive safe behaviour and work practices in the organization.

The power of the above definition is that it helps us understand where our focus as leaders should be. Changing people's values and beliefs is very hard to do and impossible if they do not want to change. However, changing work practices in an organization is much more achievable. And if you understand the concept of cognitive dissonance, you will know that people do not comfortably operate long term in a situation where their values and behaviour are not aligned. In these situations, to retain mental health, the conscious and subconscious mind creates stress to force a change to occur.

In situations of sustained cognitive dissonance, individuals will either change their values to match their behaviour or change their behaviour to bring it back in line with their values. There is a third alternative, and that is to not change and continue to live in a state of cognitive dissonance. Any psychologist or person who understands mental health will tell you this is not sustainable—something has to give. If you want to understand what this environment looks like read Sam Goodman's book *Safety Sucks!*[2] This is the World of Safety-I—frustration with this unsustainable approach was a key motivator for our 2015 article titled *It's Time for a Change.*[3]

Clive Lloyd, in *The Next generation of Safety Leadership* discussed that *"Safety Science as a discipline is about 30 years behind its parent disciplines, such as psychology."*[4]

We wholeheartedly agree with this observation. Safety as it is practiced in the conventional 3D Safety-I approach is an anachronism that is in serious need of change. It is time for Safety to embrace effective leadership practices and embrace a 4-Dimensional approach.

It seems that Safety has been in the grips of a behaviourism driven approach (see Chapter 8) since the mid 1980's which has effectively held it in a management/leadership time warp (see Chapters 3 and 5). While other areas of business, management and leadership have progressed, Safety has stagnated and festered.

We make these statements, knowing that our words will aggravate some of the proponents of BBS—let's explore why that might be. Martin Seligman, the founder of positive psychology, in his book *Learned Optimism* discussed the fight he had with the devotees of behaviourism in psychology. In Seligman's words, *"The behaviourists did not blithely surrender."* Seligman went on to describe how at *"an international meeting I was accosted by Skinner's leading disciple—in the men's room of all places—and informed that, 'the animals don't learn that anything [sic], they only learn responses'.*"[5]

It would appear that this is the nature of people who believe in a command and control approach. Their paradigm is about power and authority, and they believe in the efficacy of force, coercion, and manipulation to control behaviour. Not surprisingly, they automatically resort to this approach, instead of engaging in progressive dialogue. This polarised power play is ongoing in the field of Safety right now and is a continuation of the opposition and hostility that Martin Seligman faced 30 years ago.

The convenient and simplistic nature of the conventional, *"people are the problem,"* approach to safety means that there are still people in management roles who support this view. We hope this book provides useful information to help progress the dialogue and create a better understanding of the new view, Safety Differently, Safety-II, 4D Safety approaches which focus on safety as—a capacity for things to go well.

Let's Reimagine Safety

The principles and practices that are part of a 4-Dimensional performance approach are not unproven academic theories. They are based on the leadership philosophy and practices of some of the world's most successful leaders and innovators, blended with our own research and applications. Here is a list of some of the thinkers that have influenced our thinking and approach.

- Ricardo Semler, owner of Semco, author of *Maverick (1994)*

- Paul O'Neill, Alcoa CEO

- Tom Peters, bestselling author of multiple leadership and management books, creator of the video series *The Leadership Alliance*[6]

- Pat Carrigan, Plant Manager of the GM Bay City Plant

- Ralph Stayer, owner of Johnsonville Sausage Co. author of *Flight of the Buffalo (1993)*

- Pikes Fish Place and the Fish Video[7]

- David Marquets, author of *Turn the Ship Around*[8], creator of the video *The Submarine Commander*[9]

- Toto Wolff, Mercedes AMG Petronas F1 Team Principle

There is a common thread that runs through all the leadership philosophy and practices in the list of leaders above. Every one of these leaders would score very highly against the

20 leadership practices of the CARES Framework. Every one of these is a story of relationship based leadership and a mastery orientation focused on sustained performance.

Leadership driven performance

Semco is a Brazilian company that Ricardo Semler took over from his father who founded the company. Under Ricardo Semler's leadership, in one decade the company grew from $4Million annual turnover to over a $1Billion annual turnover. Semler's model was one of employee participation and ownership. In 2012, the Semco Group transitioned into a partnership structure as Semco Partners.

In 1993 Semler wrote a book called *Maverick* in which he outlined the philosophy and principles that guided his reimagining of the family business that he took over from his father a decade before. Even though *Maverick* was written almost three decades ago, it still makes for good reading. Semler based his approach on changing the relationship with the company's workers. A philosophy of trust and respect was a cornerstone of his approach.

In *Maverick*, Semler described how when he took the reins at Semco, they appeared highly organized and well disciplined, but they still could not get their people to perform as the company wanted or to be happy with their jobs. So Semler set about making changes. He abolished the security checks that every employee had to submit to on their way through the plant gate. He described how a senior manager in the company had justified the checks on the basis that, *"theft is so common, we need to check everyone, every day ... Besides every company does it."* was added as further justification.[10]

Abolishing the security checks was just one of many changes Semler made, he also did away with time clocks and rigid time-keeping in the factories.

His reasoning was based on a belief that, *"on average 2 or 3 per cent of any workforce will take advantage of their employer's trust. But is this a valid reason to subject 97 per cent to a daily ritual of humiliation?"*[11]

He added, *"Have thefts and time-card cheating increased or decreased? I don't know and I don't care. It's not worth it to me to have a company at which you don't trust the people with whom you work."*[12]

This is a great example of the difference in mindset and thinking between a management and a leadership approach. In a 3D management approach people are just a resource to be controlled. In a 4D leadership approach people are an asset to be developed and relied upon as the biggest store of untapped capacity in the business.

A purely 3D management approach is a cop out from people who are either incapable of, or never learned how to build relationships based on trust. Semler was correct, there will be a small percentage of people that are not reliable and cannot be trusted to do the things that they committed to and said they would be responsible for. But that's life, good leaders identify those people and address that issue, as opposed to punishing the 97 percent.

Formula One racing stands at the pinnacle of motorsport and also as an example of a highly competitive sociotechnical environment. In 2020 the Mercedes AMG Petronas Formula One Team won their seventh consecutive constructors' championship. This is an unprecedented achievement which eclipsed Ferrari's Six consecutive championships won in the Michael Schumacher era. Toto Wolff was the Team Principle of the Mercedes F1 team for all seven victories. Wolff's leadership is on display week in and week out during the F1 season. He has given several interviews and spoken about his views on the need to find purpose and to have a no blame culture.[13] No blame does not mean no accountability, Wolff explains how people need to be a good fit for the team and able to engage in healthy conflict to create the outcomes they need to stay in the lead. One of the things that he attributes this success to is their philosophy that came from their sports psychologist, Ceri Evans.[14] Evans has also been the sports psychologist for the New Zealand All Blacks Rugby Team since 2010. He has a simple philosophy of *"No D!(kheads"*, which basically means support the 97 per cent and don't tolerate the 2-3 per cent that are not reliable and trustworthy.

Paul O'Neill and Alcoa

Paul O'Neill was the CEO of Alcoa for the late 1980's and all of the 1990's. What Paul O'Neill achieved at Alcoa is a perfect example of leadership and using safety as a driver of performance. O'Neill proved that the same leadership that creates safety performance also drives all other areas of team performance – including quality, productivity, and costs.

After several years of depressed earnings in the early 90's, O'Neill took Alcoa from a profit of $4.8 million in 1993 to a profit of $1.5 billion in 2000.

Along the way, he transformed Alcoa's manufacturing process and grafted his character and his beliefs onto the lives of its workers.

On his first day, he told Alcoa's executives that,

> *They weren't going to talk people into buying more aluminium and that they weren't going to be able to raise prices.*
>
> *So the only way to improve the company's fortunes was to lower its costs. And the only way to do that was with the cooperation of Alcoa's*

workers. And the only way to get that was to show them that you actually cared about them.

And the only way to do that was to actually care about them.

And the way to do that was to establish, as the first priority of Alcoa, the elimination of all job-related injuries. [15]

O'Neill set the bar for his executive team and stated that any executive who didn't make worker safety his personal focus—more important than immediate profits—would be fired. He made good on that commitment and this helped convince his workers that he was sincere in his commitment to care about their safety.

O'Neill's commitment to safety was on show from the moment he took the reins as CEO. He empowered workers, supervisors and managers to stop the job and do what was needed to operate safely. He instigated a daily reporting program that required that each vice president report the details of every workplace injury within 24 hours of their occurrence. The report included the name and contact details of the injured worker and a description of the incident. It also included the name of the workers direct supervisor. O'Neill would ring each worker and have a conversation with them. He always started with apologising for the fact that they were injured working for Alcoa and then would ask them if they needed anything from him and what they thought could be done to prevent this happening again—what was missing or needed to be done better? He then phoned the workers supervisor and asked them the pointed question, *"What are you doing right now to ensure that this never happens again in your work area?"*

There were three other questions that O'Neill would regularly ask workers in Alcoa.[16]

1. Are you treated with dignity and respect everyday by everyone you encounter?

2. Are you given the things you need, tools, equipment, training and encouragement so that you can make a contribution that gives meaning to your life?

3. Do you get recognized for what you do?

Paul O'Neill's leadership provided the drive to make Alcoa one of the safest companies in the world and a leader in its industry. The principles of Paul O'Neill's approach are an exemplar of a 4D Performance approach.

Tom Peters – The Leadership Alliance

In the late 1980's Tom Peters created a video series called *The Leadership Alliance.*[17] In the series he takes a journey to explore the leadership practices of a diverse range of highly successful organizations including, Harley-Davidson Motorcycles, Johnsonville

Sausage and Pat Carrigan the Plant Manager of the General Motors Bay City Assembly Plant.

We have very successfully used the different stories from this Tom Peters video series, in a variety of engagements around the world to generate conversations with managers, supervisors and workers about ownership, respect, and trust.

Ralph Stayer—Johnsonville Sausage Co

One of the stories in the series is about Johnsonville Sausage owned by Ralph Stayer. Like Semler, Stayer took over the family business from his father and while the business was successful and profitable, he was not enjoying the role of boss. In his book, *Flight of the Buffalo,* he discusses his journey in leadership and changing the culture of his company.

Early on Stayer realised that, *"What I really wanted in the organisation was a group of responsible, interdependent workers."*

The book is named after the paradigm shift he went through that saw him move from the old head-buffalo leadership paradigm, to a new lead-goose leadership paradigm. That paradigm is built around the following leadership principles:

- Leaders transfer ownership for work to those who execute the work.

- Leaders create the environment for ownership where each person wants to be responsible.

- Leaders coach the development of personal capabilities.

- Leaders learn fast themselves and encourage others to also learn quickly.[18]

Pat Carrigan—General Motors Parts and Assembly Plant, Bay City, Michigan

Another story in the Tom Peters, Leadership Alliance series was the story of Pat Carrigan and the General Motors Assembly Plant, Bay City, Michigan. When Pat took on the Plant Manager role she was confronted with decades of ill feelings between management and the auto workers and their union. At the time General Motors (GM) was shutting down parts and assembly plants all over the country and outsourcing the work. The GM party line was that it was not possible to run manufacturing plants economically in America. But a telling juxtaposition to this was that Honda, Toyota and Nissan were all successfully starting up plants in the US.

The context when Pat Carrigan took over was that much of the plant was 70 years old, with old machines on wooden floorboards. It was the epitome of the 3D Management approach. Managers and supervisors controlled everything, workers had no authority and were not trusted to do anything. The workers even needed a Supervisor to sign a pass out for them to leave their workstation to go to the toilet.

Pat Carrigan changed much of that, she got out on the floor and met the workers and built relationships. She worked with her managers and supervisors and changed how they saw their role. Bureaucracy was removed. Some successfully made the change, some did not.

Ownership shifted from the supervisors to teams. In the new Pat Carrigan approach teams did everything, they planned their work, they set their budgets, they were responsible for quality control and continuous improvement. They looked after performance, they set their own measures and tracked their statistics. The Union was brought in as a true partner, with a role in joint decision making. Savings were identified and realised. Efficiencies were achieved through consultation and collaboration.

These changes highlighted the flaws of a command and control, 3D Management approach. A leadership driven approach which was based on trust and everyone acknowledging that they would sink or swim together (common purpose) created massive improvements and results.

Until you have experienced this type of change the results are hard to fathom. Instead of the 3D management approach of setting targets for cost cutting, and demanding productivity improvements, the workers created the quality improvements, rejects dropped by 44% in one year, productivity increased by over 40%, and this translated into budget savings in the millions of dollars.

The principles are simple—but the task is not simplistic
We have used this story and the key principles as the catalyst for cultural change with significant success in multiple countries around the world. It must be understood though, that every case is different. How much autonomy can be given in the early stages and how much individuals will step up and be responsible varies quite significantly depending a range of sociotechnical factors including things such as:

- the quality and integrity of leadership,

- the history of previous 'initiatives',

- how rumours and misinformation is handled,

- level of competency of the workforce,

- Union involvement and collaboration,

- the freedom or ability to address technical, operational, structural and organizational issues that confound efforts for improvement, and

- a range of external factors that are linked to the previous point including things such as tribalism and corruption that cuts across team bonds and relationships.

However, in every case it was never the workforce that was the major impediment to performance improvement. It was always leadership, combined in some cases with Union agendas. In every case, the solution hinged on the commitment and competency of leaders to work through the Six Factors that create Relationship and Achievement (see Chapter 9) was always the critical determinant of what was possible.

Putting 4D Performance into practice

To reiterate, the level of success of every performance improvement program that we have run, was in every case determined by the leadership of the organization. We are very proud to have played a part in some highly successful programs but have also had a couple that fell short of what could have been achieved. The limiting factor in each of these cases was leadership. Typically, the gap has to do with a lack of leadership skills, such as an inability to win the trust of the workforce. But in one case it came down to the senior leader simply not caring about the safety and wellbeing of their workers. We think it is important to be speak openly about this and to understand the psychology that sits behind poor performance. As Ricardo Semler said there are a small percentage of workers that cannot be relied upon to be honest and not steal from the company. There are also a small per centage that can't be relied upon to follow the rules or stop the job and ask for clarification, even though they are working in a culture that encourages and supports such behaviour. However, it is equally important to understand that there are people who make it into supervisory and management roles who just don't care about others. This type of leader is not willing to do what it takes to make sure things go well. They tolerate gaps in the organizations capacity to make things go as planned and then they blame the individual and often their supervisor when something bad happens (refer back to the SAS Blackhawk tragedy discussed in Chapter 1).

Having worked in operations on every continent, except Antarctica, we can confidently say that it was never the workers that were not capable of making the change needed to create sustainable safe performance. Outstanding performance requires that the "*No D!(kheads*" rule be applied at every level of the organization.

Great leadership and great results—OMV Austria

When I moved to Vienna and took on the role of General Manager (GM) HSEQ for global exploration and production, I knew that we could make significant improvements in safety performance. The question was where to start.

The GM of Austrian operations was Reinhart Samhaber. When Samhaber first took over as the GM the safety performance was quite poor. Samhaber had worked internationally and had created leadership driven safety performance in other operations. He knew what he wanted, but there was an issue. The workers and even most of the managers in OMV Austria had never worked internationally so they didn't know what performance in the rest of the Oil and Gas industry looked like.

Looking at Austria's performance this was the logical place to start and I found a very willing ally in Reinhart Samhaber. Introducing Reinhart to Brett and engaging Safety Leaders Group (SLG) to help us make the change was a logical progression to the work I had already done with Brett and SLG.

For several years prior to us engaging SLG, OMV Austria had been engaging a well-known, large global safety consulting firm whose solution required significant ongoing investment in layer upon layer of their safety systems including, ZERO slogans, STOP Cards and Safety Performance Curves. The result was an ever-increasing safety bureaucracy and a classic 3D Management approach when what was needed was leadership.

The approach was based on a performance orientation not a mastery orientation (See Chapter 6). For many years, OMV in Austria was only compared to other national companies, and in comparison to Austrian construction or steel production businesses, OMV's safety performance appeared to be quite good. A culture developed in Austria where Oil and Gas production was seen as a very risky business and lost time injuries were accepted as part of the job. This culture normalised the occurrence of industrial accidents and was expressed in statements such as: *"accidents happen, because it is a risky business".*

More recently, OMV had started comparing Austria's safety performance to statistics from OMV's international operations (a performance orientation)—and telling the Austrian workers that they needed to improve—however, this only created cynicism. The response from many was, *"Those numbers aren't real. They just don't report their injuries in those other parts of the world."*

From my perspective as Managing Director of SLG, the task in OMV Austria presented a picture perfect opportunity to create change. Reinhart Samhaber and Rod Ritchie, both knew what they wanted and were committed to making it happen. Their CEO was an Austrian who had not had the international experience of Rod or Reinhart, but he had been visiting the OMV International operations and had seen the difference—he knew that the gap was real and he wanted to change things.

Our approach in OMV Austria was based on the CARES Framework (see Chapter 6). We stopped referring to other parts of OMV or other companies. Instead, we built relationships with the frontline workers and focused internally. Through different approaches and dialogue, we created shared meaning through questions such as,

- *"How important is it to you that you and all of your teammates go home safely each day?"*

- *"Is that what is currently happening?"*

- *"What would you be willing to do to change this result?"*

- *"How can we make that change, what do we need to do differently, what support do you need to make it different?"*

This approach moved the focus from *"what was wrong"* to *"what was missing."* The focus was not about blame, it was about learning.

The approach with OMV Austria required a lot of work across all 4-Dimensions of performance. We established a Safety Leadership Team (SLT) that Reinhart Samhaber headed. That team, which included a cross section of key people from different levels in the business, met monthly and steered the change. Reinhart is a great leader; he instinctively understood the CARES Framework and embraced the insight of the Integral Model. He attended every Safety Leadership Team meeting, and his leadership was powerful in building the relationship base that was needed to support what everyone wanted to achieve. While he was instrumental in creating huge changes, I never saw him raise his voice or lose his patience. He would very graciously but purposefully challenge the SLT by bringing them back to their Why—which was simply put as *"People should not be injured working for OMV"*.

His leadership created the psychological safety that engaged people and made it possible for people to question and challenge how things were done and what needed to change.

The second thing we did was to establish learning teams in different departments that focused on mastery in their operations. We ran safety leadership and train the trainer programs to create internal champions who were respected by and could work with the operators on the tools to identify the gaps and what needed to change. The needs in different departments varied. In some areas it required solutions in all 3-Dimensions of business management. For example, production and schedule pressures (Dimension 1), cost or resourcing issues (Dimension 2) or inadequacies in systems and processes to manage workflow and work practices better (Dimension 3) were all identified and addressed.

But the biggest change came about through working in the 4th Dimension and developing safety leadership and ownership among frontline crews. Once the workers could see that their managers were serious about addressing the issues that were identified the pace and momentum of change ramped up considerably. RAMP became an acronym for the change we were creating.

- **R**elationship,

- **A**utonomy,

- **M**astery, and

- **P**urpose.

We knew that everything we achieved was built on a foundation of trust, but as we worked through the changes and created more engagement, we could see that there were four things we did that drove the change. We created a **Relationship** base (See Chapter 6) that supported the need for change. We gave as much **Autonomy** to the teams and frontline workers as they could handle. The more skilled and capable they became, the more autonomy they were given. We focused on **Mastery.** The frontline workers knew what was not going well and what needed to be done better. And fourth, we created a commitment to a common **Purpose** (see Chapter 8). This process became the essential elements of what we would later identify as the Six Factors that created Relationship and Achievement (as discussed in Chapter 9).

It took just under three years to create sustainable safety performance where people were not being injured working for OMV Austria.[19] It could have happened earlier but 12-months into the program a major drilling campaign started that doubled the workforce numbers. Bringing new people on board and getting them aligned, can be a challenge, but on this engagement and in subsequent work we streamlined that process (See the upcoming discussion—Rig Start-ups in a Coal Seam Gas Project). A number of the departments in our operations created safety leadership driven, injury free operations within the first 12-months of the program, some took longer. Experiencing this truly highlighted the complexities of sociotechnical systems and the subtle changes that make a difference from one situation to the next.

Safety performance improvement on a grand scale—Petrom

When we were 6-months into the safety performance improvement program in OMV Austria, Petrom which was Romania's state owned oil company and largest company overall was privatised. OMV invested €1.5 billion to purchase a 51% stake in Petrom and embarked on a vast reorganization & restructuring process investing €13.5bn between 2005 and 2017 to modernize Petrom.

As we started to scope out the size and the nature of the change required in Petrom I was busy coming to grips with the HSE performance in the company. It was essential that we make massive improvements and achieve them fast. In the year before we took control of Petrom they had 14 fatalities. As we did our research, I was dismayed to learn that they had more than 10 fatalities every year over the last decade. I had always held the view and the personal value that it was unacceptable for people to be seriously injured or killed at work, regardless of what part of the world they worked in. This now presented a major challenge that would test my conviction to that value.

We engaged SLG to work closely with our HSE department and our two teams put their heads together to scope out the recommended solution. As we analysed the situation, we made note of the following sociotechnical safety factors:

- Romania has over 160 years of history in crude oil production & refining. It was among the first producing countries and one of the largest oil producers in the world at the beginning of the 20th century. The Petrom people were proud of their history and would not take well to external parties coming in and telling them that the HSE performance was not acceptable and that change was needed, and quickly.

- Many of the facilities were very old and in varying states of disrepair. Lots of obsolete or not in use equipment was still in situ in the facilities.

- The refineries and oil fields had been bombed in both the First and Second World Wars. Unexploded bombs and other ordnance were to be expected any time we turned soil in these facilities.

- Records of repairs and changes to the facilities made after bombings were either non-existent or poor quality and not reliable.

- Petrom still operated under the Soviet business model where virtually all support services were owned by Petrom. This included schools, hotels, shops, engineering, and other support services all in regional centres. The cultural shift that a company faces when it moves from a state-owned to a corporate business model was not lost on us.

- Petrom employed 70,000 people. Many of them had nothing to do with the core business. OMV by comparison was less than a tenth of that size. The changes that were coming meant that many people would leave the company.

Based on the successes of the safety leadership program we were running in Austria with SLG it was a natural progression to run the same program in Petrom, obviously a much bigger challenge, but as the product was proven, why change.

Dealing with the Romanian culture was a challenge when it came to leadership as the country culture was heavily swayed by a hierarchical chain of command where you never challenged the authority of your supervisor, much less a manager. So many Petrom employees died thinking they were doing the best job they could for the company—not knowing what they didn't know.

Changing a culture in a company of this size with this background is like driving a super tanker, you can turn the wheel on the bridge, but the vessel will travel a long distance before a real change in direction is realised. Developing safety leadership capability across the company was a priority. But we were clear that changes needed to happen across all 4-Dimensions of performance. Understanding the integral nature of performance and the complexities of sociotechnical safety (as we discussed in Chapter 4) were essential to be able to turn the Petrom ship around. As we said in Chapter 3,

> *"Getting the first 3 Dimensions right is not enough. These 3 Dimensions are merely enablers of performance; they are based on systems thinking and they focus on compliance with that system. But they don't create commitment."*

At the risk of using too many metaphors, we would like to share an aviation analogy that we use to make the distinction between the first 3 Dimensions and the 4th Dimension of Performance. There have been many instances of pilot error that have seen a pilot fly a perfectly good aircraft into the ground. But the flipside of this argument is that having an airworthy aircraft is a prerequisite for safe operations. No amount of good piloting will allow a pilot to safely land the aircraft when the wings fall off.

Creating the structural, technical, and operational changes in Petrom needed to happen in the context of leadership that understood the integral nature of the 4-Dimensional changes needed. Once the senior leadership understood the WHY (See Figure 15. The Leadership Efficacy Chain) the Safety Leadership program was effectively cascaded down through the organization.

Addressing the deficiencies in the 3-Dimensional enablers and supporting Petrom's frontline leaders to create the change took five years before we achieved the first year without a fatality.

Furthermore, as with every other program, we saw an improvement in overall operation performance as our leaders started to *"get it"*. As they embraced the program, they opened themselves up to being challenged by their subordinates. This included STOP THE JOB, which was a major cultural change.

Rig Start-ups in a Coal Seam Gas Project
One engagement that we worked on over several years was instrumental in the development of our suite of online tools for creating and improving 4-Dimensional Performance. This engagement was a Coal Seam Gas Project in Queensland, Australia.

The project requirement was for 4,000 gas wells to be drilled in a 3 year period. The plan required 30 plus drilling rigs operated by four different contractors and started-up in the first three years. This needed to be done in the middle of a boom where several multi-billion dollar coal seam gas projects were running concurrently. The additional risks this imposed were identified by our client, so they engaged SLG to help them mitigate the sociotechnical safety issues. A list of the current challenges and identified risks were as follows:

- Our client had put on nine rigs in the past year and the project scope called for 20 plus rigs to be added to the drilling campaign. Poor safety performance was already becoming a concern. Our client and their contractors were taking a conventional approach to safety and were tracking all the usual lagging KPI's plus a few so called *"leading"* KPI's. What they were doing was clearly not working. Their Total Recordable Injury Frequency Rate (TRIFR) had more than tripled in the last year and was sitting at 29 despite managers being constantly focused on and bringing pressure to bear to reduce TRIFR.

- Investigating all these incidents was taking considerable time and resources. Operational people and safety professionals were being overloaded investigating and focusing on things that had gone wrong instead of putting the time into planning and preparation to ensure that upcoming drilling tasks were done well.

- Relationships with contractors were getting strained. One contractor had been put on notice that if safety performance didn't improve rig contracts would start getting cancelled.

- Finding qualified and experienced people in the boom to crew the drilling rigs was a major challenge.

Our solution was to move the focus from what was going wrong, to doing the things needed to make sure things went well. We did this by working at multiple levels using the CARES Framework and working on the Six Factors to strengthen relationships and align achievement goals.

We worked with our client and the drilling contractors to create a shared understanding of what was not being done well and what needed to improve. It was interesting to see the energy in the room change when our client accepted that a number of the contractor performance gaps were occurring because of things our client was doing. By focusing on creating trust and shared meaning we were able to start making improvements.

The second part of the solution was to focus on the quality of the leadership on the rigs. We were not going to be able to do anything about the lack of skilled and experienced drilling crew members. So, it was critical that we created an environment where it was psychologically and physically safe for the new crew members to learn and get up to speed on the job. This was achieved through focusing on developing the leadership practices that created and supported a team commitment to learning and improving.

Each of the current operating rigs participated in a one day restart workshop and every new rig went through a 2-day start-up workshop. The initial focus for every new rig that we started up was on learning and teamwork to develop their performance. Each new rig was given a 3 month period where they were not expected to reach schedule or budget targets. The message was that speed and for that matter safety, were not the focus. Both of those would come as individuals and teams practiced doing things well (mastery). During the first 3 months we provided on the job mentoring and coaching on leadership and work practices using the CARES Framework and the Six Factors. A range of measures of both leadership and work practices were used as meaningful leading key performance indicators.

The results were quite remarkable. Over the next two years we ran more than 30 rig restarts or start-ups. Many of the rigs hit their schedule and budget targets well inside the 3 month window while maintaining safe performance. Thomas Paine said that, *"Character is much easier kept than recovered."* And this was the attitude of the crews on each rig towards their safety performance. Of course, if there was an incident, the potential psychological reaction to this needed to be managed. But that is not difficult when there is a learning and mastery orientation as opposed to a performance orientation.

A key part of the overall approach required us to be able to cherry pick skilled individuals out of operating teams and use them as the core of a newly formed team. Some individuals proved to be exceptional leaders who were able to readily adjust their approach. They started up several teams and were highly effective in bringing a new team together and creating a commitment to excellent performance. Each of these leaders were great examples of CARES, they created the relationship base for performance to be built on. They consistently created an achievement orientation and set standards that were achievable by individuals and the team. They created endeavour through autonomy, mastery and purpose and they got outstanding results.

An interesting observation from this program was that the original rigs that were poor performers took longer to improve and often plateaued at a lesser level that the new start-ups. Our learning from this is that it is often more effective to break up and reform a poor performing team that it is to try to change that team. Team dynamics bring a level of complexity that are often better side stepped than persevered with.

Two projects, same challenge, hugely different outcome

Another example of how 4D Performance works, comes from several years ago, when we were working with two different Oil and Gas clients on projects involving the design and construction of not normally manned offshore platforms. While the companies were operating in different parts of the world, there were quite a few similarities in the projects. Both were a reasonable distance offshore, which required a 30 minute helicopter trip to put people on the platform, both experienced seasonal periods of bad weather that could mean choppers couldn't land, and crews would have to overnight on the rig unexpectedly. Both were on migration paths for sea birds and in the periods where there was no human occupation of the rigs became colonised by birds. This brought all kinds of HSE problems with fouling and contamination of equipment from bird guano.

The two companies took very different approaches to the design of the facilities. One had a small team of operations people involved throughout the project phases. We worked through the Trust Triangle (Figure 12) and the Why—How—What questions (see Figure 11) with the designers and future operators of the rig. We coached and worked with the project leadership team and team leaders to help them establish and maintain effective dialogue within and between the teams. This process identified and addressed concerns raised in a continuous process of dialogue and constructive conflict management.

The second company engaged us during project commissioning to help them resolve *"relationship and operability issues"*. They had not embedded operations people in the project through the earlier project design phases. The designers had made all kinds of assumptions that were a classic example of the failings and pitfalls that occur between work as imagined (WAI) and work as done (WAD). The design assumptions meant that they had not allowed for people routinely overnighting on the rig. They had overlooked needs regarding living conditions and accommodation, including sleeping, shower and toilet facilities, catering, firefighting and escape provisions. They overlooked many ergonomic issues, including access to and cleaning of fouled equipment and the list went on. The difference between the two company's approaches and final solutions was staggering.

Both projects experienced technology issues that resulted in the not normally manned platforms having crews on the rigs for more than 50% of the time in the first year of operation.

Because they had been proactive and recognised the need for collaboration, trust, and dialogue, the first company had worked through the vast majority of issues in design workshops. We were able to help them workshop the process which identified concerns and conflicts and addressed them constructively. One key factor that proved to be the critical difference between the two projects was that the first company identified the need for accommodation and emergency response, including a lifeboat for a crew held over as a result of weather.

The second company had not gone through the same process. In the absence of shared meaning and the understanding that is created, the design engineers had made many incorrect assumptions and overlooked multiple concerns which made it through into the construction and plagued the project through commissioning and in operations.

Jim Collins in the book *Good to Great* calls it, *"First Who … Then What."* Collins explained that when they first started researching good to great performance, they thought that setting direction and strategy would be the key determinant of great performance. It turned out that *"getting the right people on the bus"* before worrying about where the bus is going was the critical factor.[20]

By involving operations people very early in the project life cycle, the first company ensured that shared meaning and purpose was created through establishing shared reality and maintaining shared values with the people that were going to be delivering the results for the company once the new project had been commissioned and handed over to operations. This is what we mean by a 4-Dimensional approach.

Whereas, in the second company the design engineers had effectively been set up to fail. They lost credibility which as we know is a key aspect in establishing and maintaining trust. Furthermore, due to schedule and budget overruns (Dimensions 1 & 2), managers lost credibility. People were constantly battling problems, stressed, working long hours, and operating in reactive *"fix it"* mode. The focus of the work we did with this project ended up being much more about conflict resolution, avoiding the blame game and trying to keep relationships *"above the line."* The focus and level of job satisfaction between the two projects could not have been more different.

The difference between resolving issues in a workshop and being able to construct the solution in a fabrication yard during project construction versus having to retrofit work around solutions offshore, is difficult to comprehend; until you've experienced it. The cost of creating solutions in the first project was measured in the thousands, the cost of fixing problems on the second project was measured in the millions.

Final thoughts

Creating sustainable Sociotechnical Safety requires a 4-Dimensional approach to safety performance. Moving to a 4D ST-Safety approach which recognises the complex interplay between people, technology, systems, the structures, and the markets they operate in, will need a paradigm shift across industry, regulators and academia if we are to achieve the performance improvement that we know is possible. Clearly this is no minor feat, it requires us as leaders to recognise the deficiencies in the current approach and focus our resources on creating the change. Table 4 captures key elements of the reimagined view.

Sustainable safety performance is only achieved through great safety leadership. Great safety leaders are steering their team's safety performance and they are steering themselves. They do the things they need to do to make the difference they believe is needed. They are in the game; they choose to be responsible for safety and they hold themselves accountable. Of course, they make these choices within the constraints and limitations of their current thinking and their paradigms. The most effective safety leaders are aware of this and are constantly exploring what else they could do that would make a difference.

As a leader, the most powerful question you can regularly ask yourself is:

"What is shaping my thinking and my ability to improve the safety and overall performance of my organization?"

The Old View: A 3-Dimensional View of Safety		The New View: A 4-Dimensional View of Safety
Technical Systems. Performance is controlled by complicated systems and linear processes.	*Core Principles*	Sociotechnical Systems. Performance is created through navigating the complex interplay between people, technology, systems, the structures, and the markets they operate in.
As few things as possible go wrong. Managing errors to zero. Chronic unease.	*Where's the Focus*	Mastery—doing what is needed to ensure that things go well. Relationships and leading people. Constant vigilance.
People are viewed as unreliable and inconsistent—a problem to be managed and controlled.	*The Role of Humans in Performance*	People are viewed as having huge potential, people bring an inherent adaptive capacity to create exceptional levels of performance. People are not seen as problems, but as problem solvers.
Identify what went wrong and put a fix in place. Control everything to stop things going wrong.	*Loss Prevention*	Go upstream. Identify what's needed for things to go well. Get better at doing those things.

Table 4. Reimagining Performance and Safety

Next Steps

To move from the Conventional 3D View of Safety to a 4D View of Safety requires developing different capacities and capabilities in your organization. We recommend using a resilience engineering approach as per Hollnagel's four resilience potentials, discussed in Chapter 1. Here are some key things that we recommend you do to create a 4-Dimensional approach to performance and safety.

1. **Potential to Learn.** Train, develop and reward leadership practices that are in line with the CARES Framework and the Six Factors. Support leaders to create shared meaning and a common purpose from the Boardroom to the frontline. Working through the elements in Table 4 is where to start. This is best done through workshops using the CARES Framework and the Six Factors that Create Relationships and Achievement. Both CARES and the Six Factors are proprietary intellectual property of the Safety Leaders Group. We can make these available to your organization.[21]

2. **Purpose – Your Why for Safety.** Engage your People and ensure that everyone is clear about what safety means for them and what their role is in creating it. We call it, *"Your WHY for Safety."* When people have a WHY and when they share a common purpose then things start to RAMP up.

3. **Potential to Respond.** Focus on building Relationships, providing Autonomy, and tapping into people's desire for Mastery and Purpose (RAMP). We suggest you do this by having each team develop a Team Foundation document for their team. This is something they firstly, individually choose to be responsible for and secondly, are willing to be held accountable for creating.

4. **Potential to Monitor and Anticipate.** Track progress and Monitor performance against a set of meaningful leading 4D KPI's. These must focus on the thinking and the leadership practices that ensure things go well, not just tracking ineffective measures such as safety walk arounds, safety conversations, safety observations and the like.[22]

5. **Trust but Verify.** It is not correct to say that if you trust your people you don't need to verify. This view is missing the point in several ways. Firstly, people are human, they make mistakes, checks are meant to keep them safe, not catch them doing something wrong. Secondly, people are always learning, we do not all learn in the same way and at the same pace. Third, we don't know what we don't know, help your people learn and give support where it is needed.

We hope you find this book useful to help you reflect and to reimagine safety in your organization. The next step is to put this new view, a 4-Dimensional view into practice.

Endnotes:

[1] VUCA environment—short for an environment characterised by Volatility, Uncertainty, Complexity and Ambiguity. See Chapter 5 for original discussion.

[2] Goodman, S. U. (2020). Safety Sucks!: *The Bull $H!# in the Safety Profession They Don't Tell You About*. Hominum, LLC. Kindle Edition.

[3] Read, B., Ritchie, R. and Butler, C. (2015*). It's Time for a Global Rethink on Safety Performance*. [post] LinkedIn. https://www.linkedin.com/pulse/its-time-global-rethink-safety-performance-brett-read/

[4] Lloyd, C. F. (2020). *Next Generation Safety Leadership*. CRC Press. Kindle Edition. p.xi.

[5] Seligman, M.E.P. (2006*). Learned Optimism: How to Change Your Mind and Your Life*. Vintage Books.

[6] Enterprise Media (n.d.). *Leadership Alliance with Top Peters*. [online] https://www.enterprisemedia.com/product/00016/leadership-alliance-with-tom-peters

[7]The FISH! Philosophy (2012). *Best Leadership Training to improve Development Programs with FISH! For Leaders Series*. [video] https://www.youtube.com/watch?v=j3kQujxU2Bw&list=PL5SV2LUfJfllIbjOEwYLcucFJcQ nNEeCF&ab_channel=TheFISH%21Philosophy

[8] Marquets, L. D. and Covey, S. R. (2015). *Turn the Ship Around!: A True Story of Building Leaders by Breaking the Rules*. Penguin. Kindle Edition.

[9] Marquets, L. D. (2016). *Leadership on a Submarine*. [video] https://www.youtube.com/watch?v=HYXH2XUfhfo&t=62s&ab_channel=LeadershipAca demy

[10] Semler, R. (1995). *Maverick*. Century. Print.

[11] *Ibid*.

[12] *Ibid*.

[13] Wolff, T. (2020). *Leadership Styles, Finding Purpose and No Blame Culture in F1*. [video] https://www.youtube.com/watch?v=q8mGymE7bXo&list=PLVg3xp2wpU9MKU6bAppn NS6Gx5kY98V8K&index=9&ab_channel=Mercedes-AMGPetronasFormulaOneTeam Formula 1. (2020). *Toto Wolff Interview | Building Mercedes Into Seven-Time Champions*. [video] https://www.youtube.com/watch?v=DDgQEQQfYew&ab_channel=FORMULA1

[14] Dr Ceri Evans (n.d.) *Meet Ceri*. [online] https://drcerievans.nz/meet/

[15] Lewis, M. (2002). *O'Neill's List*. [online] The New York Times Magazine. https://www.nytimes.com/2002/01/13/magazine/o-neill-s-list.html

[16] Aerossurance (2020). *The Power of Safety Leadership: Paul O'Neill, Safety and Alcoa*. [online]   http://aerossurance.com/helicopters/paul-oneill-safety-alcoa-power-safety-leadership/

[17] Enterprise Media (n.d.). *Leadership Alliance with Top Peters.* [online] https://www.enterprisemedia.com/product/00016/leadership-alliance-with-tom-peters

[18] Belasco, J. A. and Stayer, R.C. (1993). Flight of the Buffalo. New York. Warner Books Inc. Print.

[19] Read, B., Zartl-Klik, A., Winter, J.D., Veit, C. and Zamhaber, R. (2011). Safety Leadership that Engages the Workforce to Create Sustainable HSE Performance. In: *SPE European Health Safety and Environmental Conference in Oil and Gas Exploration and Production.* Vienna, Austria, 22-24 Feb, 2011. [online] SPE. https://onepetro.org/search-results?page=1&q=SPE-140854-MS

[20] Collins, J. (2001). *Good to Great.* Random House. Print.

[21] We can accredit your people to use these materials and we have developed online Tools and a 4-Dimensional Performance Dashboard to help your organization track progress and monitor performance against a set of meaningful leading 4D KPI's. Contact Safety Leaders Group for details. www.safetyleadersgroup.com

[22] See https://www.4dsafety.org/what-we-do

INDEX

Made in the USA
Middletown, DE
09 April 2021